Feast Here Awhile

Books by Jo Brans

Mother, I Have Something to Tell You
Listen to the Voices
Take Two
Feast Here Awhile

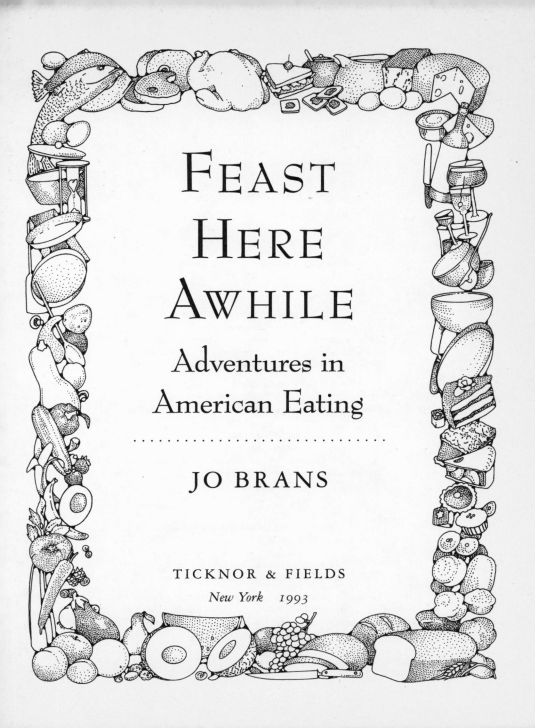

FEAST
HERE
AWHILE

Adventures in
American Eating

. . . .

JO BRANS

TICKNOR & FIELDS

New York 1993

Library of Congress Cataloging-in-Publication Data
Brans, Jo.
Feast here awhile : adventures in American eating / Jo Brans.
p.   cm.
Includes bibliographical references.
ISBN 0-395-61593-3
1. Gastronomy.   2. Cookery, American.
3. Food habits—United States.   4. Brans, Jo.   I. Title.
TX633.B69   1993
641'.01'3—dc20   93-92
CIP

Printed in the United States of America
DOH 10 9 8 7 6 5 4 3 2 1

Parts of several chapters have appeared,
in slightly different form, in *D Magazine*.

The author gratefully acknowledges permission to quote from
"Public and Private: Rabbit Pinch," by Anna Quindlen, April 15, 1992.
Copyright © 1992 by The New York Times Company.
Reprinted by permission.

To Willem

Feast here awhile
Until our stars . . . lend us a smile.
—William Shakespeare, *Pericles,* I, iv, 107

"Listen and I'll tell you what Miss Nell served at the party," Loch's mother said softly. . . .

"Ma'am."

"An orange scooped out and filled with orange juice, with the top put back on and decorated with icing leaves, a straw stuck in. A slice of pineapple with a heap of candied sweet potatoes on it, and a little handle of pastry. A cup made out of toast, filled with creamed chicken, fairly warm. A sweet peach pickle with flower petals around it of different-colored cream cheese. A swan made of a cream puff. He had whipped cream feathers, a pastry neck, green icing eyes. A pastry biscuit the size of a marble with a little date filling." She sighed abruptly.

"Were you hungry, Mama?" he said.

—Eudora Welty, *The Golden Apples*

Acknowledgments

WRITING THIS BOOK, I received so much help from all sides that what for me might have been thin gruel went down like chocolate mousse. Willem Brans, always the first reader, perused what he calls the daily rushes. Every morning, I could face the fearful blank screen with some equanimity, knowing that his unflagging interest and creative suggestions awaited me at the end of the day.

For the past decade, Molly Friedrich of the Aaron M. Priest Literary Agency has been my faithful second reader, and I hope never to lose her generous friendship, spirited partisanship, and good advice. On the third reader, Jane von Mehren, my exemplary editor, fell the largest responsibility, which she fulfilled with unfailing warmth, intelligent criticism, and enthusiasm.

Thanks also to Mark Piel and the efficient and considerate staff at the New York Society Library. Jeanne Wilensky, Ruth Diebold, Diane Harris Brown, and Peter Kump of the James Beard Foundation offered hospitality, memorable meals, and the run of the James Beard House and its library. Julee Rosso and Sheila Lukins gave me time and encouragement, as did the friendly folks at General Mills, Nach Waxman at Kitchen Arts and Letters, and such consummate cooks as Martha Rose Shulman, David Harris, Stephen Pyles, and David Bouley.

Finally, a pantheon of friends and relations cooked for me, ate with me, and confessed to me their gustatory lives: Edison Allen, Tim Allis, Michael Birdsall, Elly Brans, Jean Reid Cody, Lee Cullum, Jane de Rochemont, Michael Dunne, Ann Early, Nanette Fodell, Stephanie Helgesen, Pat and Jim Hyatt, Cathryn Jakobson, Peyton Lewis, Prudence Mackintosh, Charles Matthews, Jean and Burt Meyers, Harold Peterson, Bill Porterfield, Erin Porterfield, Winton Porterfield, Ashley Prend, Jackie Rushing, Carl Shaver, Charlie Smith, Marcia Smith, Reid Smith, Willard Spiegelman, Susan Stewart, Susan Allen Toth, Marguerite Victor, and Sarah Ziegler.

For these and all other blessings make us truly thankful.

Contents

A Love Affair with Food   1

At My Mother's Table   7

The Way We Ate   21

Kooking in the Kamera Kitchen   36

Eatniks   49

Saint Beard   62

A Servantless American Cook   76

Putting the Big Pot in the Little One   88

Gazpacho in a Sausage Grinder   103

Pipe Dreams   117

Strange Fruit   135

Nouvelle Is Swell!   153

Silver Palate in My Mouth   168

Rabbit Stew   182

How Would You Feel If a Cow Ate *You?*   196

Food Fanatic in New York   209

Notes   221

·✕·

Feast Here Awhile

·✗·

A Love Affair
with Food

. . . .

E ATING IS A DEMOCRACY. We may not know much about
"cuisine," but we know what we like. Real eaters like to talk
about food, especially at the table: what we ate yesterday,
what we will eat tomorrow, and, joy of joys, what we are eating this
very minute. In this country, our tastes have changed, both as in-
dividuals and as a people; over the past four decades, Americans
have become increasingly sophisticated about food. Yogurt. Pizza.
Crêpes. Pasta. Sushi. These concepts permeate the national consciousness, from Seattle to Savannah, as they did not in 1950.

Over the same four decades, we have also grown increasingly
afraid of food and its effects. Every woman in America, someone has
said, wants to lose five pounds. Calories. Sodium. Cholesterol. Anorexia. Carcinogen. These words, largely without currency before the

fifties, have gradually become part of the daily vocabulary of ordinary, middle-class Americans. Yet in the eighties, as never before in American history, we became a nation of food fanatics. Our terror of food has perhaps diminished but has certainly not destroyed our pleasure in food.

In the fifties, there was renewed emphasis on home life and home cooking after the upheaval of the war years. At the same time, increased national and international travel led to a growing interest in food away from home. That interest had already been provoked by the news about "foreign food" that young men from Minnesota and Mississippi brought home with them from their wartime travels, both in this country and abroad. To a Southern kid, remember, Minnesota meatballs in sour cream and dill were as exotic as Neapolitan pizza. But what was considered ethnic then, and even into the seventies, has gradually become part of our national cuisine. Pizza pie is now as all-American as apple pie. I trace the broadening of my own food horizons to a moment in 1953 when, as a college freshman, I had my first unsettling taste of Parmesan cheese. I did not like to tell my hostess that her cheese was rotten, so I swallowed it. I have been swallowing ever since.

At one time, according to James Beard, most Americans knew only the food of their own region, in my case the rural South. I may be the only person alive today who grieves for the passing of lye hominy. Where are the snows of yesteryear, and whatever happened to my grandmother's butter roll? This kind of "fading feast," to use Raymond Sokolov's term, can really be experienced now only through memory and imagination. Peculiarly alive as this feast is for me, I believe that my experience is common, that most of us have mourned the fading feasts of our memories. Many Americans of my generation, for better or worse, no longer eat the food they grew up on.

Instead, over the years, we have radically altered our menus. With typical American curiosity, we peer into each other's carts at the supermarket, crane to check out the steaming dish being brought to the next table, read the food pages in the daily paper, pay attention to what television characters eat. In the same inquisitive spirit, as I began this personal odyssey I sent a written query to about a hundred of my friends and relations, asking questions like "What memorable experiences did you have at the table as a child?" "How have your eating habits changed over the decades?" "If you cook, how did you learn?" "In a crisis, do you pig out or starve?" "Are you influenced by the Zeitgeist in your eating?"

My queries struck a nerve. Quoted throughout this book are the replies, some rich with emotion recollected in tranquility, some not so tranquil. My friends grapple, as I do, with memories of the admirable or reprehensible attitudes at their family table, the best and worst meals of their lives, and their own triumphs or catastrophes in the kitchen, as well as with their distaste for food snobbery, their earnest reflections on vegetarianism, and their guilt about cholesterol. What Americans eat clearly affects the American psyche.

And if *what* we eat has changed over the years, so has *how much* we eat. As America's food supply has swelled, so has the nation's food consumption. The average American ate 49 more pounds of food in 1983 than in 1963, according to the Department of Agriculture, and consumed 270 more calories a day. As a nation, we are eating more, and, if the proliferation of gourmet cookbooks is an indication, though we may not be cooking more, we are cooking more ambitiously.

In 1950, most households in the United States had one cookbook, if that. Typically, I grew up in a house that had no cookbooks. In their absence, learning to cook meant serving an apprenticeship, of the kind my mother had served before me, to the resident cook. My generation chafed at this method of transmission. Instead, we learned to cook from books. In the late fifties, I acquired my first cookbook, *Betty Crocker's Picture Cook Book*.

In 1960, 49 new cookbooks were published in America, and in 1961 I was given Julia Child's *Mastering the Art of French Cooking,* Volume I. In 1972, the number of cookbooks published escalated to 385; I had about a dozen. In 1988, 1,057 new American cookbook titles appeared. At this writing, I own possibly 200 cookbooks, as well as a large stack of cooking magazines.

Am I satisfied? No. My stash is small compared with the collections of some of my friends, and I recently read of a professor at New York University who has 6,000 cookbooks. Clearly there's always another book to want. I counted, on the shelves of the Minneapolis downtown public library, 37 books on French food, 34 on Italian, as well as books on the food of China, India, Indonesia, Japan, Laos, Korea, Thailand, Sri Lanka, Mexico, England, Ireland, Germany, Scandinavia, Russia, Greece, Hungary, Poland, Portugal, Spain, Switzerland, and Transylvania. Between *The Artful Avocado* and *The Zucchini Cookbook,* I saw *Bean Feast, Think Cranberries, Edible Flowers, Lilies in the Kitchen, Wild about Mushrooms, The Ultimate Peanut Butter Cookbook,* and *Peppers Hot and Chile.*

We buy these books. More than twenty-six million copies of *Betty Crocker's Cookbook* have been sold over the years, and even the books of a relatively recent addition to food writing, Frugal Gourmet Jeff Smith, have cumulatively sold more than four million copies. At the astronomical price of fifty dollars a copy, Julia Child's 1989 volume, *The Way to Cook,* became a best seller and a Book-of-the-Month Club main selection. Cookbook buyers are apparently at ease with some really tough recipes.

Americans love reading about food even if they never plan to go near a stove. In bed at night, cookbooks, like travel books or novels, soothe us to sleep, where we dream of other places, other lives, other meals. Browsing at libraries and bookstores across the country, in communities as dissimilar as Minneapolis, Dallas, and Manhattan, I have observed all kinds of people, men and women, young and old, sitting at a table and reading cookbooks, sometimes for an hour or more at a time. But they usually aren't taking notes. They plainly don't mean to rush home and construct a cassoulet or whip up a sabayon. No, they are reading in order to *imagine* the cassoulet or sabayon, to experience these delicacies vicariously, just as we learn to taste, not to cook, from reading Brillat-Savarin.

All my life, I have had a love affair with food. This book is a grateful attempt to chronicle the vicissitudes of that affair, which has made my life infinitely richer and more pleasurable. Today I'm eating better than I ever have, but still I feel sad when I think I will never eat some things again. The hot dogs at Belhaven, for example.

At Belhaven, the girls' school I attended in the fifties, the hot dogs were weird. The cook split the wienies the long way and grilled them while she toasted slices of ordinary white bread. Then she'd arrange the wienie strips on the bread, douse them with mustard, and cover them with tomato and onion relish. I'd buy a little nickel bag of potato chips, open the hot dog sandwich, and spread a crispy layer of potato chips inside for texture.

Oh, those hot dogs! The sweet of the relish, the bite of the mustard, the crunch of the chips, and the salty juiciness of the wienie! I could try to make them, but they wouldn't be the same. And how silly, anyway, to try to make a pseudo hot dog when I'm living in New York, a city where the best hot dogs in the world are available for a buck on the street corner. What can I say? I'm in love with almost everything I've ever eaten.

Maybe, reading this — this *romance* — you think you'd like more bodice ripping, more "it slid down her throat, wet, and warm, and wanton." You won't find much of that here. "Why describe, as if you were changing a tire, the most exalted human experience?"

the writer John Cheever once asked. Cheever was talking about sex, but I feel that way about eating too. I'll do my best to *suggest* the pleasures of the table, as Cheever suggested the pleasures of the bed, but a lot in both realms depends on the reader's empathy.

Like sex, like sleep, like warmth, the flavors of food appeal to a zone of elemental pleasure within us. We taste life through food, and words honor the love for food best when they express its connection with the joys and sorrows of life. So, yes, I have a passion for food. In this book, I have tried to represent the America of our time through the passionate cooks and eaters of our time, both the professionals and those numerous others who, like me, are enthusiastic amateurs in the sense of *amo, amas, amat* — people who just love food, love to eat it, love to prepare it, love to talk about it, and love to read about it. And we are legion.

At My Mother's Table

I THINK ABOUT FOOD all the time. I've always been that way. As long ago as the fifties, Connie, my college roommate, once complained plaintively, "I like you, Jo, but I don't like to eat with you. While you're chewing one bite, you're lining up the next two on your plate, and before you finish breakfast, you're already planning lunch. The truth is, you're obsessed."

If I'm obsessed with food, it's my mother's fault. When my Mississippi mother died two years ago, she left me three gifts: the china and crystal that once belonged to my grandmother and that had graced Mother's table for forty years; the dough bowl both women had used for making biscuits and kneading bread; and her firm conviction that the pleasures of the table are the dough that holds the human family together. Mother loved to feed her family, and we loved to eat her food. "Did I cook enough?" she would ask, half amused, half chagrined, as she surveyed the table at the end of a meal, with every bowl and platter emptied, every plate licked clean. "I'm afraid I didn't cook enough."

Mother never seemed to wise up to the fact that no matter how much she cooked, we were determined to eat it all. Away from home, we knew to mind our manners. "When you're company, don't gobble down every last bite on your plate," Mother instructed us. "I don't want people to think I starve you." At home, we were anything but starved. From the time we were children, my brothers and I believed that our mother was the best cook in the world. Anyone we married was required to subscribe to this belief, and our children were brought up in the family doctrine. Any doubts any of us might have entertained after a meal at, say, Lutèce, we put firmly aside. The food at Lutèce was *different* from Mother's, of course, but not really any better.

Meal after meal, living at home or back for a visit, we put our feet under the big kitchen table and ate for the honor of Mother's cooking and the Southern way of life. Most Southern food is country food, and my mother cooked country. From the enormous garden, my father's pride, came mountains of fresh vegetables. I can still see the tub of crisp, green cucumbers, the dishpan full of okra, the heaps of corn and peas, and Daddy beaming as he brings in yet another bushel basket of ripe tomatoes, while my mother rolls her eyes to heaven and says, "My soul and body! What in the world am I going to do with all of these vegetables?"

But somehow she did with them, canning, freezing, cooking, rounding out what she called "a good vegetable dinner" with fried chicken or "a mess of Mississippi River catfish." Over and over, Mother cooked the same things in the same way. "I just cook," she said when she was complimented, and just cook she did, every dish a product of culture and tradition. I can recite a rosary of her meals.

For breakfast, we had biscuits ("take two and butter 'em while they're hot"), fried eggs, bacon or sausage or both, homemade pear preserves or blackberry jam. On ordinary days, we had lunch, not dinner, at noon. For years, even after we were in high school, my brothers and I would often walk home for lunch, maybe Mother's special "goulash," which even when I learned better I preferred to the real thing, or cold baked ham with potato salad and peach pickles. On the rare occasions when Mother had to be away at lunchtime, she would leave on the neatly set kitchen table a thermos of hot vegetable soup with fresh tomatoes, okra, and corn, and a plate, covered with a damp napkin, of pimiento cheese sandwiches.

Let me pause to rhapsodize about those sandwiches. For them, made with the softest, whitest bread Wonder could produce, Mother laboriously grated extra-sharp Cheddar on the tiniest side of the grater. To the yellow mountain of cheese, she added mashed pimientos and mayonnaise; sometimes, after I was grown, I would bring home garlic and persuade her to make two batches, one with for me, one without for Daddy and everyone else. Grating the cheese is an awful, gummy job, but years later I learned from Reynolds Price, another enthusiast for pimiento cheese, that a reasonable facsimile of this purely Southern delicacy can be made in the food processor. "I think any child of the thirties and forties (from, say, Baltimore down) will recall the glory and bless my name," Price says, and he's right.

For our grand meal, Sunday dinner right after church, Mother made Swiss steak, browned and left to braise in its gravy till it was fall-apart tender. She shaped the dough for Andrews's Rolls, named for the friend who taught her to make them, and set it to rise. Green beans with a fat slice of salt pork simmered at the back of the stove. My friend Jean Meyers, another Southerner, cites these archetypal beans as her measure of changing tastes in food. "My grandmother," Jean told me, "started her green beans for supper first thing in the morning, boiling them all day with lots of salt and gobs of bacon fat for seasoning. I thought they were wonderful (and secretly, still do), but now (how dull!) I eat my green beans steamed very lightly with no salt, no bacon fat, just a little bit of margarine."

How Mother timed the Sunday meal so perfectly on her ancient electric stove I don't know, but after three hours of the Baptist religion we were greeted at the front door by the incense of food at the ready. For this once-a-week extravaganza, Mother added potatoes cooked in the pan juices, a squash casserole topped with cracker crumbs, homemade pickles. For dessert there was white cake with chocolate icing or fresh coconut cake, with ice cream or homegrown peaches from the freezer.

Another special Sunday dinner was chicken and corn bread dressing — dressing, not stuffing — rich with eggs, butter, and broth, fragrant with onion, baked in its own pan. The chicken, which Mother preferred to turkey — "a dry, useless bird, too big to be good," she would declare — was definitely the side dish in this menu. Other complements to that gorgeous pan of dressing included giblet gravy with hard-boiled eggs, cranberry relish, and candied sweet potatoes, with a cup of sugar and a stick of butter to every three potatoes.

But it was at supper every night that my mother really strutted her stuff in the kitchen. She could always pull a vegetable meal from the freezer, but on rainy winter nights there might be fried catfish instead, with hush puppies and cole slaw, or brains and eggs, or piles of fried oysters, with nothing in the world besides but crackers, ketchup, hot coffee, and lemon meringue pie for dessert. In early spring we ate greens "for strengthening," Mother's own special mix of turnip and mustard greens, sometimes with a few heavy collard leaves or shoots of poke salad thrown in, the whole "mess of greens" cooked to death with salt pork and served with their "pot likker," accompanied by homemade pepper sauce, black-eyed peas, and flat cakes of corn bread to soak up all the juices. Fried apple pies, with melted butter poured over them, followed.

Summers were best, when she would serve a big platter of fried chicken, with all the vegetables there ever were alongside it: delicate pale green butter beans, fried corn golden and sweet, crowder peas, cucumbers in ice water and vinegar, small crunchy circles of fried okra, fat red tomato slices, tiny green onions, mashed potatoes, thin, delicate, hot, moist, crisp corn sticks, and tall, beaded glasses of iced tea. Then came chocolate pie, which we always insisted we couldn't possibly eat, but somehow always did.

Mother didn't have much patience with a picky eater, and she defined as picky anyone who couldn't stay abreast of the pack through dessert. My son, Winton, who has never been a picky eater, spent his ninth summer with his grandparents and came back home twenty pounds heavier and wearing Huskies. Mother had cooked hash browns every morning to go with his sausage and biscuit. His mid-morning snack was peanut butter cookies and a big glass of milk. In his honor, she had created a special cake, ever after referred to in the family as Winky's Cake, which leaned heavily on butter, coconut, pecans, and crushed pineapple.

I heard the whole ghastly story from my brother at the end of the summer, when I drove from Texas to Mississippi to pick Winton up. "That kid can eat us under the table," my brother said, shaking his head. "It's downright inspiring. Compared with him, we're pikers." Faced with the prospect of reoutfitting my now pudgy child, I shamed Mother and scolded Winton. They were both quietly defiant. "Oh, don't make such a fuss," Mother said airily. She clearly believed she had only been doing her grandmotherly duty. Winton just smiled; I could see that he thought his summer food fest was worth any consequences, including going into the fifth grade as a little fat kid.

My father ate two strips of bacon and a fried egg every morning of his life. In his eighties, he had double bypass surgery, spent several weeks in the hospital, then came home and continued his usual breakfast. "His doctor told me to give him what he wants," my mother said defensively when I looked at her in horror. "And breakfast is his favorite meal."

This flagrant indulgence and generosity extended beyond the food to the conversation at my mother's table and to what restaurant critics like to call "ambience." Friends have told me they learned adult discussion at their parental board; they were expected to contribute a "current event" to dinner table conversation, to defend a position rationally and calmly, to talk of issues and to put personalities aside. None of these Yankee skills would have cut the mustard in our house. Northerners may talk about things, but Southerners talk about people. From an early age, my brothers and I knew what the supper table was for: it was the place to tell stories.

Both my parents loved to talk, to tell us what they knew about our Southern past and our family, and when we sat around the table, the stories circulated as fast as the corn bread. It could be frustrating for a child with something to relate; early on, I had to learn to talk well, or if not well, loudly. "Lose your breath and lose your place," my mother would say when I stumbled telling a tale and was interrupted by one of my father's set pieces. Of necessity, I also learned to listen. Over the years I came to know Daddy's yarns so well that I could, and sometimes did, recite them with him, which I suppose was good practice for telling my own stories.

Daddy's supper table specialty was politicians. "Back home in Pittsboro, Old Joe Sheffield was running for sheriff. 'Well,' he said at a stump meeting, 'I been in some sixty-odd states' " — here Daddy paused for us to catch the joke as, sotto voce, I joined in — " 'and slept with might near every man, woman, and child in Calhoun County.' "

Sometimes Daddy enlivened our meals with stories about growing up on Granddaddy Reid's farm with his eight brothers and sisters and three orphan cousins Grandmother Reid raised with her own brood. His brother, my uncle Tom Earl, had a mule that wouldn't ever leave the field after plowing. The mule would just sulk and stand, so Uncle Tom would have to get in front of him and make faces at the mule till the mule got mad enough to chase him a little way. Then Tom would make another face, then run another little way, all the way back to the barn.

Cousin Rasberry — "Raz" — was justifiably enraged at this dilatory beast. "You son of a bitch," he yelled at the mule. Whereupon Uncle Tom, Daddy said, "beat the hell out of Raz for calling his mule a son of a bitch. And the mule just stood there laughing."

I laughed too. I loved to think of my serious, grown-up uncle making faces at a mule. But when I was little I found this story puzzling. Could mules really laugh? And what was so funny? Wasn't Uncle Tom doing the right thing in defending his mule? Only in later years did I realize that the theme of much of Daddy's table talk was human folly and absurdity. It was my father's deep cynicism, a cynicism that extended even to the very Southern notion of honor, that planted the smile on that mule's face.

Mother's stories were different, gentler, more domestic. From her we heard about the big Fourth of July picnics she went to as a girl, with fried chicken and tubs of pink lemonade, with egg races and watermelon seed spitting contests. She told us about the Saturday night square dances at their house on the farm, with her uncle fiddling and her father calling the sets:

Ida Red, Ida Red, I'm a big fool about Ida Red.
Ida Red, Ida Green, prettiest little gal I ever seen.

"And Ken and I would dance just like the grownups," Mother would remember. "When we got hot and tired, we'd eat homemade ice cream so cold we'd have to wrap up in quilts to finish it."

If my family no longer danced now that Daddy had become a deacon in the Baptist church and Mother one of the pillars of the Sunday school and the Women's Missionary Union, there was one pleasure left that Baptists strongly supported: food. I don't think I ever met a Baptist preacher who wasn't corpulent, fed to obesity by his devout flock. Many of Mother's stories had to do with food and how to behave about food.

Hospitality was good; you never let anyone go away hungry. Tramps were fed in the kitchen or brought to the table. "My mama and daddy were hospitable people," Mother would begin. "Always had extra people at the table." The laws of hospitality imposed good behavior on giver and receiver, and courtly table manners were important. How not to be was like "the poor old man who wanted to thank Mama nicely. He said, 'Miss Mitt, that supper was mighty fine, what there was of it.' Then he realized that didn't sound just right, and he said, 'I mean, there was God's plenty of it, such as it was.'" From such stories my brothers and I learned mealtime rules: to bow our heads for the blessing, to say please and thank you, to keep the food moving, to wait to eat until everyone was served, to thank the cook, and to ask to be excused.

Good manners were important in storytelling too. You were supposed to play yourself down; the joke was always supposed to be on the teller. We joked about our shiftlessness, our ignorance, the meagerness of our talents. Thus Mother told about chopping cotton with her brothers for the sharecropper on her father's farm. "We didn't know that meant chopping out the *weeds* in the cotton." After watching them for a while, her employer was moved to plead with her mother, "Ole Miss, I done offered them children fifty cents to chop cotton, but I'll give you two dollars if you'll get them to stop."

This habit of self-deprecation was a bedrock attitude in my

family. If something good happened to us, we claimed to be "just lucky." But good luck made us uneasy, too. We didn't trust it, and we thought if we "bragged on ourselves," our luck would fly out the window.

For Mother, a democrat to the core, selfishness and snobbishness were cardinal sins. Moral lessons were pointed out in the stories of my great-grandmother. To my mother, her grandmother Harlan was hubristic — "show-offy," Mother would have said — in every way, even to her name: "Eleanor Elmira Judith Ann Gregory when she married my granddaddy Harlan, and there wasn't anything about her family that wasn't the best, in her estimation. She grew up on a big place near Charleston, South Carolina, and her father had a good many slaves. She had her own personal little black maid, who just laced her corset, I guess, and she never let you forget it. She was a braggart and a terrible snob. My mama was orphaned when she was eight, and Grandmother didn't want my daddy to marry her because Mama was old orphan trash. That's how she talked."

Even in death Great-grandmother couldn't please Mother. "She finally died when she was a hundred and two on the hottest day in July in 1949. I remember some of them saying it looked like any-body who had lived a hundred and two years could have picked a cooler day to die on." Inconsiderate to the last, Mother implied.

If all this table talk sounds pleasurable, even idyllic, to me now, many times during my life I rebelled against it, against the inter-minable storytelling, the ancestor worship, the code of behavior. As an adolescent, I concealed my impatience poorly when my father would launch into a twice-told tale, and I made no secret of my disapproval of Mother when she told me that my ancestors had emi-grated from South Carolina to Mississippi because "Uncle George had killed a man, got scared and ran, so the whole family followed him."

"But he was a murderer," I said, genuinely horrified. "You mean the whole family pulled up roots to follow a murderer?"

"Oh, no, honey," she said, "not a murderer. He didn't mean to do it; it was just hot-blooded young men fighting, like they will. People didn't want to break up their families in those days," she added, looking at me significantly. "That was real important."

Uncle George drew me. I felt that he and I were soul mates. In my moments of severest disenchantment, I sometimes speculated that Uncle George may have killed the other fellow just so he could run, to have an excuse to get away from the family, with no idea that they would follow him. It was a story with which I amused myself: Uncle George lighting out for the territory on horseback. His jubilation to be free at last, a lone ranger, not a son, not a brother, not a cousin. His dismay when one evening just at dusk, sitting on the porch of some little old log house in the wilds of Mississippi, smoking a cigar and strumming his banjo, a jug of bourbon at his feet, he looked up, and down the road came a whole wagonload of family.

I kept my version to myself, but it was an omen of some kind. Predictably, the time came when I pulled an Uncle George. I wasn't allowed to leave the state for college — the idea was literally unthinkable — but I could have gone to Ole Miss, thirty-five miles away, and zipped back and forth. Instead I chose a school in Jackson, two hundred miles away. I made the trip home a few times a year in glamorous style, living it up with my friends in the club car of the City of New Orleans. Surrounded by attentive waiters, gleaming silver, and starched white linen, we drank something very pink and sweet called a Pink Lady, ate hot open-faced turkey sandwiches, and smoked like maniacs. I always wanted to stay on the City and go all the way to Chicago; instead I got off in Memphis, where my parents met me.

After I graduated from college, I couldn't wait to shake the whole bloody South off my feet and hightail it to Texas and eventually to points north. I never really escaped, of course, any more than Uncle George did. As long as I live, I suppose, I will carry that wagonload of family wherever I go.

Still, running was not a bad idea. It gave me, you will forgive me, some distance, and, oddly enough, a stronger appreciation for what I ran away from. I'm not the cook my mother was, or the woman either. In the South, cooking often reveals character: "She's so mean her rolls won't rise." When Cora Tull in *As I Lay Dying* makes cakes she can neither sell nor give away, Faulkner is commenting slyly on her grudging heart. My mother was steeped in this tradition. Food, family, and God were the major preoccupations of her life. Above her overworked stove hung a sign that read GOD BLESS OUR HOME, and she strove to earn that blessing by feeding her family well, physically and spiritually, at the big kitchen table. Oh, she had other gifts. She sewed beautifully; she knew the Bible backward and forward; she was a wise counselor and a faithful friend; and I have seen her enthrall a three-year-old with "Itsy Bitsy Spider" and a Sunday school class with the Book of Job. But as a cook she was inspired.

When she married in 1933, she learned to bake my father's favorites by watching Grandmother Reid in the kitchen. "Take your hand, honey," Grandmother would say, "and feel how much baking powder I've got here. Add that to your flour, then pour in buttermilk — see here — till it's creamy, but not thin, like this. Here, you stir it; get the feel." From such elementary lessons, Mother advanced naturally and instinctively. She could make a perfect piecrust in minutes. She rolled out egg noodles and tossed them on the backs of kitchen chairs to dry; dropped into bubbling chicken broth, they said affirmative things about the meaning of life. Her meringues rose sky-high, with little tender, peaky points that waved at each other in a friendly fashion. Her fried corn could have colonized the moon and her cakes brought about world peace.

• The only cookbook Mother ever owned was a Time-Life book, *The Cooking of Provincial France,* which I bought for her when she was in her fifties and which she never used. When she died, however, I found a few recipes she had clipped from magazines or written down from friends' instructions, full of Cool Whip, miniature marshmallows, and the like. I found them embarrassing. But then Mother often embarrassed me. She knew nothing about food, I thought, but just happened to be a fabulous cook — a happy accident, like playing the piano by ear or remembering the numbers on boxcars. Her thirty-year-old set of spices gathered dust; she used only salt, pepper, and occasionally cinnamon for baking. She used no liquor in her cooking or at her table; apple slices, not brandy, preserved her fruitcake, and iced tea was the drink of choice, indeed the only drink, at her table.

Also, I thought Mother was incredibly messy, every pot and pan piled in the sink and full of wet vegetable peelings, flour on the floor, and her face as often as not smudged with flour too. Once, after I had left home and married, I decided on one of their visits to cook a sophisticated supper with wine in a neat way to show her how it was done. I stuffed pork chops and browned them, carefully wiping the stove afterward, and put them on to simmer in gravy with a dash of Madeira. With them were a rice pilaf with pistachio nuts, a spinach soufflé, a cleverly dressed green salad, and a pleasant domestic red. I'd have liked to get fancier, but I wanted to be sure that she and Daddy would eat what I cooked. I forget what dessert was — something not messy and not Southern, for sure. All afternoon I toiled over this meal, cleaning up as I went, firmly determined to get my message across. Mother was never slow with a compliment. "Oh, honey," she exclaimed, as I put it on the table and poured wine all around, "it looks just wonderful. But it's taken you so long! You should have let me just throw something together for us!" I could have killed her.

I'm not alone in these mixed feelings about my mother's cooking, nor are the feelings peculiar to Southerners. "Certainly, always, anything I know about cooking is from my mother," Molly Friedrich, who grew up on Long Island, told me, "and it's been forever an intimidating experience." She describes her mother, a woman with five children, as "the first (and possibly the last) on her block to have a pasta machine and a Cuisinart." But the cook in this case is not defined by her machines. Mrs. Friedrich also "made yogurt from scratch before Dannon ever existed — some housekeeper from Albania taught her about cheesecloth — and made Finnish ryes, sourdoughs, Christmas stollen, and other breads before any of these passions became remotely fashionable."

Molly, a literary agent, is the daughter of the historian Otto Friedrich, so her own adult world and her parents' world connect. The sense of intimidation is, she says, "not at all helped by the fact that a man in publishing once lovingly described every course of a meal my mother had served ten years previously."

But now that she herself is able to put together a dinner party for twenty with aplomb, surely Molly has outgrown her My Mother, My Self terrors in the kitchen? "I go into a cold chill when my mother comes to my house for supper, though she always calls afterward to say how lovely it was. Recently her burst of enthusiasm went something like this: 'So wonderful! Of course, the ham was overcooked and the scalloped potatoes were undercooked, and the cherry pie seemed, well, a little viscous. But none of that mattered, dear! We had such a lovely time!'"

Two women can't share a kitchen, folk wisdom teaches. Not always true, but in my case it was. No, Mother never taught me to cook. Perhaps it's more accurate to say that I couldn't allow her to teach me. Eudora Welty once wrote that to learn to make her mother's spoon bread, she had to sit in the kitchen, watch, and take notes. For some reason, when the time was right for me to behave that way, I couldn't.

In the kitchen, Mother was an autocrat, I thought. Bristly and protective of my dignity and independence, I couldn't apprentice myself to her, couldn't bring myself to inquire into what her smidgen of this and pinch of that meant. So, from the time I was thirteen or so, we worked out a compromise: she did the cooking, I did the dishes. Later, on my own, I learned to cook from books. Now, when it's too late, I'm sorry.

·✕·

The Way We Ate

. . . .

D ON'T HARBOR THE ILLUSION that all was peaches and
cream at our family dinner table. For example, I remember
quite well a period — it seemed like years but was probably
only months — when, routinely, my little brother spilled his full
glass of milk. Usually we had just sat down and said the blessing.
"Well, snookums, what happened at school today?" Daddy began.
And over tumbled the glass.

Daddy jumped up, swearing, guarding his shirtfront. Mother
ran for a dishtowel. I stuck out my tongue at Sonny, and he burst
into tears. This happened about every other night, but not regularly
enough to be predictable. We all sat on the edge of our chairs until
Sonny spilled his milk and we could relax.

My parents tried everything they could think of. They coached
him — "Take the glass in both hands, now pick it up slowly, that's

right, careful." When that didn't help, they sent him away from the table. At length, they spanked him. Nothing worked. Finally a ritual developed.

"It's all right, sweetheart. I know you didn't mean to," Mother would sigh, as she moved all the dishes, mopped up the table, spooned milk out of the peas, and refilled Sonny's glass. But the meal was spoiled. Daddy muttered darkly about "damn kids," Mother kept patting at the tablecloth, big tears rolled down Sonny's cheeks as he tried to swallow, and I'm sure I sat there with an odious smirk on my face.

Family togetherness.

"What memorable experiences did you have at the table as a child?" I asked my friends and relatives, who were surprisingly eager to call up the past. In their vivid recollections, the family dinner table signified, variously, a proving ground for identity and hierarchy, the stable center of family tradition, or a place where the needs for both food and love were satisfied.

Still nursing their wounds or jesting at old scars, some of my friends recalled the family dinner table as a battlefield, with ambushes, minor skirmishes, search and destroy missions, and hints of Armageddon to come. Among those in this camp were sneaky or skimpy eaters, who tried to overthrow the enemy forces of order and control. Peyton Lewis, a playwright who grew up in Tennessee, confessed to sneaking Neapolitan ice cream from the freezer, eating the vanilla and chocolate sections, and leaving the strawberry untouched, a practice highly unsavory to her parents. Peyton's daughter Ashley credits her discriminating palate to a childhood even more finicky than her mother's, when she refused all food except Pop-Tarts, peanut butter, and SpaghettiOs. Threatened with a painful death if she didn't eat her squash, Ashley eventually developed "a highly skilled technique of feeding our dog under the table when no one was looking."

I can't believe the numbers of people I know who began as skimpy or picky eaters. Jane de Rochemont, who grew up in Philadelphia and New York, didn't want to eat at all as a child. "The only thing I really liked was milk," Jane told me. Her lack of appetite may have had something to do with the company. Until she and her siblings were over eight years old, they ate not with their parents but with a succession of mean nurses and governesses. Whenever possible, Jane fled to the welcoming region downstairs, the kitchen. Under the kindly auspices of the family cooks, first a Southern woman named Lydia, who made a fourteen-layer cake, and then Mary Fox, whom Jane adored, Jane learned to like food and "picked up what I know about cooking by osmosis."

The worst tale I heard from my friends about the way they ate as children came from Cathryn Jakobson, whom I first met in a New York writing class several years ago. Cathryn read a story to the class about a dreadful family dinner. She seemed overwrought as she read. Why, I wondered? Did she fear, as we all did, a verbal assault from our teacher? That unnatural man had told us emphatically that he disliked food, and had once made me a public example for the barest mention of crème brûlée in my story. Or could the horrific scene she described be fact, not fiction? After class, I asked her if the story was autobiographical. It was.

"My experiences at the table as a child were horrible," she said. "My mother and stepfather, who had usually had a couple of drinks by the time we hit the dining room, spent dinner picking on whoever seemed most vulnerable. That made it almost impossible for me to eat. I *still* hate formal meals and have trouble sitting at a table for a long time."

Picky eaters abound even in happier circumstances, where they develop devious childhood tricks for disposing of unwanted food. My husband, Willem, remembers keeping a soggy bite of cod in his mouth for most of an afternoon — "because I was told not to waste food, but I couldn't bear to swallow it" — until it finally slid down his throat when he forgot about it on the school playground.

Willem was not really picky, he insists. He just hated fish, a dish palatable to many children only in microwaved fish sticks. Lee Cullum was a tougher case. "I simply wanted to get away from the table having ingested as little as possible," the Dallas newswoman told me, "so I would hide food in my napkin to discard later, or on a little ledge beneath the tabletop."

One place where Lee did eat well, however, the Oak Lawn Restaurant, "changed from the Italian Restaurant during World War II, when the Italians became 'not our friends.' My parents would drape me in napkins, and I would indulge myself in spaghetti with tomato sauce and meatballs. Pure heaven."

Do you suppose parents *make* picky, skimpy eaters by some of their own military tactics? I mean, here was Lee, who could no doubt have lived, even thrived, on just spaghetti and meatballs. Here was Ashley, cheerfully scarfing up Pop-Tarts (fruit and carbohydrates), peanut butter (protein and fat), and SpaghettiOs (most of the above, plus tomato, which is a vegetable, sort of). A big glass of milk and you've covered the fifties food groups. And the thought of a mouthful of soggy cod makes even unpicky me gag. So why not leave these children alone to eat what they would until they change their stripes or leave home, whichever comes first?

In the ongoing battle of the dinner table, fifties parents also mistakenly batted their poor kids over the head with something called the Clean Plate Club. I can understand the frustration of dealing with a child who wants only spaghetti, but I am willing to bet that eventually even the most recalcitrant will yield a little. My cousin Reid Smith recalled a time when, as a boy of twelve, he was at dinner at a relative's house with five or six cousins and sisters, and the children began a litany of the foods they hated.

"I hate eggplant," Reid stated emphatically. "I could never eat eggplant in any way, shape, or form." As he ate, Reid fiercely continued to hold forth on the nastiness of eggplant, while one by one around the table the other children began to giggle. The empty platter in front of Reid, before he had gobbled up the contents and polished the dish to a gleam, had held eggplant. "I thought I was eating fried green tomatoes," he told me. "The truth of the matter was that I had never tasted an eggplant until that day because the name sounded so awful. *Eggplant* — phooey!" If the eggplant had been urged on Reid and he had been forced to clean that platter, he might hate eggplant to the present day.

Often the enforced membership in the Clean Plate Club is hereditary, or so Marguerite Victor, who grew up in California, sees it. Marguerite's memories of the family dinner table are not great. Martial law prevailed; Marguerite had to keep quiet so that the family could listen to Walter Winchell. After that, what Marguerite remembers most vividly is that her father made her eat everything on her plate because "when he was a child, he was forced to eat everything on *his* plate. Even as an adult, he made himself do the same thing."

Not until ten-year-old Marguerite got away from home to a Girl Scout camp in the mountains did she develop an appetite and begin to love food. She ran around all day, slept outside under the stars and the fir trees, and had no one around at meals to shut her up or force her to finish food she loathed. Left alone to eat or not, she began to appreciate the pleasures of the table. "I think having an appetite, and being able to satisfy it, is one of the greatest joys of life."

In some families, the dinner table became the scene of subtle power struggles between the parents themselves, like those at the Matthews home in Oxford, Mississippi. "I was rinsing off a bunch of raspberries the other day," Charles Matthews said, "when it occurred to me that as a kid I always wanted two things: a machine that would play movies and enough raspberries. Now I've got both."

In Palo Alto, where Charles lives now, fresh raspberries are easy to come by. In the fifties in Mississippi, as far as I know they didn't exist, certainly not for most people. Charles first tasted them in their frozen form when frozen foods became popular not long after World War II. He was seven or eight, and his mother made a raspberry parfait pie from a recipe "that probably came on a box of Jell-O — or else she clipped it out of *McCall's*."

That pie was the overt flag Charles's mother raised in an ongoing, largely covert, conflict with her husband. Charles's father loved country eating, like collard greens cooked with fatback. Mrs. Matthews, whom her son described as "one of those Southern women who hated being thought 'country,'" liked to experiment with recipes from the women's magazines, "lots of horrid stuff with Jell-O and canned fruit cocktail."

"Horrid stuff" is the grown-up Charles talking, the magazine editor with a Harvard doctorate. The child Charles felt differently. A budding aesthete, he sided with his mother, "probably oedipally," he told me. "I adored raspberry parfait pie. That pie may be my earliest food memory."

In sharp contrast to the children of battling families, other friends spoke with amusement or respect, or both, of the dependable sameness of family meals; for them, the dining room was the center of family tradition, with tribal rituals children were expected to learn and maintain. Eating alone at his little red table, Harold Peterson enjoyed his solitary meals and the steady round of pork chops, Campbell's soup, and Franco-American spaghetti cooked by his nanny. But his family had standards, and eventually he had to be "dragged screaming into an orderly middle-class world."

Very soon, Hal, now a librarian in Minneapolis, was captivated by the pleasures of this new realm. First of all, the food was better. Plentiful milk, eggs, and butter were delivered fresh to the door, meat was sent to the house by an obliging butcher, and chickens came from local farmers. Even more than he liked the food, however, Hal liked the grown-up dinner table manners and conversation, especially those of his rather grand aunt in Chicago. Hal has always enjoyed ceremony; his friends joke that he would like to revisit Brideshead and *live* there. The Chicago aunt would permit him to light candles even at breakfast and let him cook anything he wanted at any time of day.

Hal loved ritual; so do many children. Family rituals offer children a sense of stability and security, anchors in the flux of experience. "If you grow up in a family with strong rituals, you're more likely to be resilient as an adult," Dr. Steven J. Wolin, a psychiatrist who has done research on the subject, told the *New York Times.* And the bellwether of family ritual is the family dinner, sacred to families of an earlier time as it is not to many families of the nineties.

But there's dinner, and there's Dinner. The meaning of the word is by no means universal across the country. To me, growing up in Mississippi, dinner was a big meal in the middle of the day, usually on Sunday after church. On the other hand, until he went away to college, Willard Spiegelman, the son of a Philadelphia doctor, had never heard of "this tradition called Sunday dinner." Willard's parents *had* warned him, as he set out for higher education, that, as he puts it, "Jews eat and Goys drink." But they had neglected to prepare him for Sunday dinner, which, in the school cafeteria, involved "the proverbial brown mystery meat, or turkey, plus mashed potatoes, and other elaborate, heavy fixings, which one was supposed to eat upon arising at one P.M."

For Willard, this uncouth meal underscored a major difference between Wasps and Jews, a difference heightened when sometime later he was asked to partake of a Sunday evening meal at the table of one of his professors. "Informal, a Sunday at-home," the invitation went. His host was an eminent classicist, Skull and Bones, the brother of a Supreme Court justice; his hostess was the daughter of an Irish peer; the other guests, male and female, were blond, blue-eyed, "Leslie Howardish." In spite of his parents' warning, Willard expected a good feed.

After the preliminary glasses of champagne and something spread on crackers, the company proceeded to the dining room, which was arrayed with all the right crystal, china, and silver. Willard honed his taste buds. Out came the first course, a very rich and delicious soup, an oyster stew, in fact. Soup, nevertheless.

Willard exercised his powers of discipline. "I went against the grain and refused seconds, feeling certain that a saddle of something was coming up next." Instead, what came up next was a green salad, then cheese, then something sweet. "Among the Wasps, such a meal," Willard said ruefully, "was the appropriate Sunday evening supper. In true Wasp fashion, they'd already had their roast at Sunday dinner, after church."

For many traditional families, the evening meal came right out of "One Man's Family" and "Leave It to Beaver." Pleasing the man of the house was the cardinal rule in Robinsdale, a suburb of Minneapolis, when Stephanie Helgesen was a child. "Oh, my husband will *never* eat casseroles!" Stephanie remembers hearing a neighbor say, with all the other women murmuring agreement. Stephanie "took it for granted that men never ate casseroles. What men ate is what families ate."

What the Helgesen family ate, six nights out of seven, was the same: meat, potatoes, salad, and milk. The meat was beef roast, pork roast or chops, or chicken. When Mr. Helgesen had steak, the rest of the family ate "hamburger steak." Real or ersatz, all of the steaks were doused with A.1. sauce. "We were not into derivations. Steak sauce *was* A.1. sauce; it was generic."

The Helgesen children found eating at someone else's table a gamble. They didn't like visiting friends for dinner because they might be served forth a heresy, something they thought of as "funny food," like lasagna or tuna fish casserole, or some strange vegetable. "Potatoes were our vegetable, any way my mother cooked them," Stephanie told me. The Helgesens ate iceberg lettuce and tomato salad, and drank milk by the gallon; cream, butter, and eggs were "good for you."

On the other hand, David Harris, a musician who also grew up in the Midwest, never indulged as a child in butter or cream, again in order to please Father. David's father was involved in some of the original research on cholesterol, so family members were allowed only one egg a week. In other respects, however, the Harris family ate much like the Helgesens. Six or seven dishes were rotated as dinner entrées: pot roast, roast beef, stewed chicken, meat loaf, hamburgers, and occasionally spaghetti.

Was dessert as predictable as the rest of dinner, I wanted to know? "What dessert?" Stephanie retorted. The Helgesens never ate dessert, though just before bed they might each have a bowl of ice cream, "at least a pint apiece." The little Harrises were pensioned off after dinner with fruit and one pathetic cookie. In Mississippi, with our legendary Southern sweet tooth, we often considered everything else at the meal a preamble to that raspberry parfait pie. Lapping up my favorite banana pudding, I would have felt awfully sorry for those Yankee kids.

We were generally allowed a lot of leeway in the way we ate at my house. Bedtime snacks, for example. I was always the last person in the kitchen every night. Often after my parents and brothers had gone to sleep, I would gather up whatever was left of dessert to eat as I read in the comfort of bed, which is still in my mind the best place to eat. In Heaven, I'm sure the dining room will also be the bedroom. Tiptoeing through the quiet house, I would carry the pie plate with the last piece of pie to my lair. When two pieces were left, I might have pie for breakfast. There is no better breakfast than chocolate meringue pie and a tall glass of milk.

If a Southern mother would have grieved for the poor little Helgesens, who never got homemade pie, an Italian mother from Brooklyn would have marveled at their pasta. On Friday nights, which were meatless for the Catholic Helgesens, Mrs. Helgesen made spaghetti by a simple but extraordinary method. To the cooked noodles, she added a melting mountain of butter. Then, in a separate saucepan, she heated a can of tomato juice until it thickened slightly. Finally she poured the tomato juice over the noodles. "We *loved* it," said Stephanie. "Everybody loved my mother's spaghetti — cousins, neighbor children. My aunt tried for years to duplicate it."

Middle-American eating habits, especially the ritual of family dinner, went through a big change in the fifties, when frozen food became readily available. Charles Matthews's frozen raspberries were the tip of the iceberg; before long there were whole dinners, with meat and vegetables in the tidy little compartments of foil trays. These TV dinners, with every individual dinner heated in the oven and served on TV trays in front of the TV set, were the essence of modernity. Many Americans were enchanted with the new freedom.

Mother never went in for ready-made frozen dinners. However, she was happy to relinquish the drudgery of canning, of hot summer mornings in her steam bath of a kitchen, with a big pot of peas simmering and the sterilizer full of jars clanking in boiling water. She and Daddy bought a big chest of a freezer, which she stuffed with neat packages of homemade soup, garden produce, sugared fresh peaches and berries, and from our own trees pecans and black walnuts, which Daddy laboriously picked out during long winter nights. I still remember, on a dark February night, virtually standing on my head to dig out the last bag of tiny okra rounds or corn on the cob, coming up frostbitten and triumphant with my summer miracle.

In many households, the instant frozen meals led to experimentation with other innovations, such as instant mashed potatoes. Aficionados of exotic gourmet food sometimes forget the very real appeal bland and predictable tastes hold for millions of people, especially children. Someone has advanced the reasonable theory that the jaded taste buds of adults can tolerate stronger flavors than the tiny virginal taste buds of children. "I know food was fairly tasteless when I was a child," Stephanie told me, "but we liked things like soft white sandwich bread."

A touch of white bread makes the whole world kin, I guess. Sonny and I smeared oleo onto slices of bread so soft they crushed with the weight of the knife. We rolled up and ate dozens of little white bread pellets from the soft center of half a loaf. When I read *Heidi,* the story of a Swiss mountain girl who sneaks white bread from a middle-class table as a treat for her peasant grandfather, I felt a spasm of identification with her. We ate sliced tomato and mayonnaise on soft white bread. Canned pineapple slices and mayonnaise on soft white bread. Mashed banana and peanut butter on soft white bread. Our bread of choice was Wonder, and it was Wonderful.

White bread and certainly white bread tastes are still going strong in the heartland today. A year or so ago, Stephanie thought it would be a lark to serve the classic "white bread" salad, Waldorf, with, you will remember, apples, walnuts, celery, and mayonnaise, at a dinner party. "I meant to be funny," she told me ruefully, "but Waldorf salad turned out to be a great success." Maybe Lin Yutang was right: What is patriotism but the love of the good things we ate in our childhood?

My father had white bread tastes, and like other fifties mothers my mother always considered the man of the house first when she planned a meal. But Mother was willing to bend, to lend an ear to cajolery. Daddy didn't like garlic, so officially Mother never cooked with garlic. But when I discovered I adored garlic, Mother could be persuaded to sprinkle garlic powder in mashed potatoes or pimiento cheese just for me.

Marcia Smith, a Dallas teacher, had a stepfather who introduced strange dishes to the family table. But Marcia's mother, a Southerner, like my mother had the breed's characteristic quality of — call it what you will. Some say laxity, but I call it diplomacy. For the stepfather, a Yankee, Mrs. Smith gamely cooked Italian food, corned beef and cabbage for St. Patrick's Day, even a duck instead of turkey one Thanksgiving. But the children were not expected to change their tastes, and there was something to appeal to everyone. "Certain favorite dishes were associated with all the members of my family," Marcia told me. "When I was old enough to notice, I understood how menus were tailored and rotated to please each of us." Marcia was never forced to eat anything she didn't like. She had a child's distrust of vegetables, and so was grown and married before she learned that black-eyed peas, pinto beans, fried okra, and stewed potatoes weren't what most people meant by vegetables.

Eating eccentricities abounded in this laissez-faire environment. One of Marcia's grandmothers poured orange juice on her corn flakes. The other grandmother Marcia described as having "two eating styles: the Martyr and the Invalid." As the Martyr, she took the back, the neck, or the wing of the chicken, the scrappy, fatty pieces of roast, the heel of the bread. As the Invalid, she refused onions, tomatoes, and other foods that "hurt her stomach." Perhaps this grandmother's strangest penchant was her coffee substitute: baking cocoa mixed with sugar and hot water, so strong that the spoon would stand up in it.

In 1980, when Marcia married Charlie Smith (economically keeping her same last name), she treated her newly acquired step-children as she had been treated, like her mother equating food with love. The nine-year-old twins would show up on weekends, and "they had to be fed three times a day," Marcia said. "I didn't know how modern moms use microwaves and McDonald's; I tried to do it the way my mom did. I made their favorites."

So Marcia made, over and over, blueberry muffins for breakfast and a meal of fried pork chops, macaroni and cheese, and applesauce for lunch and dinner because that's what the kids liked. She kept the refrigerator full of snacks, and cooked a big pot roast on Sundays. They seemed indifferent at the time, but now in their early twenties they feel free to drop by for Marcia's soup and banana bread or to call and schedule a "pot roast night."

Food and love. Does it work? Take Sonny's milk spilling. What toppled that glass of milk over, night after night? Was it a bid for attention? A mutiny? A way *not* to eat? With that nightly cascade of cold white liquid, Sonny achieved all these goals. But mostly he tested and proved my parents' love. With remarkable restraint, Mother and Daddy did not murder him, and it is a fact that at sixteen he no longer spilled his milk.

But we had our more pleasant rituals too. Beyond my mother's table, which was the center of our family feeling, stretched the even wider expanse of my grandmother's wide oak table with all the leaves in. At that table, from the turn of the century until the late fifties, when Grandmother Reid had died and the family home been abandoned, congregated all the nine Reid children, their spouses, and umpteen grandchildren and great-grandchildren.

Close my eyes and I can still see the house where both my father and I were born. A white antebellum farmhouse, country comfortable, it sat all by itself on top of a red clay hill that rose steeply half a mile from the county road. In summer the hill was covered with honeysuckle, wild grapes, rambling roses, and huge shady oak trees. In winter the hill was almost bare, and the long driveway at the side had deep mud gullies and gulches. When I was a child, we sometimes had to leave our car in the ditch and walk the last curve on foot, summoning my five uncles to lay down boards and gunnysacks and help pull us out.

But in my mind the house always stands in summer brightness, surrounded by daylilies and bridal wreath, by zinnias, jonquils, and irises in season, with a tall flight of steps leading to the wide veranda and the welcoming front door. A favorite activity for my cousins, to me the scariest thing in the world, took place on Sunday afternoons after the watermelon cutting. One uncle would stand on the veranda, way, way, way up off the ground, and another uncle would stand way below in the yard, and the first would throw the willing children, one by one, high in the air, screaming with delight, down to the arms of the uncle below, while the next child clamored, "Me too, me too!" hanging on the pants legs of the uncle above, and I watched, wide-eyed, safely behind the screen door into the library.

My own favorite activity, then as now, was dinner, especially Granddaddy's birthday dinner. The Reids were kin to everybody in Calhoun County, and when my "little granddaddy," Mr. Willie Joe, had his birthday dinner every year on the middle Sunday in August, people came to Pittsboro from as far away as Banner and Sarepta, bringing food to help him celebrate. Granddaddy lived to be ninety-four, but his birthday celebrations continued for a decade after his death.

Reid Smith, who as the oldest cousin attended more of them than I did, remembers Granddaddy's birthdays well. "The food was served outside under a big oak tree on a table maybe twenty feet long. The table would be loaded with fried chicken, chicken pie, chicken and dumplings, ham, fish, pork chops — you name it, and it was there. And vegetables enough for a cafeteria. The desserts! Pecan pies, apple pies, peach cobblers, angel food cake, chocolate cake. I still see all our uncles standing, talking, telling the tallest yarns you can imagine. Now that is what I call festive!"

Me too.

·✗·

Kooking in
the Kamera Kitchen

. . . .

I T BEGAN WITH CURRY," Nora Ephron wrote in 1968, "it"
being America's plunge into food snobbery. "In the '50s, suddenly, no one quite knew why or how, everyone began to serve
curry. Dinner parties in fashionable homes featured curried lobster.
Dinner parties in middle-income homes featured curried chicken.
Dinner parties in frozen food compartments featured curried rice."

Wherefore all the curry, Nora? Would you believe Betty Crocker?
Just look, here it is, at the dawn of the decade, in my 1950 edition
of *Betty Crocker's Picture Cook Book:* beef curry, chicken curry, shrimp
curry, lamb curry, veal curry, and, yes, curried rice, all squeezed
into two society-spicing pages.

The *Picture Cook Book* even suggests social distinctions. Curried
shrimp is "especially elegant in a ring of Green Rice" colored with

spinach and parsley — clearly a dish for the haut monde. Upper-middles must make do with "a glamorous buffet" of chicken curry, surrounded by "little dishes of relishes: sieved hard-cooked eggs, India relish, chopped salted peanuts, chutney, pickled onions, grated fresh coconut, crumbled crisp bacon, sautéed bananas," accompanied by "fluffy rice" whitened with lemon juice. And for the plebs who preferred creamed chicken or ham like Mom used to make, there was the only slightly snobbish "highlight" of curried rice.

There's a why and how for you. In the beginning was not curry. In the beginning was Betty Crocker.

Professional foodies today feel sorry for you when you admit a debt to Betty Crocker. Considered the Queen of Square, she merits some attention in Jane and Michael Stern's *Square Meals,* but their *American Gourmet,* which deals with "classic recipes" and "swank company food" of the fifties and sixties, never once mentions Betty Crocker. Even by the Sterns' lighthearted standards, even in those early, innocent days, gourmet Betty Crocker was not. With all her rice rings and relishes and curry, poor aspiring Betty never made it into the ranks of, as the Sterns put it, "those who fancied themselves a cut above middlebrow America" in culinary matters.

To this day the gourmet door remains firmly closed in Betty's face. On October 1, 1991, the seventh edition of *Betty Crocker's Cookbook* was published, forty years and twenty-six million copies after the first one. A couple of days later, I called Nach Waxman at Kitchen Arts and Letters, the only bookshop in New York City just for cookbooks. "Have you received the new *Betty Crocker?*" I asked.

"Oh, is it out?" asked this most knowledgeable of cookbook mavens. "I suppose I'll get a few copies, but I don't know exactly when. You see," he went on, in the indulgent tone we use for three-year-olds, "most of my customers want the latest Ethiopian or Baltic cookbook. Could I interest you in something else?"

"I'm just an ordinary cook," I babbled, lifting a line from Professor Higgins, "an ordinary cook. I learned to cook from *Betty Crocker.*"

He was tactfully silent.

Please, Mr. Waxman, let me explain. There are twenty-six million stories in Betty Crocker's Kamera Kitchen, and this will be one of them.

After leaving Mother's Mississippi table, I spent four years at a dining room table at Belhaven, the small Presbyterian college for women I mentioned earlier. There, scraggly schoolgirls compelled to be ladies by the watchful eyes of teachers at head and foot, we sat in our assigned places, four on a side, while three times a day bountiful and delicious meals much like Mother's miraculously appeared before us. I particularly remember the fried chicken, perhaps because our demon of a dean, Miss Purnell Wilson, a.k.a. Prunella, ate it with a knife and fork.

We girls changed tables once a month, and how we dreaded landing at Miss Wilson's table! At her table I once distinguished myself and plunged my tablemates into painful silent hysterics by eating twelve rolls at a single sitting. I vividly recall Prunella's frosty glare, but I wasn't being a smart aleck, as she thought. I just couldn't resist another, and, as the basket went around, another, and yet another, of those sweet-smelling, steamy, yeasty rolls, oozing with honey butter. Like much of the food at Belhaven, they seemed well worth any penance. But, except for the once-a-year occasions before the Christmas holidays, when the black cooks circled the dining hall and sang spirituals as we ate, I never thought about how the food got on the table.

On Sundays, because of a strict Calvinist reading of the New Testament, students in residence at Belhaven weren't allowed to spend money. Townies could. So after church we would often inveigle a town friend to take us out, handing her our share of the bill in case there were spies. All dressed up in the hat and hose which were required whenever we left campus, a group of us would take the bus up North State Street for lunch at Primo's.

Always the food fanatic, I relished these outings greatly, too greatly for my friends. Once, plagued by my excessive anticipation, they dared me to stand up and tell the busload of strangers what I was boring *them* with: what I planned to order for lunch. So I did. "Primo's fried chicken," I recited, "moister and greasier than my mother's but nearly as good; Primo's famous Italian salad; Primo's equally famous French bread with garlic; and Primo's knockout fudge cake with a scoop of ice cream on the side." My friends pretended they didn't know me, but I liked betraying the ladylike veneer I was forced to wear.

After Belhaven came what all Belhaven girls ignorantly longed for, the real world. In the late fifties I was teaching seventh-grade English in Texas for thirty-six hundred dollars a year and subsisting on cold cereal, Cheez Whiz on crackers, and a gallon jug of Mother's pickles. Forget eating out. Oh, sometimes, after not having eaten all day, I would stop at a drive-in on the way home from school and scarf down breakfast, lunch, and dinner — a hamburger with fries and a chocolate shake. But on take-home pay of two hundred and fifty dollars or so a month, with rent and a car payment to make, the hamburger seemed a mad indulgence.

I will confess. On one occasion I was a mother's nightmare, the Grinch Who Stole Lunch. A seventh-grader accidentally left his lunch behind. I found it under his desk after he trotted off to the cafeteria. Mooning and homesick over the bologna sandwich his mother had packed, the tidy bag of potato chips, the homemade brownie, I wolfed it all down. Guiltily stuffing the remains in the desk drawer atop my lesson plans, I lied to the kid when he poked his head in the door to ask about his lost lunch.

I told myself a kid could borrow lunch money from the school office, but a teacher couldn't. I told myself next time the kid would be more careful. I told myself I was hungry.

My new home, a two-room walkup behind a venetian blind factory, had a kitchen complete with stove, refrigerator, and linoleum-covered table, but to my surprise I discovered I couldn't cook. Having seen Mother toss the food on the table with such abandon, I figured cooking was as easy as pie — her pie, that is. When you were grown-up, in your own kitchen, you just went to the stove and cooked. I was wrong.

The spinach at my table was full of sand, the chicken bled at the bone and made me gag, the peas were like pebbles. Sitting alone in my own kitchen at my own table with a plate of nasty sandy spinach and nasty bloody chicken, I thought of my family sitting down to supper and I called home and cried.

Mother blamed herself. "I should have made you learn to cook," she said.

"Yes," I agreed. Of course it was her fault. What wasn't?

So, back to the market, this time to the mixes. First I tried Swanson frozen chicken potpies, a fabulous all-in-one treat; you had your meat, your vegetable, your bread, in one shiny, disposable container. I ate one every day for a month.

Then I experimented. Though I had only dimly heard of pizza, I next tried a Chef Boyardee pizza mix. Add water to the dough packet, then spread out the dough. Smear on the tomato sauce from the neat little can and sprinkle the envelope of cheese on top. Can you buy this — that lacking a cookie sheet I baked my pizza in a coffee can? I swear. Never having eaten pizza, nevertheless I had moved instantly to deep-dish. Emboldened by success, I bought two packages of Chef Boyardee spaghetti dinner and invited a friend to dine.

In the fifties, I wasn't alone in the pleasure I took in shortcuts to gracious dining. Orange juice concentrate, Minute Rice, instant potatoes, and frozen cheesecake had been around since the forties, but it was 1954 when I first tasted frozen orange juice. I still remember the miracle of that first glass, extravagantly tall and generous because it hadn't had to be squeezed. Gradually, the whole country fell in love with such convenience. By the end of the fifties, a party might begin with Lipton onion-soup dip and end with a cake made from Betty Crocker yellow cake mix, lemon Jell-O, and Wesson oil.

Harold Peterson, today an excellent cook and host, remembers that his first attempts at entertaining, like mine, involved individual packages of Chef Boyardee spaghetti, one per guest. "If I invited six people to dinner, I bought six packages." He prepared each package separately. "The real breakthrough came one evening," Hal said, "when I realized that I could *pool* the little cans of sauce and cook all the pasta from the packages together in one big pot."

Tiring at length of Chef Boyardee, I grew bolder and asked for recipes. Why I didn't buy a cookbook I can only speculate — I suppose because I'd never seen anyone cook from a book. Mrs. Howe, an older, motherly teacher, told me how to roast a roast. From a carpool friend came instructions for soup made with hamburger meat, onions, and canned beans and tomatoes. Burt Schorr, a *Houston Press* reporter who lived in his own tiny pit below my walkup and complained that I sounded like a herd of water buffalo walking on his head, demonstrated his beef heart stew. Then Mrs. Howe bought the second edition of *Betty Crocker's Picture Cook Book.* She passed her 1950 edition on to me, and Betty Crocker took charge of my kitchen.

Who was this welcome interloper, anyway? In 1921, Betty Crocker was conceived by Sam Gale, the advertising manager for the company that would become General Mills; she was named

Crocker for a company director, Betty because it had the right, comfortable sound. Initially, her sole purpose in life was to answer questions by mail about baking with Gold Medal flour.

In 1924, Betty began to talk, as the featured expert on "The Betty Crocker Cooking School of the Air" on WCCO in Minneapolis. Within a year the cooking school became a network program successfully launched on radio stations across the country, from New York to Los Angeles. Over the next thirty years, Betty Crocker enrolled over one million listeners in her school and received an average of four thousand letters a day from her radio audience.

By 1936, Betty had a face. Neysa McMein, a New York artist, was commissioned to do a portrait that blended the features of several General Mills employees into a motherly image, which remained Betty's official likeness for nearly twenty years. Betty wore a red dress with a white fichu. Her warm brown hair was lightly touched with gray. Her expression, slightly severe, looked to the writer Jane Simon as if she'd caught a child with his hand in the cookie jar.

But her mouth was the cupid's bow of beauties of the time, and her blue eyes were kind. Across America, women were looking to Betty Crocker as a model of good sense in personal as well as culinary matters. Nine out of ten housewives surveyed could identify her. Women sent her Christmas presents, and men were actually falling in love and proposing marriage. "Dear Miss Crocker," one proposal ran, "You are my ideal woman. I can tell by your eyes that you are warm-hearted, feminine and pleasant to be with. Your voice, which I've heard many times on the radio, makes my heart beat with happiness. It's my dream that we might meet, and if you are willing, engage in courtship." As an advertising ploy, Betty Crocker was successful beyond her creator's wildest dreams.

General Mills found itself in the position of Dr. Frankenstein;

it had made a benevolent monster which had taken on a life of its own. Betty Crocker was fast becoming a powerful symbol of American femininity, and the company was delighted but alarmed. What had it wrought? If one of the fictional Betty's admirers, disappointed in love, should hurl himself off a bridge, was General Mills responsible?

A crisis of conscience followed, which erupted in 1938 in a sharp internal conflict at General Mills between the advertising department and the legal department. The advertising department took the position that "the effective use of BETTY CROCKER in advertising required personalizing BETTY CROCKER as a woman." To limit this use "would largely destroy the effectiveness," they declared recklessly. Send Betty out, full speed ahead, and the devil take the hindmost.

The legal department worried that the Federal Trade Commission could raise holy hell for "deceptive acts and practices and false advertisements." They contended that the name BETTY CROCKER could only be used honestly (and safely) to personify willing members of the General Mills Home Economics Staff, Betty's division of the company.

O innocent age! In this day of composite portraits and fabricated testimonials, the brouhaha seems like a tempest in a teapot, or musings in a muffin pan. But to General Mills, the issue was a serious one. The contretemps was finally settled, in favor of advertising, by executive fiat. Over the next ten years, however, "a complete policy statement concerning Betty Crocker herself and methods of portrayal" was carefully developed by the company.

The core of the policy was the "singular sympathetic personality" of Betty Crocker, of what we might call Betty's heart. Most essentially, Betty was to overflow with warmth and human kindness. Over the years, General Mills has kept a careful measure of her emotional temperature, particularly through the holiday gifts Betty receives. When the number of presents goes down, Betty's warmth and humanity are revved up.

Like any model parent, General Mills has laid down firm and consistent guidelines for Betty Crocker's behavior. First, Betty must be unselfish. To use the company language, Betty's stance is always to be "What can I do to help you?" rather than "What can you do to help me?" Not "What I think" but "What you asked."

Second, Betty must be reliable. All recipes and cooking tips must be triple-tested, no goofs allowed. In addition, Betty was created to be versatile enough to move through life with you, a reliable presence in the kitchen, not dazzling but dependable.

When you needed a romantic dinner menu, you could look to Betty for hamburger beef Stroganoff, a cinch even for beginners in the kitchen. Later, when your husband's boss came to dinner, Betty would see you safely through an evening of salmon mousse and filet mignon. And when, in due time, the children came along, it was Betty who helped you with the birthday cakes and homeroom parties and graduation celebrations. Betty was your friend.

Finally, there was Betty's carefully circumscribed attitude toward men and sex. "Where the male factor is predominant," company policy insisted, "it is vital to remember that Betty Crocker is and must always be 'A Woman's Woman,'" implying somewhat unfairly, it seems to me, that without constant vigilance Betty might run amuck.

Like Belhaven girls, who in the fifties were required to wear hats and hose on the street and who couldn't single-date in a car, Betty obviously lived by strict rules. Just looking at her pictures, you can tell she endures a dress code. Her collars are high, her sleeves and hemlines modest, her jewelry unremarkable, her hairstyle short and neat — no hairs in her soup! Give or take a curve or two, she's about as seductive as June Cleaver, and even less threatening to other women.

In behavior, Betty was required to be chaste, if not downright celibate. Though unmarried, Betty Crocker doesn't sleep around, never has, never will. "Keeping a personal relationship with women without developing a private life" for herself, she is a sort of Mother Teresa of the kitchen. "Man may come and man may go," General Mills intoned, "but Betty Crocker goes on forever."

Perhaps the secret of Betty's longevity has been her willingness to bend with the wind. During the Second World War, Betty Crocker was a supreme patriot, realizing only too well that a country, like an army, fights on its stomach. Under the auspices of the War Food Administration, she delivered a series of broadcasts with the jazzy title of "Our Nation's Rations," telling cooks how to make the best use of the country's restricted food supplies. In grocery stores across the United States, she distributed seven million copies of "Your Share," a booklet with wartime menus and recipes. Like Kilroy, when America needed her, Betty Crocker was here.

After the war, Betty busied herself with cake mixes, piecrust mix, even a new line of home appliances. But her most phenomenal postwar accomplishment came in 1950, when she published an instant best seller, *Betty Crocker's Picture Cook Book*. With total sales of three hundred thousand copies that first year, the *Picture Cook Book* was the number-one nonfiction best seller of 1950. Only the Bible and Anne Morrow Lindbergh's *Gift from the Sea* exceeded it in yearly nonfiction sales over the entire decade.

In 1956, with the second edition of the *Cook Book,* Betty Crocker burst into what today we call rap: "It's best to use ingredients the recipe recommends; / But if you have to substitute, this list solution lends." Fortunately, Betty the Rapper didn't last long. In the third edition, in 1961, Betty had reverted to her old prosaic self.

Other editions followed in 1969, 1978, and 1986. With twenty-six million copies in print even before the advent of the seventh edition in 1991, *Betty Crocker's Cookbook* — "Big Red," the nickname earned by its cheerful cover — is to date the best-selling cookbook of all time.

Success agrees with Betty Crocker. In each of the six portraits that have followed the original, she grows younger. In the most recent portrait, in 1986, the gray in her hair has, like that of many of her admirers, turned to soft highlights, and she is dressed for success in a smart suit with a white bow at her neck. But still familiar and still feminine, oh, yes, still feminine — the suit is the Betty Crocker red, her eyes the Betty Crocker blue, and she wears tiny gold hoops in her shapely ears. She looks young enough to be her own granddaughter.

Betty Crocker continues to be on hand when we need her. She responded to the influx of women into the work force with such convenience foods as Hamburger Helper, Tuna Helper, and Potato Buds. The national interest in better nutrition led her to bring out fruit snacks, such as Thunder Jets, Garfield, Shark Bites, and the Berry Bears, as well as the Nature Valley granola bars. When America wanted to lose weight, Betty was on the spot with two microwave popcorn products, Pop Secret Light and Pop Secret.

In the fall of 1992, Betty moved from bites to bytes when she put compilations of her recipes on eight floppy disks. Use these recipes and you'll never have to triple two thirds of a cup in your head again or search for a pencil and paper with floury hands. These computerized cookbooks double, triple, or quadruple recipes automatically at the stroke of a key or two. Betty hopes to teach the computer-savvy, cooking-illiterate children of the nineties with such seductions. Annual sales for Betty Crocker products gross well over a billion dollars.

And I still treasure my old *Cook Book*. When I looked through the latest edition I was pleased to discover some of my former favorites are still there. I'm glad to know Starlight Cake, Welsh rabbit, Waldorf salad, and of course the ubiquitous curry will be available to the kitchen novice at the end of the century as they were to me in the middle. And, like a daughter proud of her mother's progress, I am also pleased to find herb vinegars and nut-flavored oil. There's life in the old girl yet.

Not everyone who uses Betty gives Betty credit. In the first edition, for example, there's a hot fudge pudding cake. The recipe calls for pouring hot water over the cake batter and setting the whole thing, unstirred, in the oven. The hot water makes a sauce under the cake which can be ladled over it. It's a serendipitous mixture of pudding and cake, and very distinctive. In two recent cookbooks, which shall be nameless, I've run into the same recipe, with only minor changes and without acknowledgment of its source.

I suspect there are a good many closet Betty Crockerites, people who aren't off like dogs after the hare for the newest Ethiopian or Baltic cookbook. These people take comfort in the thought that, as Anna Quindlen once wrote, "In winter people eat stew and mashed potatoes, and in summer they eat chicken and potato salad." Some of us love dependability.

So let's go back to the fifties, when I first became acquainted with Betty. Let's open the 1950 *Picture Cook Book* and look at the pictures. Most are maple in tone and homey in texture. There's Betty Crocker's Early American Dining Room, a blur of brick, old wood, fireplace, and pewter. There's the cozy Tasting Bar, with five June Cleaver clones nibbling happily together.

And there are the kitchens, four of them. In the Kamera Kitchen, with red-checked tablecloth and ruffled curtains, photographers take pictures of Betty's cooking creations. From a "patiolike terrace," whatever that means, through a floor-to-ceiling window, visitors can spy on the cooking in the Terrace Kitchen. The Kitchen of

Tomorrow, for experimental baking and product testing, is vaguely Scandinavian, with light wood and stencils. My favorite, the Polka Dot Kitchen, has stainless steel counters, washer and dryer, and bar stools covered with, you guessed it, red and white polka-dotted cushions.

Then there are the color pictures of food, not many or grand by today's more elaborate standards, but impressive to a girl who had never, to my recollection, looked at a cookbook before. A two-page spread of cocktail canapés. Three full pages of gaily decorated cookies, darling little horses and gingerbread men. Christmas breads. Fresh coconut cake like my mother made. Two pages of pies with fancy crusts. Baked ham, its fat cut into diamonds, surrounded by daisies and Easter eggs. Roast tenderloin surrounded by whole potatoes and stuffed onions. Rib roast surrounded by — what? — fluffy potatoes in their jackets topped with *strawberries?* Plate dinners of four varieties, with meat, starchy vegetable, green vegetable, and yellow vegetable, arranged on burlap mats and surrounded by pine cones and brown leaves.

Clearly a girl had a lot to think about here.

Eatniks

S O THERE I STOOD at my single girl's stove, wearing a
pretty dress with a full skirt and a little apron to protect it.
Intent on the niceties of Betty Crocker's Six-Layer Dinner, I
was planning to make her Strawberry Delight for dessert. Then all
of a sudden in rolled Jack Kerouac, and I realized, reading *Time,*
that I was a member of the Beat Generation. At last, a club I wanted
to join. My college friends and I had been made guiltily aware that
we belonged to the Silent Generation. Beat was better, I thought;
it offered more room for imagination.

Not that I was a real beatnik. Beatniks were "beat" in a special
sense — beaten down by disillusionment stemming from the "police action" in Korea and the middle-class conformity of American
society. They were also "beat" as in "beatitude" — blessed with
some vague mystical powers. In neither sense was I, a junior high

school teacher from a small town in Mississippi, truly beat, or Beat. My only contact with Korea had been letters from my high school boyfriend while he was overseas, and the cheongsam he'd brought back for me — not real silk, it's true, but hardly a serious disillusionment. As for mysticism, any potential I had in that direction was stifled by being a Baptist; Baptists didn't go in for mysticism.

But middle-class conformity I could and immediately did abjure. I had never felt precisely middle-class anyway. I'd felt Southern, which was somehow classless, like my mother's cooking; everybody in the South, high and low, ate the same way, just as most of us, high and low, learned a similar code of behavior. But I saw clearly enough that my cooking teacher Betty Crocker was middle-class, so I bade Betty a rueful good-bye. As a member of the Beat Generation, I had an obligation to get out of her neat, safe bailiwick, with its Early American artifacts and its Polka Dot Kitchen, to get out of the kitchen and into the world. To be disillusioned, seasoned, and transformed into a real beatnik, I had an obligation to Experience Life.

Already I fancied myself a fringe bohemian. From my reading I knew a bit about bohemian life in the Village — about Maxwell Bodenheim, about "Professor Seagull" Joe Gould and his oral history, about the old Waldorf Cafeteria, about the Cedar Street Tavern, where the artists hung out, about the San Remo. Very worldly, I thought myself. Determined now to be Beat, after school and on weekends I put on the costume of the beatniks, the requisite black turtleneck and jeans, the black eyeliner, the green eye shadow, the white lipstick. In old photographs, I look like a refugee from wartime Poland.

Thumbtacking magenta and green William Steig prints to the living room walls, I beatniked my pad. "Who are all those others?" one wispy Steig character asked, hiding behind a tree. My sofa cum bed I covered with a madras spread, tossed Indian pillows on the ratty green Morris chair, and stripped the kitchen of Betty Crocker by naming the views from the two windows. One, which overlooked the tile roof of the venetian blind factory, I dubbed "Paris Roofs"; the other, a close-up of the brick wall next door, was "Zenfinity." Both were beatnik concepts.

Next I acquired the right kind of boyfriend, no "frail don smelling of water biscuits" (a favorite line from my recording of *Dylan Thomas in America*), but Bill Porterfield, a newspaper reporter for the *Houston Chronicle*. Like Burt Schorr, he lived downstairs in my building. Unlike Burt or anyone else I knew, Bill combed his curly hair in a pompadour and a ducktail and wore black muscle shirts, black pants, and no underwear. We got acquainted over a couple of Mexican babies.

At about nine o'clock one early October evening, I was slumped in the Morris chair reading *The Myth of Sisyphus* and transfixed by the absurdity of existence. "There is no sun without shadow, and it is essential to know the night. The absurd man says yes. . . ." I looked up, exalted. Someone was rapping lightly at my door — Bill, hair curlier and T-shirt blacker than usual. Two of his old friends were visiting from South Texas, and they wanted to go dancing. Would I sit with the babies while he cha-chaed with the mamas? Like the absurd man, I said yes. I carried Camus downstairs and watched Bill whirl off with two pretty young señoras. His disorderly apartment smelled like pee and perfume, a very Beat mix, I decided.

What did beatniks eat? With my food obsession, this question was never far from my mind, and it was Bill who suggested an answer. Not long after that first evening, he asked me out for Sunday dinner. "I'll pick you up early," he promised. Sunday dinner meant one thing to me. At that point, I was a Baptist beatnik, so at noon, after attending services at the big Baptist church on San Jacinto, I took off my nice printed silk dress, put on my black sweater and eyeliner, and sat down to wait. And wait. And wait. By six o'clock, when he finally arrived, I was furious. When he understood the reason, Bill laughed so hard he could barely choke out an apology. "But — Sunday dinner!" he would exclaim, and burst out again as I sat in starved and injured calm. To hell with him, I thought; to hell with Texas, to hell with Mexican food, to hell with being Beat.

Texas had a stern liquor law in those dark ages, so first we went to a private club and drank margaritas, which I believed to be some sort of Mexican fruit punch. Nervously, I gulped several glasses of the stuff in short order. By the time we got to the restaurant, the old Spanish Village on Almeda, I was feeling much better and finding Bill extremely nice. Whatever he offered me, I tried: guacamole, chiles rellenos, burritos, tacos, chilaquiles. By the time I reached the green enchiladas, I was greener than they were. I spent the remainder of the night in prayerful contemplation of the porcelain god, and two or three days passed before I fully recovered.

Bill and I became friends, then more. Dylan Thomas had only recently introduced alliteration to America, seduced virgins on college campuses, drunk himself into a stupor at the White Horse Tavern, and died the perfect romantic death. I was mad for his memory and for all things drunken, priapic, tragic, and poetic. Bill and I read Thomas's poems aloud, resolving to let "the force that through the green fuse drives the flower" drive us. I dismissed the Baptists and all their talk of Hell from my life. We taught each other. Ignoring my obvious tin ear, Bill taught me to tolerate Dave Brubeck and to look knowing about progressive jazz. In return, I taught him prosody, condescendingly assuring him he could never be a poet till he mastered the double dactyl. But we also held hands and shared populist surges listening to Cisco Houston, Woody Guthrie, and Jimmie Rodgers, the Mississippi brakeman. As the West Alabama Amalgamated Poets and Artists League, membership of two, we read Jack Kerouac's new blockbuster novel, *On the Road,* and Allen Ginsberg's long poem, *Howl,* in the little City Lights dollar paperback. From Europe, a friend brought a copy of *Naked Lunch,* William Burroughs's Beat extravaganza. Thoroughly unsavory, I thought it, but that didn't keep us from biting off big chunks of it. We were trying to prove we had the stomach to be sure enough beatniks.

What did beatniks eat? What didn't beatniks eat? Beatniks weren't fussy. They didn't mess about with Betty Crocker and Strawberry Delight. In 1991, Pat and Jim Hyatt decided to pay tribute to the Beat Generation with a literary dinner. They offered their guests a can of spaghetti or pork and beans and a spoon. The whole point about being a beatnik at table was to eat anything and everything, to go at food as you went at life, omnivorously. The ideal life made good book jacket reading, like Kerouac's — high school football star, Columbia dropout, gas station attendant, sportswriter, merchant marine, roustabout, hitchhiker, fighter, lover, novelist.

Do everything, eat anything. As Kerouac put it in *On the Road,* be prepared to devour

all the food of San Francisco. There were seafood places out there where the buns were hot, and the baskets were good enough to eat too; where the menus themselves were soft with foody esculence as though dipped in hot broths and roasted dry and good enough to eat too. Just show me the bluefish spangle on a seafood menu and I'd eat it; let me smell the drawn butter and lobster claws. There were places where they specialized in thick red roast beef *au jus,* or roast chicken basted in wine. There were places where hamburgs sizzled on grills and the coffee was only a nickel. And oh, that pan-fried chow mein flavored air that blew into my room from Chinatown, vying with the spaghetti sauces of North Beach, the soft-shell crab of Fisherman's Wharf — nay, the ribs of Fillmore turning on spits! Throw in the Market Street chili beans, redhot, and french-fried potatoes of the Embarcadero wino night, and steamed clams from Sausalito across the bay, and that's my ah-dream of San Francisco.

That was my ah-dream of life. It would be impossible to exaggerate the influence that beatnik dreams had on young, imaginative provincials of the kind Bill and I were in the fifties. Primed with the stories we'd read of Greenwich Village in the thirties, we dreamed of "a little Italian place," with red-checked tablecloths and candles in Chianti bottles, or an all-night diner where, elbows propped on Formica, heads wreathed by smoke, intellectuals planned social overthrow. We longed to go to San Francisco, or to New York, or to Paris, anywhere On the Road. Bill was offered and gleefully accepted one press junket, only to have it turn out to be the National Boy Scout Jamboree in Valley Forge, Pennsylvania. He came back "down at winged heel," as he put it, another Dylan Thomas line. So there we were, stuck in Houston, Texas, prepared to be as Beat as we could.

Bill was easily, by nature, more Beat than I. He pulled down the curtains in his one-room apartment to use for blankets when his college friends came to visit and offered them pages of the *Chronicle* as toilet paper. My refrigerator contained vestiges of Betty Crocker; his held a six-pack of Carta Blanca and something furry. When his car stopped one night, he pushed it to a Humble station, left it, and never went back. For twenty-one days that winter, a banana peel lay in the middle of his kitchen floor. I finally scraped it up.

But he was generous; he shared his Beatness. With him I learned to eat Beat, and we prepared to devour all the food of Houston. After Kerouac, we knew what beatniks ate. First of all, they ate standard American fare. Hamburgers and fries. Beans and franks. Chili. Milk shakes. Pancakes. Meat loaf and mashed potatoes. This was Kerouac's diet as he circumnavigated America in *On the Road,* and it was ours as we circumnavigated Houston. Kerouac particularly liked apple pie and ice cream, which he ate at bus stations, roadside stands, and diners all the way across the country. "I knew it was nutritious," he says, "and it was delicious, of course."

Instead of "a little Italian place in the Village," we had the Spanish Village. Bill was working the night police beat for the *Chronicle,* as all cub reporters did in those days, and the police pressroom became our equivalent of the all-night diner where intellectuals planned social overthrow.

Many evenings I went down to the police station with Bill, carrying a stack of student papers to salve my conscience. Putting revolution on hold, in the pressroom we would play gin rummy with the reporters from the *Press* and the *Post* and wait for some story to break. We drank a mixture of gin and grapefruit juice called Salty Dogs, and somebody would go out for barbecue. Hours went by while we waited for something, anything, to happen. When, at about that same time, I saw *Waiting for Godot* in an early production at the Alley Theater, it reminded me of nothing so much as those nights at the police station. Waiting for Godot, waiting for something to happen, waiting for Life to come along and let us Experience it.

While we waited, we found diversions. I remember crowding in to the late show for *And God Created Woman,* the country's first glimpse of Brigitte Bardot. The movie shocked me, and Bill made me angry, so obviously was he salivating over her. I had some satisfaction from the review in *Time,* which described BB simply as a luscious dish. Her "rear glows like a peach" in the Riviera sun, the reviewer said, and the camera seemed to follow it, "waiting for it to ripen."

Bill loved to dance. Sometimes I got out of my all-black garb and we went to Rosalie's, a beer joint on South Main, where we drank Champale and had huge arguments about my dancing. Accustomed to the dark-eyed verve of a lithe Lola or a cha-chaing Chiquita, Bill was dismayed by my Scotch-Irish reserve. "Where's your lilt, José?" he would demand as I sashayed decorously in my pink Springolators under the blue lights that turned my white dress ultraviolet. Of course, his question immediately drove my poor beleaguered lilt into hiding, like a holed fox. Dancing was not our best thing; anyway, I wasn't sure beatniks danced. At dawn, tiredness gray in our mouths, giddy and exhausted with the jokes of the night, we would go to the One's a Meal on Bissonet and eat scrambled eggs, biscuits, and sausage.

We attended a few poetry readings, but coffeehouses felt artificial in Houston, a mutant from San Francisco with humorless poets and lousy poems, no Ginsbergs or Ferlinghettis here! Jazz was better and mandatory for the Beat Generation, so on Sunday afternoons we went to a jazz club downtown for a jam session. I remember stepping out of the white hot Texas sunshine into complete blackness, standing still in the doorway until shapes gradually emerged. Often black musicians played alongside white; these groups attracted mixed audiences. At a time when Texas still had miscegenation laws, when a white man driving his black maid home could be stopped by the police, black and white together we sat at small tables in the dusky room, eating salted peanuts and drinking Cokes that we spiked with bourbon from a bottle we brought with us in a brown paper bag. We joked back and forth between tables. Bill and I applauded riffs in a "cool" fashion, while our new black friends sighed "Yeah!" and "Hit it, Raley!" For me, who had never before sat down with blacks who didn't work for my family, this mingling was as exciting as the music.

When the jam ended, we might go to Gaido's for a fried shrimp fix or, if Bill had just had a payday, to Kirby's for steak. Baked potatoes with all the fixings had just been invented. "Everything," I always said recklessly when the waiter came around with the condiments, and I watched blissfully while into my huge hot potato in its foil shell he piled two pats of butter, a large scoop of sour cream, bacon bits, chives, and grated Cheddar cheese. I far preferred the potato to the steak — still do, for that matter, though my conscience would strike me dead today if I piled on "everything."

In retrospect, though I developed a lifelong passion for Tex-Mex, I realize that none of the food we ate as budding beatniks was very good. In fact, some of it would probably appall me now. But that didn't matter. Then, we liked it. Jim Hyatt remembers that he and his wife, Pat, who were students at the University in Austin, ate Fritos pie — canned chili over Fritos, topped with cheese — directly out of the Fritos bag. At that time everything tasted wonderful: scrambled eggs at One's a Meal, a double cheeseburger at Whattaburger or Forever Amburger, rare roast beef at Morrison's cafeteria, steak, barbecue, it was all the same.

Food tasted good because we were hungry. Out in the hinterland, our whole generation was hungry, the sort of hunger Dean Moriarty has in *On the Road.* "All my New York friends were in the negative, nightmare position of putting down society and giving their tired bookish or political or psychoanalytical reasons," says the narrator, "but Dean just raced in society, eager for bread and love; he didn't care one way or the other . . . 'so long's we can eat, *son,* y'ear me? I'm *hungry,* I'm *starving,* let's *eat right now!'* — and off we'd rush to *eat,* whereof, as saith Ecclesiastes, 'It is your portion under the sun.'" I don't remember any of our fifties food being really bad.

Other people do, however. Following the Kerouac tradition, C. W. Smith was racking up jacket credits for the novels he would go on to write by working in the yard of a trucking company and eating across the street at a place called Runt and Dot's Cafe. "It was about the size of a one-bedroom frame house," Charlie told me, "which it had been quite recently, and it was furnished with chrome-rimmed dinettes with Formica tops, tubular chairs with vinyl pads whose rips had been duct-taped. There was always a cirrus cloud of tobacco smoke about three feet under the ceiling. For breakfast I would have three eggs fried hard so that their grease-soaked fringes were tattered and brown, four pieces of bacon and a couple patties of sausage, undercooked biscuits and lumpy gravy, a short stack of leathery pancakes topped off with margarine and Aunt Jemima syrup, watery grits, and bad weak coffee in a thick brown mug."

This food had a lasting effect on Charlie. Because he took such abuse at the hands of Runt and Dot, on the road he's rarely willing to pass by a dependable chain restaurant in favor of a place with "individuality" and "charm." Charlie went on, "When we take that gamble and choose a mom-and-pop café over a more pedestrian but dependable Wendy's, we're invariably sorry. The worst food offered to diners in America is made by none other than the likes of a Runt and Dot."

The trouble was, in the fifties, Wendy's didn't exist; the first Wendy's opened in 1969. Standardized food and self-service were not unknown, however. New York and Philadelphia had highly successful Automats, but somehow Automats never caught on elsewhere, even in Chicago and Boston, and they never made it to the highway. Cities also had chains of fast hamburger joints, tiny lunch counters like White Castle in the Northeast or Krystal in the South, where a miniburger cost, as I remember, about a dime. Krystal hamburgers had a distinctive flavor, largely because the onions were *cooked*. They were fun but seemed synthetic, and of course a hungry man could easily eat ten of them.

Across the South there were also chains of cafeterias — Britling's, Wyatt's, Morrison's, Luby's — which still flourish today. Southerners like cafeterias — have ever since the first one, Britling's, opened in 1918 in Birmingham. Every fall, when my mother and I bought my school clothes in Memphis, we treated ourselves to lunch at Britling's, where we ran into other girls and their mothers doing the same thing; lunch at Britling's was a back-to-school tradition. As John Mariani says in *America Eats Out,* "The cafeteria concept struck just the proper balance of formality and traditionalism, serving a solid, old-fashioned Southern cooking — hot biscuits and gravy, fried chicken, turkey with corn-bread dressing, fried catfish, mashed potatoes, numerous vegetables, and congealed salads." In short, you could eat out and hardly know you weren't at home, except for the luxurious selection. Cafeterias were usually located in town or in shopping centers, however, so they weren't easily accessible for the highway traveler.

By the end of the fifties, a time of general prosperity, with the proliferation of automobiles, low gasoline prices, and two-week family vacations, more Americans than ever before were on the road. And for millions, the need for a clean, inexpensive, dependable place to eat had been met with spectacular success: all they had to do was drive through the Golden Arches of the nearest McDonald's. In 1961, McDonald's had sold five hundred million hamburgers, but that was only the beginning. In the thirty years since, it has become one of the most profitable companies in the country's history and has carried the reality of American entrepreneurial genius to the four corners of the earth.

Before McDonald's, plenty of places to eat could be found along the highway — diners, drive-ins, ice cream parlors, barbecue stands — but their quality was uneven. Never mind gourmet. Other standards, like simple cleanliness, were not always met on the road. "When I was an impoverished young newsman," Edison Allen, who lives in Atlanta, told me, "I used to frequent a place called the Sanitary Cafe. Methought they did protest too much. Duncan Hines once remarked, 'I've run more risk eating my way across the country than in all my driving.'" It's perhaps no accident that at the conclusion of *On the Road,* Kerouac's narrator has been laid low with a severe case of dysentery.

Beat died an inglorious death, its knell tolled by Kenneth Rexroth in *The Village Voice:* "As for the Beat Generation. Let's all stop. Right now. This has turned into a Madison Avenue gimmick. When the fall book lists come out, it will be as dead as Davy Crockett caps."

As a young married couple, Bill and I hung on the cusp of Beatdom as long as we could, until it all began to look pretty silly. Lots of others were out there on the cusp with us. For example, I remember going to a happening (or is that term from another decade?) in the late summer of 1960, when I was about eight months pregnant with our daughter, Erin. Earlier in the evening, we had been to a dinner party given by *Chronicle* brass and we decided to stop off for a little while at a beatnik affair on the way home. As we walked up to the door of the apartment building, we met another couple in the full Beat regalia of black sweaters, torn jeans, moccasins, and beads. They took one look at us in coat and tie, heels and hose, looked at each other, then turned and left. About thirty minutes later, as we were leaving, they came in again — *and they were dressed as we were!* That put the Davy Crockett cap on the Beat Generation for me.

Bill and I were afraid all along we would lose our lilt. Getting married had not been an easy decision for us. Although we knew Kerouac had been married several times, as had Neal Cassady, on whom the messianic Dean Moriarty was modeled, we both equated marriage with settling down and dulling our beatnik edge. Our dilemma was summed up aptly in an agonizingly funny poem called "Marriage" by Gregory Corso, another of the Beats, which begins, "Should I get married? Should I be good?" Corso continues the argument with corny scenes from old fifties movies and pulp magazines — the terrors of telling the family, the dread of the ceremony, the final obscenity of the honeymoon. After all our efforts to be bad, the two of us felt we would be terrible sissies if we succumbed to marriage and unrelenting goodness.

But, "All the universe married but me!" Corso screams. Besides, when you got right down to it, beatnik or not, Bill and I were nice, wholesome, small-town kids. Marriage was what you did. We capitulated. On our terms, we insisted. The press reported on a party the newly wed Mike Todd and Elizabeth Taylor gave for "a few friends," twenty-five hundred, to be exact. "She's very domestic," Todd marveled, as Liz climbed on a ladder to cut the cake, which was eleven feet high and weighed nearly a ton. With this horrific example before us, Bill and I declined a big wedding and a honeymoon. Still, the gifts arrived. Sheets. Dishes. Silver. Pots and pans. What Zorba the Greek calls "the full catastrophe." And, before I knew it, I had come full circle, right back to Betty Crocker.

Saint Beard

. . . .

"A TERRINE of white chocolate ice cream and white peach sorbet," Leah Stewart says into the phone, "drizzled with bittersweet chocolate sauce." She pauses, listens. "Oh, *to-night*," she says. "Cold apple soup, followed by gingerbread mousse with caramel ice cream and dried cherry sauce. Certainly. See you then." Leah, in charge of membership relations at New York's James Beard Foundation, replaces the receiver with a rueful look. "I've been working here a year and a half," she sighs, "and I've gained twenty-five pounds." A sign behind her desk reads, IT'S LONELY AT THE TOP BUT YOU EAT BETTER.

It's the afternoon of the last day of 1991. Elsewhere in the city, people are having their nails manicured and their hair blow-dried; they're shopping for silk cummerbunds and lace camisoles; they're buying boutonnieres and Baccarat, whiskey and whistles, champagne, caviar, and confetti for the hundreds of parties, small and large, that will dismiss the year they're all tired of. Here, in the James Beard House at 167 West Twelfth Street, preparations are under way for its 168th party of the year. Tonight's gala black-tie dinner features homemade duck prosciutto, lobster-stuffed Belgian endive with caviar sauce, loin of venison, and of course the ginger-bread mousse. All very ritzy (the guest chef, Tom Parlo, is from the Ritz-Carlton), all very American, all very, very James Beard.

I first discovered James Beard in the fifties, so I place him here in my orgy through the ages. But many food historians see him as the most important figure in American cuisine from the forties until his death in 1985, and after. If the desire for good American food has taken on in some quarters the fervor of a holy crusade, James Beard is its patron saint, spontaneously canonized by the general consent of the faithful. This four-story brownstone in Greenwich Village, where Beard lived, cooked, taught cooking, and wrote many of his twenty-two cookbooks and hundreds of articles, has become a culinary shrine. Julia Child, who helped to organize the Foundation soon after Beard's death, has said, "The Beard House is like having Beethoven's house as a center for musicians, because Beard is as important to food people as Beethoven is to the music world."

Like the shrine of Bernadette, the Beard House provides a gathering place for the disciples, who flock to its classes, workshops, lectures, and exhibits, read its monthly newsletter, and joyfully eat at its ten or fifteen tables. The Foundation now has more than two thousand members, both food amateurs and professionals. To the first and only such culinary center in North America, its most respected chefs come to cook demonstration meals. Sometimes these chefs are moved to tears, Leah tells me, as they look for the first time at the map-of-the-world wallpaper the great man had installed on the walls of the kitchen, as they take their place at the center of the semicircular wooden counter where Beard stood, as they eye *his* stove, *his* refrigerator, *his* whatever. *They are cooking in James Beard's kitchen.* "It's a combination culinary Mount Vernon and Carnegie Hall," Peter Kump, the Foundation president, has explained. How do you get there? Practice, practice, practice. A cook who is standing in James Beard's kitchen wielding a spatula knows he's made it.

The kitchen is quiet early in the afternoon this December 31. Parlo and his helpers have not arrived yet. Leah Stewart has gone back to her telephone in the cluttered third-floor office she shares with the Foundation's executive director, Diane Harris Brown, and the other staff members. Clay Triplette, Beard's houseman for thirty years and now house steward, is checking off cases of wine and champagne on the terrace. Plants in pots on the brick floor and healthy ivy in copper window boxes around the second-floor balcony enjoy the extravagance of light that pours in to this two-story high, glass-walled and glass-roofed room behind the kitchen. I look out at the wintry garden behind, then mosey on upstairs behind José Silva, Clay's nephew, who is hoisting big bags of table linens to the second-floor dining area, once Beard's bedroom, living room, library, and bath.

The bath is the quirkiest room in the house. The entire second-floor balcony, with chrome shower fixtures, is completely open to the rest of the house and, with glass on all sides and glass above, to the world. In the heart of New York City, Beard must have felt as if he were showering outdoors.

The interior rooms, a library and Beard's living room, both now filled with tables, offer a contradiction. With walls painted a red that Beard called "really good cream of tomato soup," these rooms are as warm and cosy as the bath is open. Surrounded by a mirrored bar, Beard's raised sleeping alcove, just big enough for a large bed, now houses a table for four.

Over the mantel hangs a large portrait of the presiding genius of the house, Saint Beard himself, with his laugh-crinkled eyes full of affection and fun, his mischievous grin, his bald pate. As in a good medieval painting, the saint is surrounded by his icons. With his striped shirt and characteristic bow tie, he wears a chef's white apron; behind him is a copper pot into which he perhaps plans to plunge the bunch of asparagus he is holding.

As I study his homely, kindly mug, I think back to the fifties and the event that led me to become a Bearded lady. You rarely meet a saint at a cocktail party, but that's how I met James Beard. Not that he was there in the flesh, all six feet four of him, you understand. But his spirit, equally big, attended me and performed a miracle. The year was 1959, Bill and I had been married about six months, and we decided to show ourselves off in our new state. We invited about fifty people, all the people we knew and their dates, to a party.

A cocktail party, of course. America was still in the throes of cocktail party madness at the time. Three times more gin was being sold than in 1950, some nineteen million gallons. Sales of vodka, once considered certain death by the hoi polloi, were ten times higher. Predictably, aspirin sales had increased as well, by six million pounds during the decade. Only a cocktail party, we agreed, would suffice to reveal our sophisticated domesticity. There was only one difficulty. Nothing in our past had equipped either Bill or me to give a cocktail party.

He would do the liquor and I would do the food. Bill, a good old Texas boy, drank quite a lot of bourbon on the rocks and quite a lot of beer. Period. To set up the bar, he threw himself on the mercy of the experts at the corner liquor store and came home with not only bourbon and beer, but also with gin, vodka, rum, Scotch, vermouth, olives, tonic, Cointreau, cognac, bitters, crème de menthe, maraschino cherries, something called Cherry Heering, little striped straws, and a worried expression. As I always do in a crisis, I went to the library.

"I don't know what people expect to eat with cocktails," I confided to the man at the information desk, who wasn't surprised to hear it. "Is there a book?"

"Do you know James Beard?" asked the librarian, who was "older," perhaps all of thirty, and suave.

"Know who?" I looked around hopefully, expecting maybe a genie.

"James Beard. His book on hors d'oeuvre. Has drinks in it too. Just what you need. Applied sciences, upstairs."

And Saint Beard materialized to guide us through.

Cocktail parties were an early Beard specialty. In fact, his career in food began, in 1938, at a cocktail party on Manhattan's Upper East Side, where he met Bill Rhode. Rhode was a man about town with ideas as well as valuable social and press connections. Beard, with Bill Rhode and Bill's sister Irma Rhode, made plans to "astonish the bellies of New York." They calculated that some 250 cocktail parties were held on the Upper East Side of Manhattan each day and that the food served was usually awful, consisting of what Beard called "doots," little dabs of something on soggy bread bits. Beard and the Rhodes opened a catering establishment called Hors d'Oeuvre, Inc.

Peculiar kind of saint, you say? Maybe. But the American food world still talks with adoration about his phenomenal energy and generosity. When I lucked into him in the fifties, his career had moved well beyond the cocktail party circuit. Once I became aware of him, he showed up everywhere: on radio and television, in books and magazines. He taught classes and flew all over the globe to give demonstrations. A Janus figure in American cuisine, Beard harked backward to early cookbook writers like Eliza Leslie and Fannie Farmer, and forward, through the seventies and eighties, to advance the careers of cooks like Alice Waters of California's Chez Panisse and Larry Forgione of New York's An American Place. When Beard died, the loss to American cuisine of his all-embracing spirit was the pilot light that ignited the James Beard Foundation.

If today the bustling Beard House centers on food, so did the life of James Beard. From the beginning, his enthusiasm and tastes were extraordinary. He tells the story in his autobiography, *Delights and Prejudices,* of his "first gastronomic adventure. I was on all fours. I crawled into the vegetable bin, settled on a giant onion and ate it, skin and all." His independent mother had run a hotel in Portland, Oregon, before James, a thirteen and a half pounder, was born in 1903, when she was forty-two. "Forceful and fearless," as her son describes her, with "an international approach to food that would have been considered revolutionary" even decades later, Elizabeth Beard encouraged the development of her only child's palate. When he was five, she took him out for champagne and oysters; at home he ate white asparagus with homemade mayonnaise and foie gras, as well as all the seafood, game, fruit, and vegetables indigenous to the Pacific Northwest.

As you might imagine, he grew up and out. At his peak, Beard weighed 310 pounds. He had the build of Pavarotti and ambitions for a career in theater or opera. In 1921, he enrolled at Reed College, but was thrown out in his freshman year, he told Barbara Kafka in an interview, for his liberal politics and a suspect "attachment" to one of his professors. Off he went to London to study singing, where, at twenty, he made his musical debut before deciding that he wasn't cut out for an operatic career. Back in Portland, he studied acting and went with a touring repertory company to New York, where he remained.

The food world and the theatrical world are closely related in Manhattan. Broadway hopefuls wait tables and uncork wine all over town. "Oh, actress," a man hails his waitress in *Eastern Standard,* a hit play of 1990. Pursuing his theatrical ambitions, Beard became what he calls "a gastronomic gigolo." He cooked for his friends' parties, exchanging his culinary skills for his own dinner and for tickets to the theater and opera. At length he realized that Broadway was not for him. With his enormous size, he was too dominant a stage presence for bit parts, yet not handsome enough for a lead. He turned full-time to his first love, food.

Out of his experience as a caterer for cocktail parties came, in 1940, his first book, that same *Hors d'Oeuvre and Canapés* which I clutched in my nervously sweating hand almost twenty years later, as Bill and I prepared to make our debut to society as a married couple. Beard's first cookbook may in fact be less important for its recipes than as a guide to social navigation such as ours. Without ever mentioning the repellent word "etiquette," for us two country bumpkins the little book performed a miracle. Here were the cool drinks that our cool friends would request: martini, Manhattan, daiquiri, screwdriver, vodkatini, old-fashioned, Tom Collins, sidecar, stinger, and whiskey sour. Here was the food that would keep them sober and satisfied: ham rolls, mushroom caps filled with Roquefort, shish kebab, and salami Parmigiana.

Beard taught me that cream cheese goes with everything. I made marble-sized balls of cream cheese and chopped ripe olives, and rolled them in chopped walnuts. I made other balls of cream cheese, chutney, and curry powder, and rolled them in coconut. As a variation, I topped cucumber rounds with cream cheese and horseradish. Following Beard, I made onion sandwiches with parsleyed edges. I souped up deviled eggs with spices, then, breathless at my own creativity, surrounded them with radish roses, carrot sticks, and green onions.

Bill meanwhile had sliced limes and lemons, set out bitters, Tabasco, booze, and mixers, and loaded our wedding present silver ice bucket for its maiden voyage. Checking over Beard's opening list of dos and don'ts, we felt that we had fallen into the hands of a kindly but worldly mentor, his role to instruct, ours but to obey right through: "And now, the table is set, the bottles laid out, the glasses gleaming, the flowers in their places, the cigarettes and ash trays arranged, food for the eye and the body and the soul ready. Adjust your tie or powder your nose, forget cares, let your best smiles come out, and on to a gay and happy adventure."

More actor than saint, you might argue, reading those words that might be preceded by stage directions: *A modest apartment, furnished in Early Married. Bill and Jo are obviously nervous. As they wait for their guests to arrive, they survey the party preparations.* Caught up in beatnik "sincerity" as we were, Bill and I profited by the implicit suggestion that a successful party, like civilization itself, depends on a certain amount of stage management and skillful social pretense. In reality nervous and ignorant, to give our guests a good time we had to pretend to be cool and smart. The stage was set; now it was our turn.

I will always be grateful to Beard for the never-to-be-forgotten lesson that a party, whether a dinner for six or a bacchanal with a cast of thousands, is a production similar in almost every way to a stage production. Taking up a career in food, Beard hadn't really given up the theater, he told an interviewer forty years later. "Food is very much theater. Especially cocktail parties per se."

Nevertheless, to continue my steadfastly mixed metaphor, in those forty years Saint Beard pursued his vocation with the devotion of the true acolyte. Several of his books, especially *The James Beard Cookbook, American Cookery,* and *James Beard's Theory and Practice of Good Cooking,* are classics of the genre. He wrote a weekly syndicated newspaper column. The first cooking show on television was his. Though he continued to love theater and opera — James Villas has written a touching vignette of an "opera dinner" the two had, with Beard, like Bottom, taking all the roles — American food was his life and the object of his deepest commitment.

"I can close my eyes and see him forever at the end of one class," the food critic Gael Greene has written, "slicing a juicy, jiggling piece of beef brisket, picking up a piece of fat, and popping it into his mouth. 'I'm just a fat boy,' he said with a magical laugh. And that's what separates a born foody from the mere mortal. An appreciation of fat. A passion for leftover pasta cold the next morning. The ability to weep over the perfect ripeness of a Chambery peach, scarlet inside of its prim green skin. And that's the secret Jim brought us. What fun it is. How lucky we are."

One could argue with some validity that Beard died a martyr's death for the sake of what he loved. He didn't care much for sweets, but he loved fat, from pork skins to sweet cream butter. "I'm a butter boy," he was fond of announcing. No doubt his diet killed him; he finally died of a heart attack. On the other hand, he was almost eighty-two years old and had eaten almost everything he'd wanted almost all of his life.

For some reason, in his will Beard had left the brownstone and its contents to Reed College, the school that had kicked him out over sixty years previously. The house was put up for auction but was slow to sell. With the triple oddities of an oversized kitchen, no bedroom, and a shower open to the eyes of the world, it was "worth a gawk," as Peter Kump puts it, but not the asking price of a million five. At Julia Child's instigation, Beard's friends in the food world offered to buy the brownstone. If they could raise a down payment of $250,000 in thirty days, they were told, the asking price would be cut in half.

Under this deadline, the first Beard Birthday Celebration, now an annual affair, was held as a benefit. Chefs, cooking teachers, and friends held additional benefits in their restaurants, schools, and homes. The benefit proceeds and other donations saved the day — and the James Beard House. Thus the James Beard Foundation was born.

"The key word that distinguishes the saint is 'heroism,'" according to my Penguin dictionary of saints. "The saint is the man or woman who gives himself, herself, to God heroically." For God, substitute "a belief" or "a vision," and you come up with a working definition of a secular saint like James Beard. And I'm only half joking, because Beard was a man with a vision. His vision, espoused most clearly in *American Cookery,* is that, contrary to international food dogma, this United States of America does have a cuisine of its own, a cuisine which includes such disparate elements as lobster thermidor, loin of pork teriyaki, cracker pie, and Nantucket fireman's supper.

Raymond Sokolov, who initially jeered at Beard's philosophy and seems never to have been entirely convinced, nevertheless explains the theory better than the master himself, and, furthermore, sees its significance:

> I have come to realize that Mr. Beard did not think that johnny-cakes and kielbasa fitted into a seamless whole. He meant that they were the survivors in a winnowing process that had left large parts of traditional cuisines behind in their homelands. Here in this unmelted pot some very disparate things had floated to the top and looked to be staying there for the duration. He meant that America's cuisine, like America, was not to be understood by referring to an Old World model of coherence and longevity, which didn't exist anyway. American food's coherence was in its incoherence. Diversity made it whole.

"If you detect a mystic tone there," Sokolov adds cryptically, "you are not mistaken."

Like other mystics, James Beard left a body of legend behind him. Much has been written about him, including the full-scale biography *Epicurean Delight* by Evan Jones, whose wife, Judith Jones, was Beard's editor at Knopf for some thirty years. In spite of obvious advantages with source material, however, *Epicurean Delight*'s avuncular tone gets between the spirit of James Beard and the reader. A much better revelation of the man is a sort of Festschrift, as academics call such an effort — *The James Beard Celebration Cookbook,* a collection of memories and recipes by nearly 150 of Beard's friends, published in his honor by the James Beard Foundation and edited by Barbara Kafka. *Celebration* gives the lie to the legendary clawing and backbiting which supposedly are endemic to the food world. But perhaps only Saint Beard could have spurred such a massive group achievement. The affectionate stories of his friends and students in *Celebration* reveal Beard to be a many-sided man, visionary, pragmatic, irreverent, self-reliant, democratic, proudly American in character as well as cuisine.

A democrat with the American gift for selling, who appeared on television with Elsie the Borden Cow, Beard has been labeled a huckster in some quarters. Not by me, I hasten to add. Far be it from one overjoyed in the fifties to have discovered Chef Boyardee and Swanson's chicken potpies to criticize Beard for touting shortcuts, from canned beef consommé to packaged mixes. Just pragmatic: he needed money and the products worked. He laughed at criticism, embraced everything he considered his country's contribution to world cuisine, from cured meats to cornmeal, and spawned a generation of cooks as self-reliant as he was himself. Sampling an ambitious dish from Christopher Idone, Beard commented, "This is quite delicious, but remember — you are an American. The foie gras and truffles can go."

"Thereafter," says Idone, "the foie gras and truffles were gone."

Beard liked to shock. An omnivore himself, he regaled his student Mark Caraluzzi with tall tales, which Caraluzzi suspected might have been Beard inventions. In Shanghai, he told the horrified Caraluzzi, he had been served monkey brains. The live monkey's head poked up through a hole in a special table, the top was then sliced off, and guests were invited to scoop the brains out. He had to sample the delicacy, Beard said; duty to his profession demanded it.

Shocking indeed, but in the late fifties, on the eve of our big event, some of the recipes now considered tame in *Hors d'Oeuvre and Canapés* shocked me. Smoked tongue? Fish eggs? Snails? Where did the man get these ideas anyway? Time would change my opinion, as it did America's. Tongue I've never tolerated, but caviar and escargots — well, I forgive my youthful self. How could I know that steak tartare, which Beard included under the particularly unattractive name of Raw Beef Paste, would become a cocktail party favorite across the country, until years later the fear of cholesterol and salmonella killed it? For that matter, how could I possibly have envisioned the craze in the eighties for sushi, for which Beard's Raw Beef Paste might have prepared the American palate?

And when I saw Beard challenge Garry Moore on national television to sample chicken cooked with *forty* cloves of garlic, how could I know, novice that I was, that with long cooking the garlic had melted into a tender sweetness and the dish was entirely edible and savory? But the fun for Beard was the shock of what he liked to call "acres of garlic."

Beard liked food with clout. Down with precious little "doots." Down with Domestic Science, calorie counting, and potato chips with onion soup dip. Down with congealed salads, canned peas, and tasteless white bread. Up with hearty homemade bread, fresh vegetables, an array of cheeses, satisfying stews, spicy sausages, mashed potatoes. Down with the pretentious contrivances of haute cuisine. Up with good cooking.

"Gourmet has become a hideous term," he told Jane and Michael Stern in the eighties. He complained to them "that most people who called themselves gourmets were nothing but food fetishists who would rather talk about a four-star meal than cook or eat a tasty plate of food."

Behind the scenes in our life, James Beard continued to influence Bill and me. Early in his career, he took food off the stove. With his second book, *Cook It Outdoors,* Beard enhanced the notion that cooking could be a manly art for ordinary American men as well as for French chefs, a notion that, for the fifty years since the book's publication in 1942, has put millions of suburban husbands into funny aprons to grill hamburgers and steaks. Bill didn't read the book, but a couple of years later, when we moved to the suburbs with our one and a half babies, he joined the exodus to the back yard.

Beard also claimed to have introduced into American cuisine a dish which, word has it, "real men don't eat," but which all the men I know did and in some cases still do: quiche. Because he was eclectic, James Beard made food trends that became part of American life. He "cooked the way he dressed," as the restaurateur Joe Baum, with whom Beard worked at the Four Seasons and elsewhere, says. "He'd combine plaids, stripes, and prints, and it worked — and he'd do the same with food."

Flamboyant, yes, full of zest and courage, Beard was fearless in the kitchen. His friend Ann Seranne remembers buying her first truffles at the exorbitant price of ten dollars a pound — this was the forties — and rushing with them to Beard. "He practically said so what," she told Evan Jones. "He heated some goose fat in a big sauté pan, sliced in some potatoes, then threw in my truffles. I couldn't believe what he was doing to my truffles — my very first! It turned out to be the best dish ever."

"Was it fun?" he would ask Larry Forgione, after tasting a dish Forgione had been slaving over. "What he meant, I realize," Forgione writes in *Celebration,* "was that cooking should be fun, that it shouldn't seem labored." Opening the Four Seasons in 1959, Beard and Joe Baum hired an inexperienced cook to make the soufflés. They reasoned that the cook, ignorant of the perils usually associated with making soufflés, wouldn't be afraid, so the soufflés wouldn't fall.

Fear was any cook's enemy; fun was every cook's goal. Like so much else in Beard's life, the theory worked.

Eating should be fun, too, and nowhere that I've eaten in Manhattan is it more fun than at the James Beard House. "You really must come back in the evening," Leah Stewart tells me when I leave on the afternoon of December 31. "You've come into a bare theater. All the magic is gone. You have to see it when the stage is lit and the show is on." I can't accept her invitation to the New Year's Eve gala — my husband is out with all those others buying champagne and caviar for our own party for two — but the following week we are there for a dinner by Best Hotel Chef Daniel Bruce of the Boston Harbor Hotel.

More than three decades have passed since Saint Beard came to the rescue of those two innocents planning their first party. And now I'm with a different husband, in a different town, and I like to think *I'm* different, full of savoir-faire and smarts. But that old Beard party magic is still alive and everywhere — in the busy kitchen with the guests wandering through as they drink apéritifs and nibble hors d'oeuvre, in the fresh flowers, the candlelight against the red walls, the indescribably sensuous aromas that drift throughout the house from whatever is cooking on the stove. My husband and I share a table for six with two journalists, a hospital administrator, and a financial analyst. A different wine and a new, fresh-from-the-oven homemade bread arrives with each course, and the talk is as heady as the wine, the laughter as warm as the bread. The dinner features white cornmeal–wrapped New England smoked salmon and sturgeon caviar, Jonah crab cake with lemon pasta, seared pheasant with smoked bacon and caramelized vegetables, and, for dessert, dark chocolate with Vermont mascarpone and fresh raspberries. All very ritzy, all very American, all very scrumptious, all very, very, very James Beard.

A Servantless
American Cook

. . . .

WHEN I THINK OF THE SIXTIES, that turbulent decade, I don't instantly recall race riots, bra burnings, and antiwar demonstrations, but food, particularly the French food that came out of American kitchens by way of Julia Child. The dichotomy of the decade, culinarily speaking, was between convenience and complexity. On the one hand, the women of Middle America, back in the job force in steadily increasing numbers, wanted the availability of McDonald's and the convenience of frozen food. On the other hand, middle-class working women, stay-at-home mothers, and often the husbands of both wanted, after the publication in 1961 of *Mastering the Art of French Cooking,* Volume I, to be discriminating in taste, to be connoisseurs, epicures, gourmets, you name it — to be *French.*

As the Beatles might have put it, for French we needed a little help from our friends. Pat Hyatt got married in the Julia Child heyday. Pre-Julia, her first chocolate chip cookie dough wound up on the floor of the oven because she overlooked the "add flour" step. Evelyn Friedman believed, pre-Julia, that you could just pour raw egg whites on the top of a lemon pie and they would rise miraculously into meringue on their own. Susan Stewart's mother made baked Alaskas for a luncheon, pre-Julia, put them in the oven on a board, and the varnish from the board melted and smelled up the luncheon. Then came beautiful American Julia to give us the little help we needed to get by.

Martha Rose Shulman, today the author of marvelous healthy cookbooks such as *Mediterranean Light* and *Entertaining Light,* cites Julia Child as the biggest influence on her cooking and writing. In the sixties, when Martha asked her stepmother to teach her how to cook a particular dish such as boeuf bourguignon or blanquette de veau, "Often she would merely direct me to the page in Julia Child's book."

In this country, Julia Child's name has, rightly, become synonymous with fine food, but one should keep in mind that *Mastering the Art of French Cooking* was a popularizing effort that intended to make the techniques of haute cuisine comprehensible to ordinary American cooks using ingredients available in ordinary American supermarkets. Child and her coauthors, Simone Beck and Louisette Bertholle, deliberately omitted "cobwebbed bottles, the *patron* in his white cap bustling among his sauces, anecdotes about charming little restaurants with gleaming napery," all of which "put French cooking into a never-never land instead of the Here, where happily it is available to everybody." Reading these welcoming words, Middle America embarked on a love affair with Julia's France.

Our Francophile palates had already been stimulated. One influence was M. F. K. Fisher, who had learned about food in France in the thirties. Fisher's books had been around for twenty years, but in the sixties her food pieces appeared frequently in *The New Yorker,* which of course we all read. The *New Yorker* pieces were vernacularly American, with references to Bisquick and Coke, and free of the plethora of "cobwebbed bottles" and "charming little restaurants," which to my admittedly irreverent taste sometimes grows wearisome in Fisher's earlier books. But French phrases — *les crudités, tapenade, potée Normande, oeufs mollets* — and French food lore slid voluptuously and suggestively from Fisher's American tongue and sent some of us to her 1954 collection, *The Art of Eating,* where we sampled vicariously the food of Aix-en-Provence and Dijon. If we weren't prepared to plunge immediately into making tournedos or ratatouille, if, as she says, the foie seemed still a little too gras for us, at least we learned such dishes existed.

Another Francophile influence, perhaps the greatest in numbers of converts, was Jackie Kennedy. Camelot had begun. Though we didn't call it that then, we were aware in our wistfully democratic American hearts that Jacqueline was a queen. When she conquered de Gaulle and all of France in 1961 and Jack declared himself to be "the man who accompanied Jacqueline Kennedy to Paris," we felt that was a fair analysis of the situation. Slavishly we studied Jackie's clothes, her coiffure, the menus of the French chef she installed in the White House. All across Middle America, les girls hemmed up their skirts, teased their hair, and courted Julia Child and her cohorts.

Although almost everyone does it, it's not quite fair to call *Mastering the Art of French Cooking* Julia's book. Julia Child met her French collaborators Simone Beck and Louisette Bertholle while she and her husband, Paul, a member of the foreign service, lived in Paris from 1948 until 1954. After bringing her college French up to speed, to please her food-loving husband Julia attended classes at the world-famed Cordon Bleu cooking school and eventually became a member of a gastronomic society for women, Le Cercle des Gourmettes. Soon she, Beck, and Bertholle founded their own cooking school, L'Ecole des Trois Gourmandes, which met in the Childs' apartment on the Left Bank, at five dollars a lesson.

Beck and Bertholle had been considering writing a French cookbook for Americans, but neither knew English. Julia Child joined them in the project. The first draft of *Mastering the Art of French Cooking,* which included eight hundred pages on poultry alone, was deemed unpublishable by one house and had to be completely rewritten. The book was hailed as a masterpiece when it was at length brought out by Knopf and has gone through many editions since.

In 1960, I still had only one cookbook, *Betty Crocker's Picture Cook Book.* The library copy of James Beard's *Hors d'Oeuvre and Canapés* had seen me through a difficult patch of first-married entertaining. My sister-in-law taught me an all-purpose dish, cooked in a pie plate: a "crust" of rice, a "filling" of browned hamburger meat, celery, and onion, and a "topping" of undiluted tomato soup from a can. Sometimes I served Hormel's canned Gourmet Foods of the World, fancy dishes such as chicken cacciatore and beef Stroganoff, remembered by my friend Michael Birdsall of St. Paul as "the very stuff of romance. I'm sure my mother's meat loaf was much better than Mrs. Hormel's Swedish meatballs, but to me there was no competition." So armed, I decided it was foolish to buy another cookbook until I had cooked all the Betty Crocker dishes, which might take years.

I did fall for Peg Bracken's *The I Hate to Cook Book,* irresistibly small, cheap, and funny. Bracken expressed a comically rebellious sentiment appropriate for a borderline beatnik wrapped in domesticity. Her black, or at any rate dark brown, humor was a welcome antidote to Betty Crocker's wearisome sunniness. Bracken recipes like Sweep Steak swept the country because they worked for even the least skilled cook, like me. Who could go wrong with a package of onion soup mix sprinkled on pot roast, wrapped in foil, and baked for three hours or nine hours? ("It really doesn't matter" how long, the recipe says.) A far cry from mastering the art of French cooking.

I remember very well my own introduction to Julia Child in 1961. I had been happily married just over two years and had a baby daughter. For my birthday, my husband brought home a pair of mink eyelashes.

I was devastated. Bravely I tried to put them on. "They feel just like bugs on my eyes!" I cried. I muttered darkly about a decadence in Bill's character, which a few years earlier had led him to slobber over Brigitte Bardot; which still caused him to bring home *Playboy,* claiming he'd "found it" at the washeteria or bought it "for the Playboy Philosophy"; and which now inspired him to ask me — *me,* beatnik, intellectual, poet, wife, and mother (I took myself very seriously) — to wear false eyelashes. Finally, from the bottom of my young idealist's heart, I broke down and sobbed. How could he think me so foolish, so trivial, so vain?

Whereupon poor Bill took the offending bits of fur back to Foley's and traded them in, I'm convinced, for the next object his eyes fell upon — *Mastering the Art of French Cooking.* At long last let me tell the truth: I was none too thrilled about that gift either. I had two cookbooks. What I wanted with a third was not immediately clear to me. What was clear was that, after the fussing and fuming I'd done over the false eyelashes, I had better pretend gratitude for Julia's book, or else. So I pretended, and, as pretense often does, it turned into the real thing.

Although the idea for the book and much of the expertise that went into it belonged to Beck and Bertholle, it was Julia, the intrepid American, whose voice I heard throughout. It was a confident, pragmatic, jubilant, slightly giddy voice that charmed me into believing I could cook real French food in my Texas kitchen, as it charmed us all a decade later on television.

The voice began with a sentence that was as reassuring for young cooks as the opening sentence in Dr. Spock's *Baby and Child Care*, "You know more than you think you do," was for young mothers. "This is a book for the servantless American cook," said the voice — and I smiled happily, for I was certainly that — "who can be unconcerned on occasion with budgets, waistlines, time schedules, children's meals, the parent-chauffeur-den-mother syndrome, or anything else which might interfere with the enjoyment of producing something wonderful to eat." Well, okay. I could try.

What the voice didn't say, what I learned on my own as the decade passed and I acquired other cookbooks and could make comparisons, was that you really do need a servant to clean up the ungodly messes that Julia will have you make in your kitchen. She never uses one pot if two will do, and a third is even better. She's a little like my old friend Tom, who, once complimented on his walnut torte, said, "Oh, it's fun. You get to use the blender *and* the mixer." At the time, I didn't have a mixer, much less a blender, much less still a food processor, that mechanical saint, but I did have a certain — the French have a term for it — *joie de vivre,* or perhaps I should say *joie de cuisiner.*

I cuisined up a storm. With the greatest will in the world, I sifted and measured and minced and grated and creamed. I made soufflés, whipping up the egg whites with a fork. True to James Beard's theory, I didn't know they might fall so they never did. One whole winter I spent working on pastry, until my husband, still no doubt longing for mink-laden eyes, acquired a decidedly porcine shape and begged off quiche and tartelettes in order to survive.

Quel fun! The recipes were terrifyingly long and looked formidable on the page, with their French titles and English subtitles, like the pretentious "films" (never "movies") we watched: Coquelets sur Canapés (Roast Squab Chicken with Chicken Liver Canapés and Mushrooms). The boldface lists of ingredients and equipment were haughtily specific: "1½ cups sauce Mornay (béchamel with cheese), see p. 61" and "A lightly buttered baking dish about 8 inches in diameter and 2 inches deep." The recipes took thought, and, with one and then two small children to care for, I was remarkably short on thought in the daily round. Each completed dish was a victory in the campaign waged against the forces of boredom and laziness and colicky babies.

"I started cooking because I was housebound," the cookbook writer Leslie Newman said in an interview in *The New York Times.* "If you got married in the '60s, one of the few things you could do as you were going crazy sitting home with your new baby and your college education was cook. . . . Everybody loved you for cooking, and they got to eat it at the end of the day. Of course, it was also a little like falling down a rabbit hole, because there was no end to it — there was always another cuisine."

Under Julia's tutelage, I learned not to use canned soup for sauces, or at least to lie about it in company if I did. But I never really mastered *Mastering the Art of French Cooking.* We were too poor in the beginning, when my ambition was highest, for lamb, veal, or filets. Goose and duck I regarded as bizarre, though I liked to read about them. So it was cheap cuts of beef, chicken, cheese, eggs, and vegetables that Julia taught me to cook. I fixed hamburgers, not on a bun with mustard but with cream sauce. Sometimes we had *fricassée de poulet à l'ancienne,* sometimes roast *poulet* with tarragon. Julia was quite severe about fresh vegetables instead of frozen or canned, so we sampled the joys of tiny green peas cooked with lettuce, of spinach mold and ratatouille. I made crêpes, floating island, and galettes au fromage, wonderful little cheese wafers that could turn Gallo and the Dave Brubeck album into a classy party.

Although I'd eaten brains and eggs at my mother's table, I balked at the very idea that I might serve forth kidneys or sweetbreads. Only half wanting to know, what are sweetbreads anyway, I asked? Before I was faced with the onerous necessity of finding out, I took off after another cuisine, or at least another cookbook, Craig Claiborne's *The New York Times Cook Book,* which also appeared in 1961. Claiborne, it is generally recognized today, was the first serious restaurant reviewer in the country. At the time, he was also the highly esteemed food editor of *The New York Times,* and his book contains some fifteen hundred recipes from the ten thousand or so that had appeared over the years in the *Times.* Julia's book, though it encompasses the major techniques of French cooking, is small in comparison. Julia Child had opened the world of good cooking to me, but I felt a lot more at home with Craig.

For one thing, Julia's cooking methods are impeccable, but slow and messy. I'm tiresomely neat. One of my grievances with my mother's kitchen habits, you may remember, was her messiness. I was relieved to realize that the *Times* methods were faster and neater than Julia's. Craig didn't leave you to discover too late, as Julia did, that you could have sautéed everything in one pan instead of three. He suited my personality, and I alternated between Craig and Julia for the next couple of years.

What did I cook from *The New York Times Cook Book?* To start with soup, like a good hostess, there was the minestrone, pure, aromatic, and very vegetably; the only meat allowed is a smidgin of browned salt pork. We ate the fantastic cream of mushroom, which at the first taste and for years afterward I regarded as the best soup ever. I will never forget my shock when eventually I heard someone badmouth it because the mushrooms are sliced. For a cold soup, I favored the Senegalese, creamy chicken broth seasoned with curry, or the redoubtable vichyssoise à la Ritz, accompanied by a French lesson: "Vichyssoise is not pronounced veeshy-swah! It is veeshee-swahze." As we served the soup, Bill and I used to announce haughtily to bemused dinner guests, "Eet ees veeshee-swahze."

Then we might have the herbed meat loaf with the snappiest of fresh tomato sauces, or pork chops with basil and Marsala, or, a dish I particularly relished before I knew about pasta, the sherried chicken with green noodles. Yes, yes, there was curry, Chicken Curry Jaipur. "Jaipur" threw me, but no matter; the dish contains such fillips as lime juice and fresh mint, and is delicious. Or there was Moussaka à la Grecque, replete with lamb, eggplant, and ricotta seasoned with cinnamon and nutmeg, which made a super buffet dish; it can be made a day ahead, in fact should be, and served warm or cold, as temperature and temperament dictate.

Or I might try one of the numerous seafood recipes, since in Houston we lived near the water, and fish, undesirable to Texas beefeaters, was dirt-cheap at the time. Sayur Lodeh, a spicy Indonesian dish that I never pronounced with any confidence, would serve ten people with two pounds of shrimp and a mélange of vegetables.

If I'm sounding more and more like a hostess, there's a reason. We had fallen down another rabbit hole, which opened into a world wider and more wonderful to me even now, all these years later, than anything Alice found in Wonderland. We had begun asking people to come to dinner. When I cooked my first pot of coq au vin, I realized it was something I could feed friends triumphantly and joyfully, and I have been feeding family and friends pretty steadily ever since.

Guests do not always love dinner parties, I have heard with some mystification. What's not to like? I agree with Peg Bracken: turning down a dinner invitation "is like telling a small boy to turn down a free ticket to the circus. Too well you remember the golden tranquility that bathes you, all day, when you know that *somebody else* is going to be doing that fast samba from pantry to sink."

That the samba is often dreaded by the cook is more understandable. But from my very crude beginnings, and even in my sometimes crude present, giving dinner parties has been the stuff of life to me, high on my list of pleasures. Looking back, I can see that my mother's influence was probably surfacing. What better way to while away your span on earth than by sitting around a big table eating good food and telling stories with the people you love?

For these parties, like any cook whose reach exceeds her grasp, I had my kitchen disasters. I remember chupe, described by Craig Claiborne as "a splendid buffet dish." Chupe is supposed to be a Chilean seafood casserole thickened with bread soaked with milk, but it wasn't. Thickened, that is. It wasn't thickened when I baked it for the twenty minutes the recipe called for, or for the next hour, or even when our guests banged their knife handles on the table while I poured the excess gooey milk toast into the disposal, meanwhile trying to hold back the crabmeat, shrimps, scallops, and lobster chunks with a big spoon. Take my advice. Skip chupe.

Probably I deserved this experience. I had gone too far. In the *New York Times* interview with Leslie Newman, the interviewer Nora Ephron talked about competitive cooking, always the greatest danger awaiting the eager host or hostess.

> There was an unbelievably elaborate recipe in Julia Child for something called veal Orloff, and the night I had it in about 1968 always seemed to me to epitomize the moment when it was clear Things Had Gone Too Far. The hostess had spent nine hours in the kitchen making this *oeuvre*, which nobody at the table could possibly appreciate enough to make up for the time and effort that had gone into it, and it was clear that after we left, she and her husband were going to have a fight, and five years later they would be divorced, and it would all be because of the veal Orloff.

Suffice it to say that I chose chupe for our party only because Craig Claiborne claims in his introduction to the recipe that it was served for dinner parties in the New York home of Leonard Bernstein, at that time the conductor of the New York Philharmonic, by Bernstein's beautiful wife, Felicia, who was born in Montevideo. New York! Leonard Bernstein! The Philharmonic! Felicia! Montevideo! I suppose I thought that if I served chupe, I too would be a beautiful cosmopolite.

Thin as it was, we ate the chupe, and like the South I rose to cook again, eventually throughout the sixties for friends here and there across the country. Turbulent as the times, my newspaperman husband and I moved from Houston to Detroit to the Texas hill country to Chicago to Austin, from a ticky-tacky tract house in the lower burbs to the wraparound windows and black tile floors of a Mies van der Rohe townhouse, to an eighty-year-old farmhouse on two hundred acres, to an imposing two-story with library and sun porch, and, to see the decade out, to a modest white frame in a university neighborhood. Our neighbors were variously garage mechanics, executives, doctors and professors, ranchers and good old boys, retired couples, young marrieds, students, and hippie dopers. How to remember all those changes in setting and cast? Simple, says my subconscious; use an objective correlative. Food.

So, when Bill covered James Meredith's march through Mississippi and I went along to get local color, I came away with a haunting memory of the crispy fried catfish and biscuits as big as a state trooper's fist we ate at a tarpaper shack outside of Oxford. Mention the Cuban missile crisis, and I recall, stockpiled high along one wall of a Houston bomb shelter, with the beans and Spam, the powdered milk and eggs, the Cheerios, sugar, and ten-gallon can of water, numerous cans of my favorite Vienna sausages.

In the event of a nuclear attack, ran the ethical question of the day, did the shelter owner have a right to use bullets against his neighbors to protect his precious stores? My question was different. "How can you stand to leave them alone?" I asked, salivating at the thought of the little fat, salty wieners, smooth to the tongue outside and crumbly and juicy inside. A chipper grasshopper to my friend's prudent ant, I found distant fears less compelling than pleasure so near at hand.

·✕·

Putting the Big Pot
in the Little One

. . . .

A GOOD MANY OF US went too far in the sixties. Before the decade was over, I suppose you could argue, the whole country had gone too far. Personally, I wouldn't argue it. As a former would-be beatnik, I relished the wake-up elixir the country concocted for itself after the stuffy, comatose Eisenhower years. Let's face it: Mamie Eisenhower in the White House was neither a challenge nor a model, and Jackie Kennedy was both. But, what with trying to outdo our mothers by being French à la Julia and elegant à la Jackie, what with trying to be perfect wives and raise perfect children and give perfect dinner parties, some of us undoubtedly went too far.

We were very young — Mort Sahl quipped that Kennedy had to have Lyndon Johnson on the ticket with him because they wouldn't let Kennedy into Washington without an adult — and we thought we could do everything. We entertained each other madly. Let's call it potlatching. When I first learned in college of potlatching, the custom among American Indians which caused a host to wipe himself out completely, to lay waste to his most precious possessions and all his family resources, in order to show his guests a good time, what flew into my mind was an image of my mother, brushing the hair back off her sweaty, floury forehead, knocking herself out getting ready for company. I disapproved heartily, with no idea that in a few years I myself would become a potlatcher *extraordinaire*.

Mother called it "putting the big pot in the little one." Ordinarily my mother "just cooked," but sometimes, when she invited the preacher for Sunday dinner or all our kin for a big get-together, she would sigh and say, "I guess we'll have to put the big pot in the little one." We all knew what that meant. I would be assigned the jobs of polishing the silver, ironing the best damask napkins, and arranging flowers from the garden. Instead of the big table in the kitchen where we propped our elbows every day, the round table in the dining room would be laid with Mama Harlan's crocheted tablecloth and set with several generations of family china and crystal. And Mother would cook, and cook, and cook.

"Make just one big dish of something," I would urge accusingly, irritated because when she got tired I felt guilty. While I hung around the stove poking my finger in pots and haranguing her like some surly adolescent out of a Flannery O'Connor story, she single-handedly prepared fried chicken and baked ham, peas, green beans, butter beans, squash, fried okra, mashed potatoes, corn on the cob, sliced tomatoes, dill pickles, sweet pickles, peach pickles, pickle relish, hot rolls, corn bread, German chocolate cake, and pecan pie, all for one company meal.

"I like to have a variety," she would defend herself, minutes before the guests arrived after she'd spent hours in the kitchen. Putting the big pot in the little one, I thought, was just another kind of potlatching.

Then I learned to cook, but of course I resolved to cook nothing like my mother. In the early sixties, country was undeniably, definitely out, finished, passé. So was Beat, with its nod to apple pie and canned spaghetti. If we were living in Camelot, we would maintain its standards. Would Guinevere eat hot dogs? Would Jackie settle for Sweep Steak? Gourmet had arrived. Prudence Mackintosh, a writer friend from Texas, remembers serving, alongside her beef Wellington, "some pretentious mashed potatoes molded like a cake with slivers of carrots and haricots verts striping the sides." For several years, she and her husband, John, spent each New Year's Eve rolling tiny ham and cheese crêpes for their huge New Year's Day open house.

Someone, I forget who, has said that the mother of every fabulous cook was either a terrible cook or a terrific cook. Prudence, whose mother was of the terrible school, ruefully recalls her saying that "the worst day of her life was the day that I learned that other children did not eat breakfast cereal for dinner. We ate for survival at our house." If the food was terrible, the talk was terrific. Both parents worked for the local paper and always knew the inside story, which proved an admirable distraction from canned spinach.

But at her own table, Prudence wanted both good talk and good food. So she chose to marry a university English instructor, later a lawyer, with an eye to the good talk. She and John passed up a fancy wedding, and instead traveled across Europe for several months on five dollars a day. Back home, influenced by the wonderful European meals, she began to learn to cook. She read cookbooks voraciously and thought "if I could read it, I could do it. I didn't know the most basic things. Was a head of garlic one pod or the whole elephant foot?"

Unlike Prudence's mother, Jane de Rochemont's mother entertained in grand style, but Jane's mother had a cook. When Jane and her husband, the food historian Richard de Rochemont, entertained in the sixties, Jane herself was the cook. Nevertheless, she told me that a typical sixties dinner party menu at the de Rochemont ménage would include gigot d'agneau, flageolets, ratatouille, and a delicious pear dessert baked with sugar, butter, and heavy cream.

As my mother's heritage tablecloth and polished silver indicated, dinner party potlatching doesn't necessarily have to do with food. My cousin Jean gives her table as much attention as the menu. She adds an immediate visual fillip by using silver place settings she has acquired, all of different patterns. Brides of the fifties and early sixties were not disadvantaged in this department. We often received such gifts as silver candelabra, silver flatware, crystal, and china in the chosen pattern — "What's your pattern?" we asked, at the first sign of an engagement ring — as well as chafing dishes, a damask tablecloth and a dozen napkins to match, not to mention all the monogrammed items: ashtrays, candle snuffers, drink glasses, guest towels, and cocktail napkins. We had plenty to potlatch with.

Camelot called out for glitter, for style and grace. Appearances mattered. To Harold Peterson, the dining accoutrements were more important than the food. Hal had been sent off to college with an apple green tea set ("So had Cecil Beaton") but with no knowledge of cooking. In the sixties, out of school and larking it up on Manhattan's Upper West Side, Hal jubilantly entertained a wild mix of guests, from members of the Social Register to the faithful of Warhol's Factory. Although Hal had discovered Julia Child, "along with all of gay New York," for a dinner party he might serve Dinty Moore's canned stew doctored with cheap wine and dried herbs. Sometimes he made "grunts," canned chicken dumped in a roux and served on Minute Rice. His potlatching at the time had to do with possessions. "Our table looked like something out of Tiffany's."

To this day, though he no longer serves up doctored stew, Hal feels the same way about dinner parties. "I love the setting. Billy Baldwin said, 'No one wants a big meal.' That's so true. A good meal, yes. Flowers, booze, candles, views, hours free to enjoy it, and talk about something other than the food."

For home cooks in the early sixties, talking about something other than the food we served was not so easy. The service, the cleverness or beauty of the table, the special effects like Jean's mismatched silver and Hal's apple green tea set, all mattered, all gave us cachet. But what mattered most were the elegant dishes that we created from scratch. We cooked to prove something to ourselves — for many of us, most simply, that living in those incredibly civilized days before November 22, 1963, we had outgrown our mothers. "Look at this, Mother," we shouted. And with every consummate coq au vin or wonderful Wellington, our shout grew more confident. "See what we can do!" That shout was worth a lot of bother.

This is not to say that we didn't cook for other reasons too, to please our husbands, to rise to the challenge, to compete with our friends, or that we didn't come to love the creativity of cooking for its own sake. And make no mistake, we were creating — no "just cooking" for us, or, I suspect, for my mother either, if the truth were known. Good cooking involves ego — call it creative self-expression. And what could be more satisfying than a creation others appreciate enough to eat?

If Susan Allen Toth, most recently the author of *My Love Affair with England,* has found writing to be ultimately more satisfying than cooking, she still remembers her sixties kitchen adventures with pleasure. Susan grew up in the Midwest, in the shadow of her mother's cooking. After graduate school at Berkeley, living in California with her new husband, Susan began experimenting with Japanese cuisine — needless to say, the technique most alien to her mother's meals — to discover that cooking was "not simply an arcane art whose secrets were held by my mother," she recalled. Inspired by her success with Japan, she took *The New York Times Cook Book* in hand — "anything with the *Times* logo, I thought, would be the ultimate in intelligence and sophistication" — to become a serious cook.

Susan's approach was scientific. First she acquired what she calls "the tools for my laboratory," Julia Child's "batterie de cuisine." For an omelet she was convinced she needed an omelet pan, for a soufflé a soufflé dish, for an apple charlotte a French charlotte mold. "How could I whip egg whites properly if I didn't have a copper bowl and a large whisk? The fact that Mother had always used her Mixmaster merely proved my point."

Stored today in her Minnesota basement, of not much use to a woman who since those California days has published some half dozen books, are a steamed-pudding mold, a Crock-Pot, popover pans, and springform pans. Still in use, today for her second husband's signature fish stew, is the large orange Le Creuset pot Susan purchased in the sixties, specifically to make "a proper boeuf bourguignon (I would never have referred to it as 'beef burgundy')." She chose her equipment so carefully, in fact, that much of it outlasted her first marriage.

Growing up, Susan had always been designated "the scholar" in her family, and her older sister "the artist." Susan wasn't supposed to be artistic. But in the kitchen, in spite of her scientific approach, she too could be creative. "I could turn out culinary works of art — perishable, but certified by the *New York Times.*"

Seduced by those subversive pleasures, here's what Susan eagerly went through for a major creation in her new art form. She devoted two full days to prepare for a dinner party, even though her guests were just old friends from grad school. The first day she decided what she would serve and shopped for the ingredients. The second day she made out a timetable and began her elaborate preparations.

"I didn't have the sense to limit myself to one difficult or fancy dish per meal; no, I was determined to have A Menu," she told me. It might begin with fresh cream of asparagus soup, go on to an entrée of boeuf bourguignon, followed by a mandarin orange, avocado, and fresh spinach salad, then conclude with a floating island.

Susan knew no kitchen skills, like how to cube beef or how to stir custard, so she "fussed and worried as time sped by." By dinnertime, the kitchen was a mess and so was Susan. Too tired even to notice how the food tasted, she was still proud that she had produced a passable facsimile of the dishes in the cookbook. She compares her "surprised pride" to that she felt as a child when she could actually wash her hands with the soap she had concocted from her toy chemistry set.

Looking back on her "High Gourmet phase," Susan sympathizes with and admires her aspiring youthful self. "I did learn to cook, I loved creating culinary masterpieces (ah, you should have tasted my plum pudding! my Finnish cardamom-seed bread! my Hungarian goulash!), and I thought I would continue cooking that way forever."

So did we all in those early married days. It wasn't just the cooking, however. It was all of marriage, or, as we saw it, Marriage. Many of us, our own "selfish" ambitions — for so we thought them — frustrated by domestic circumstances, tried to be perfect wives. I remember Jackie Kennedy telling an interviewer at the time that she allowed herself only a salad or cottage cheese for lunch so that she could "eat dinner with Jack." Even her daily calories were an item in the perfection of married life.

In Michigan, Lois Grant served as hostess to her lawyer husband's business associates several times a month, at events that ranged from casual midweek dinners to very elaborate parties. She routinely took, not Susan's two days, but *three* days to make a dinner party — a day cleaning, a day shopping, the third day cooking. There wasn't any food that she couldn't produce, "the world's greatest cheesecake,

Napoleons from scratch. And after the dinner was over, I would entertain them — play ragtime, or we would all sing around the piano." Dinner parties often are performance art in which everyone present is a member of the cast, but in the early sixties, for women like Lois and me who were submerged in marriage, the dinner party became a bigtime Broadway play for which we were single-handedly producer, director, stagehand, and star.

Even in a tract house on a Texas prairie, potlatching was possible. When our daughter was born, I quit teaching and my husband and I left our downtown pad. For nothing down, we bought a house with three bedrooms and a picture window on trailless, waterless Trail Lake in a new Houston suburb. We furnished the house with Salvation Army treasures, family loot, and a few heavy oak pieces purchased on time. I hung red burlap in the windows of the den, and Bill hung an antique door to add flavor to the vanilla living room. Out back, in the baking heat of the Texas sun, we splurged on a six-foot-high cedar fence, sod, and one tiny frail tree. Bill made a patio, spading the groundwork so earnestly that our neighbor asked if he were digging a well.

Every morning Bill drove our only car forty-five minutes up the freeway to the *Chronicle* newsroom, leaving me in the middle of nowhere for the whole long day, with my daughter and, after a bit, her baby brother. He loved his job, ready-made for him. I invented mine as I went along. To the pleasurable role of mother and the unavoidable one of maid, I added those of party thrower and chef. Thus the idea of the "real" dinner party was born.

We often had friends in on Friday nights after work, mostly other reporters and their wives, to eat boiled shrimp with curry dip or hamburgers, which Bill grilled on our somewhat sunken patio. My favorite companions for these encounters were Evelyn and Saul Friedman. Saul, a New Yorker, covered police for the *Chronicle;* Evelyn was a court reporter with mind-boggling stories to tell about the cases she heard. Often till three or four o'clock in the morning, we would sit around the kitchen table talking. Saul and I argued endlessly and futilely about Faulkner's social responsibility (or lack of it: Saul's position) and the significance of women in history (or lack of it: Saul again). After months of such all-night seminars, Bill and I eventually realized that Saul's Saturday shift began at five A.M. and he preferred not to go to bed before work. So I cried uncle about Faulkner and women, and we got more sleep.

These evenings were great fun, but they weren't "real" dinner parties. I still remember vividly the first I gave of those, which I potlatched in every way known to man (or woman). Bill had won the 1963 Ernie Pyle award for fine feature writing, with a check for a thousand dollars. A thousand dollars! We were rolling in it. To celebrate, I invited six friends for a real dinner party.

We had no dining room, so that week I made one. I donated the ugly den furniture to the Salvation Army from whence it had come. For the den floor, I bought a red rug to match the burlap curtains. From Mexico, by way of Pier One, came a dark wooden table, eight matching chairs, and a hand-carved buffet trimmed with painted saints and gilt. Also at Pier One, I bought hand-blown Mexican glass, gorgeous turquoise and royal blue goblets and dessert plates. I stitched up turquoise and blue napkins, made turquoise and blue paper flowers, bought turquoise and blue candles, and wrote blue names on turquoise place cards. When the table was a symphony of turquoise and blue, I turned my attention to the food.

Yes, I still remember the menu. Veeshee-swahze. Rock Cornish hens stuffed with wild rice, currants, and pecans. Fresh asparagus with, natch, hollandaise. Caesar salad. Coconut chocolate cake topped with hot fudge sauce and whipped cream. To drink, a Chilean riesling, followed by champagne for the toasts. I had very definitely put the big pot in the little one.

What I also remember, with some mortification even today, is that one of our female guests was wearing a new dress in a tender shade of soft pink. When she stood up, after hours of feasting and toasting, an ugly brown stain from one of the new chairs was smudged across her pale pink behind. I didn't say a word, but the next day I shellacked the chair seats.

Those chairs and that table came to symbolize something important to me. First of all, they were my idea. As I remember, I bought them all by myself without even consulting Bill. Never before had I bought something so big, so expensive — I think for everything, including the candles, I may have spent three hundred dollars — just because I wanted it. I was proud of my dining room, and I continued to be proud of it for the next twenty years, wherever it was transplanted. For me, it was always the setting for one of the most enduring pleasures of civilized life.

A big table and eight matching chairs impose a responsibility. Not to be taken care of, I don't mean that. Because the table soon became battered and scratched, I never felt as if I had to protect it. In honor of Saul and Faulkner, call what I felt a social responsibility. This furniture cried out to be used. I think that big brown table may also have helped to preserve my sanity, such as it was, in the mad potlatching days to come. Something about its peasant reality anchored my aspirations toward elegance, kept me aware that common sense had to govern even so ambitious a task as putting the big pot in the little one.

As the years passed and the kids grew up, I felt confident that whatever treatment that table got, it could take. When my son scratched his name on it with a knife, I left it; when my daughter's tempera paints ran off the paper, I didn't worry. When I scorched the surface with a hot pot of stew, the burn marks remained. On its uneven surface, I rolled pie dough, chopped vegetables, cut out dresses, typed graduate school papers, filled in tax forms, wrote

letters, pasted up Bill's clippings. And I sat at that table, eating
fish sticks and SpaghettiOs with the kids, while I watched Jack
Kennedy's funeral procession on television — Jackie's black veil,
the riderless black horse, the end of Camelot.

The table was so big and clumsy, so badly made, that as it got
more and more scarred and worn it was often mistaken for a valuable
colonial antique. To clean it, I scrubbed it with steel wool and
rubbed it with lemon oil. The lousy paint job softened and streaked,
and the wood acquired a patina and sheen I loved. People seeing it
for the first time would often stroke the wide dark boards reverently
and say, "This is the real thing, isn't it?"

"Yes," I would always answer. After all, I told myself, it was as
real as anything else, and realer than most.

Throughout the sixties and seventies, we gave the table and
chairs what they so blatantly asked for, the table to be loaded with
food and wine, the chairs to be sat upon by friends who laughed and
talked and argued. From Houston, the table and chairs went with
us to Detroit and sat in the front dining annex of our Lafayette
Park townhouse. Our neighbors on one side were Ramesh and Alma
Chand, an Indian professor and his Filipino wife; the smell of their
vegetable curries completely overwhelmed our pork chops as we sat
at supper in the evening. The Chands had named their son Krishna,
which fascinated me; I marveled that they had dared to name a child
"God." This was before some American rock star — was it Grace
Slick? — did just that.

On the other side were Charles and Betty Brown, who were
American blacks. To a white Mississippian, the Browns were even
more exciting neighbors than the Chands. Betty's sister was a vet-
eran of the Martha Graham dance troupe in New York, and little
Beverly, who was our daughter's age, seemed headed in the same
direction. I was amazed and grateful that our children played together. In a fog of sixties good feeling, I watched my son and little

Phil Brown take turns on the slide and envisioned an easy solution to all racial dissent.

My best friend in the neighborhood was Renate, a German woman married to a Dane. A good cook of German, Scandinavian, and Eastern European dishes I'd never heard of, much less eaten, she introduced me to the big downtown farmers' market, open year-round. In the depths of a bitter Michigan winter, I bought corned beef to simmer for hours, under her instructions, with red cabbage and juniper berries. While the children were in school, we drove out to Hamtramck for Polish sausage and experimented together with a dish called bigos, made with sausage, sauerkraut, and apples.

Along with our new friends, Bill and I saw old friends as well. Saul and Bill and a couple of other Texans had been hired at about the same time by the *Detroit Free Press,* and we all moved into the same ten-block radius. One night in particular I remember. Van Sauter, whose wife, Pat, had helped us locate our townhouse, had just returned from Vietnam. The Sauters, the Friedmans, and Bill and I had dinner with Yolanda and Mort Persky, who edited the *Free Press* Sunday magazine, in the Perskys' high-rise apartment at the edge of the park. We ate the first paella I had ever had, and Yolanda, a Cuban, made a wonderful, tart salad, which I still serve, of lettuce, garbanzo beans, red onions, and olives, dressed only with lemon juice and salt. I think we all hoped to hear war stories from Van; instead he talked about the mythic dimensions of whaling which he had absorbed during the several years he and Pat had spent in New Bedford, an old whaling town in Massachusetts.

From Detroit we took the big brown table and eight chairs to Chicago, where we moved them into the very proper dining room, complete with crystal chandelier, of a two-story red brick at the end of a tree-shaded street in Evanston. Soon after we arrived, Bill's new boss at the *Chicago Daily News,* Bill Steven, and his wife, Lucy, invited us to their spiffy apartment on the Loop for dinner, just us two, an immensely flattering invitation. In gratitude, I presented Lucy with a bouquet of paper flowers I had made by gluing petals on pipe cleaners. She seemed to like them, though why she should have I don't know.

Nevertheless, encouraged, we in turn asked the Stevens to be our first dinner guests in our new house, an occasion that called for mad potlatching on my part. Though I don't remember the entire meal, I do recall the dessert. I hollowed large oranges, leaving a wide mouth, and filled them with a sort of jury-rigged spumoni — softened vanilla ice cream into which I stirred sherry, bits of chocolate, maraschino cherries, coconut, whipped cream, and nuts — before putting them back into the freezer to harden.

In Chicago, we got on a regular dinner party circuit for a while with a fairly terrifying group of Northwestern faculty members, whose potlatching knew no bounds. Handwritten invitations, with little enclosed acceptance cards, were sent out to five or six couples from a number of three-story houses on Lake Michigan. Place cards, décolletage, five courses with the right wines, a nanny to look after all the children on the third floor while the parents partied on the first — I suppose I was thrilled but too scared to notice. The conversation swirled around my head — fair employment, DNA, that damned Daley — as I listened with one ear for shrill cries from the children two floors above.

Several months later, when my duty to reciprocate could no longer be ignored, I gave the group chili and corn bread, beer and brownies, my latent pretensions held firmly in check by the big brown table and clunky chairs, as well as a cold realization of the limits of my ability to put on a competitive bash. I counted on the Texas quaint factor to make it okay. But what had really disenchanted me with all such ambition and pretense, with ruinous, self-destructive potlatching, what had made me perhaps too conscious for a time of the gap between appearance and reality on such occasions, was a party I had recently attended.

The party was a coffee given by — I'll call her Martha Posy — who lived with her husband and two children in the most impressive house on our street, a handsome white Georgian with a gable roof. As I gazed out the window in the afternoon, watching for my daughter to come from school and trying to get a sense of the neighbors, I hit on a nickname for Martha: Wonder Woman. Martha was thin, with a sharp nose and crisp, short hair. She wore tweeds, pearls, a good cloth coat, sensible shoes. Every afternoon from four to seven, she left, came back, left again, shuttling the kids in and out of the house like automatons. She stood at the car door hurrying them, "Eleanor! Brian!" as they came out arrayed in a series of costumes — Camp Fire Girl, Cub Scout, ballet slippers and leotard, school clothes, all visible under their heavy coats slightly too large for them to allow for growth, the choice of a prudent, conscientious mother.

One day Martha rang our bell, presented me with a loaf of homemade bread, and issued an invitation. "Come over Thursday," Martha said, "to meet the neighborhood," so I thought coffee klatch. But on the day appointed the street was lined with big, sleek cars from which a steady stream of well-dressed women made their way to Martha's door. So I dressed carefully in my best brown pumps and the nubby brown suit that back in Texas had seemed to me the sort of thing Yankee women probably wore — ugly but smart.

Martha was a prudent, conscientious hostess as well. The scene that greeted me is still hard for me to reconcile with the sixties of marches, race riots, and love-ins. Martha, wearing a blue silk at-home dress with her usual pearls, presided at a large silver tea service, and her stately mother, also in silk and pearls, poured coffee. The linen was pale pink and starched; we used the wedding Spode and the family silver and dabbed our mouths with tiny starched napkins adorned with posies. We ate watercress and cucumber finger sandwiches, homemade poppy seed cakes, sand tarts, madeleines, strawberries with kirsch. Calligraphed name tags attached to individual small posies lay around the centerpiece, a large posy of gardenias, tea roses, and baby's breath. And in the rooms the women, all in Villager and Shetland and Country Set and Sadlers of Boston, moved around quietly, sipping coffee, exchanging information about children's names and cleaning women's wages. Martha Posy had not *outgrown* her mother, I decided. She had *become* her mother, or was trying to, putting the big pot in the little one exactly as Mama had always done.

But, as it turned out, not quite. I mention this party because of its aftermath, and because of something the fallout taught me about the danger of trying to be perfect. Not long after her coffee, Martha took her children to a birthday party one Friday afternoon, arranging to have them spend the night because it was her wedding anniversary. Then she came home, put the car away, bathed, and dressed carefully in a silk dress and her pearls, taking pains with her makeup. Sometime in that hour she sat down, wrote a note to her husband on her monogrammed stationery. "I can't do it anymore," she wrote in her careful Palmer Method script. "I'm a failure at everything, everything. You'll be better off without me."

Then she went out to the car in which she had spent so much time being a perfect mother, and arranged a perfect death for herself. She was thirty-two years old and had been married ten years.

Bill and I moved back to Texas not long afterward, and in all the years since I have not returned to that quiet tree-shaded street in Evanston. But Martha's death remains with me. What caused her to lay waste to all she had, I wonder? Her standards were so high that her life was hard. The apparent ease with which she slipped over the edge into the perfect order of death haunts me.

There but for the grace of God, Who alone is perfect.

Gazpacho in
a Sausage Grinder

. . . .

DURING THE TWO YEARS my husband and I lived in Detroit's Lafayette Park in the middle sixties, many of the neighbors — Indian, African American, German, Danish, Hungarian, Norwegian, French, British, and Filipino — gathered around our table at one time or another to eat and drink, as we in turn gathered at their tables. We were a close-knit community, citizens of an urban renewal project that had carved out, from the heart of a black ghetto in the inner city, two hundred green acres, dotted with high-rise apartment buildings and modern townhouses. Lawyers, journalists, doctors, professors, we huddled together, smugly feeling simultaneously progressive and safe. Our small children trotted confidently back and forth to Chrysler Elementary, which sat on East Lafayette at the edge of the park. A colorful flock, these lucky infants didn't even have to cross a street to get to a racially integrated school. After the isolationism of a Texas suburb, I found myself living in the enlightened atmosphere of the United Nations.

Eating together, living so closely together that the fragrances of our food mingled, naturally we wives of Lafayette Park exchanged recipes, which tended to be, like us, international in scope. In doing so, we were in good company, I realized, studying *The Cookbook of the United Nations,* which was just out that year, 1965. Sandwiched between the United Republic of Tanzania and the Upper Volta was the United States of America, with "Mrs. John F. Kennedy" listed as a recipe contributor. Jack was dead and Lyndon Johnson was in the White House, but Lady Bird was nowhere present in the United Nations cookbook, and Jackie was. Which of the blind recipes had Jackie contributed, I wondered? Surely not the plain roast turkey or the eggplant casserole. Maybe the seafood chowder — but with *canned* shrimp and crab — a woman with a house on the Atlantic? Finally I settled on the veal sauté as Jackie's, and tried it out on my neighbors.

Contributors to *The Cookbook of the United Nations* were amateurs. That same year, a major accomplishment in professional cuisine began, with the publication of the first volume of the Time-Life Foods of the World series. I bought these books, or some of them, as they came out, pleased by their promise of one-worldism. But I might have been more excited if I had not felt the promise had been anticipated in my neighborhood. We were ahead of the game, eating together and swapping recipes in Lafayette Park.

For my corn bread dressing and fried chicken, Alma Chand gave me her genuine Indian vegetable curry. For some reason, Alma, a Filipino, threw in the instructions, which I never used, for a slew of decorative cookies made with Jell-O; I decided that Filipinos must be as fanatical about Jell-O as Southerners are about Coke. Connie, married to a Finn, taught me how to make Finnish raisin dumplings, which we cooked in the juices of a rich pork stew. From my German friend Renate came a recipe for flank steak sliced thin and pounded, rolled up with bacon and dill, simmered in a little beef broth, and served with a sour cream dressing. Rouladen, she called it.

When the last volume of Foods of the World appeared in 1971, some three thousand recipes had been tested. The books were translated into seven languages and distributed in twenty-seven countries. Our project was more modest, but my neighbors and I wrote a cookbook too, the proceeds of its sales to go to our children's school. I have long since parted company with my copy, but as I recollect it was a thin, white volume, mimeographed and spiral-bound. Each cook was identified below his or (usually) her contribution and sometimes had penned a brief introduction. I contributed a recipe for corn bread, prefaced with a snotty little claim that "purists never use sugar," and another recipe, heaven knows why, for gazpacho, which, lacking a blender, I was in the habit of making in a sausage grinder purchased at a garage sale. *The Lafayette Park Cookbook* gathered together a miscellany of recipes revelatory of the peculiar heterogeneous charm of the sixties community from which it came. It must have been weird.

To Nach Waxman of New York's Kitchen Arts and Letters, who has judged contests for community cookbooks, for such books *place* is everything. Mr. Waxman says that most community cookbooks don't measure up to discriminating professional standards. "I'm interested in these books, to the extent that I'm interested in them at all, when they are unmistakably of the place they come from," he told me. By this theory, Southern books like *Talk About Good!* or *Charleston Receipts* are usually the best because the South has a greater tradition of regional food specialties than the rest of the country.

Talk about strict! But he's right about the South, I guess. Take *Charleston Receipts,* the stately great-grandmother of all Junior

League cookbooks. First published in 1950, this South Carolina book certainly has its charms, from its understated, tasteful format with line drawings of old Charleston buildings to its authentic recipes (or "receipts") for John C. Calhoun's lobster Newburg, benne (sesame seed) brittle, the sweet bread called Sally Lunn, and Hampton Plantation shrimp pilau. Less charming, to me at least, are the indecipherable comments in Gullah, an Afro-English dialect peculiar to the Carolinas, interspersed throughout the text: "Dis-yah de way de buckra like he bittle su'b-tuh-um." That's rooted in place with a vengeance.

But wait just a cotton-picking minute. Am I the only person bothered by that archaic — and cloying — use of "receipts" instead of the currently favored "recipes"? That's not all that's archaic. The contributors in my copy, from the twenty-second printing in 1979, are identified by their married names, with their full maiden names following in parentheses. Thus: Mrs. Henry P. Staats (Juliette Wiles). Looking at this bizarre signature, I remember the genealogy gauntlet Southern children used to run, perhaps still do. On the porch after church or at the Masonic picnic, any adult might suddenly ask me — rudely, I think now, though I accepted it then as the mysterious practice of grownups — "Now what was your mother's maiden name, honey? And which one of Mr. Willie Joe's boys did she marry?" These Charleston women — so sorry, *ladies* — are showing off their bloodlines. And then I smile, recalling my mother's description of my great-grandmother Harlan, who was a Charlestonian, as "a braggart and a terrible snob." For three or four generations, the women in my family have worked toward another way of life. Are we to backslide for a cookbook?

As for the ethnic strength of *Talk About Good!* which is published by the Junior League of Lafayette, Louisiana, I can only conclude, puzzling over the Waxman theory, that Lafayette, Louisiana, is a far piece from Lafayette Park, Michigan, in the sixties. What were we in our hodgepodge, melting pot, smorgasbord of a community, to do — forbear to publish because we lacked a sense of place? But we had a sense of place, not one place but a dozen or more. We had come from all over the world and all over America to gather peacefully together in Lafayette Park. So we published.

Like Walt Whitman, Americans go forth. They stay a little bit. They go forth again, and after a year or two they go forth again. All this going forth changes people and palates. You might say there's an essential culinary rootlessness as well as social rootlessness in many American home cooks. Even Southerners move around — a common family name in the South is, in fact, Goforth. Everything we taste, north and south, east and west, becomes a part of us. That's the American way, as James Beard understood so well.

Susan Stewart, who has lived in Texas and Pennsylvania and now lives down the road from Lafayette Park, has explored the question of her food identity at length. "I'm not sure where I stand on the socioeconomic food ladder," Susan told me. "Right now, there's some fresh ginger in the refrigerator, plus beets and kale, and yesterday there was arugula. But there are eight boxes of Velveeta Shells 'n Cheese in the cupboard. Perhaps this is because there are two preschoolers in the house. Perhaps not."

Yet Susan was brought up with a strong sense of place, a very good place for very good food — Virginia. As a child, she feasted on Smithfield ham, scalloped oysters, and baked shad. Today Susan still cooks like her mother, "And I *garnish* just like she does. I bet there is a garnishing gene."

But, typically, the development of Susan's palate did not stop at her mother's table. Her first cookbook was from All Saints Episcopal Church in Richmond, which featured such fare as chicken breasts with mushroom soup and sour cream, spinach balls, and canned artichoke hearts with mayonnaise and Kraft Parmesan. "Church cookbook food," Susan said, "is as ethnic as any dim sum recipe."

Where have these conflicting — and enriching — experiences left Susan? Confused. "Do I teach my children their Southern heritage with fat-soaked greens and fried chicken, or do I train their tiny palates with eggplant marinara sauce? They love fried chicken, which will kill them. Eggplant sauce is sophisticated and healthy, and they pick all the eggplant out of it before taking a bite." It's no wonder that cookbooks produced by groups of women who all grew up with disparate influences lack the sense of a stable culinary heritage.

Sometimes a community, however well knit, has a resident heretic, like Mickey (Mrs. Gerald) Sandridge, whose Best Ever Rum Cake considerably enlivens *Sharing Our Best,* the publication of Bethel Presbyterian Church in Olive Branch, Mississippi. Here's the recipe:

Best Ever Rum Cake

1 or 2 qt. rum	baking powder
1 c. butter	1 tsp. soda
1 tsp. sugar	lemon juice
2 large eggs	brown sugar
1 c. dried fruit	nuts

Before you start, sample the rum to check quality. Good, isn't it? Now, go ahead, select a large mixing bowl, measuring cups, etc. Check the rum again, it must be just right. To be sure the rum is of the highest quality, pour one level cup of rum into a glass and drink it as fast as you can. Repeat. Now, with electric, beat one cup of butter in large, fluffy bowl. Add one seaspoon of thugar and beat again. Meanwhile, make sure rum is of highest quadidy. Add 2 argeLeggs, 2 pucs fried druit, and beat until high. If druit gets stuck in beaters, pry it joose with a drewscriver. Sample the rum again, checking for highest conscisticity. Next, sift 3 cups pepper or salt (it really does not matter which).

Sample the rum again. Sift ½ pt. lemon juice. Add 1 Babble-
spood brown thugar (or whatever color you can find). Wix mell.
Grease oven and turn cake pan to 350 gredees. Now, pour the
mhole wess into the boven and ake. Check the rum again and go
to bed.

None of us in Lafayette Park was as daring, or as witty, as Mickey
Sandridge, whoever she is. Our little cookbook, though we were
proud of it, I'm sure was indistinguishable from the common
run of the literally thousands of fund-raising collections of recipes
brought out by American organizations between the Civil War and
the present day. How many thousands? I don't suppose anyone has
come up with an exact figure, as many of these cookbooks go unre-
marked beyond their own locales. (I've certainly never seen a list
that includes *our* cookbook.) But to give you an idea, records show
more than three thousand such cookbooks between 1861 and 1915,
and surely many more were lost in the shuffle. With modern methods of printing, copying, and desktop publishing, after 1915 the
number has grown to uncountable, and astronomical, heights.

And these books sell, first of all because cookbooks sell, year
after year outpacing in sales everything but the Bible. Of the
perhaps one hundred million cookbooks sold in this country in
the eighties, over one fifth were these community labors of love,
compiled by committees to benefit local endeavors like churches,
schools, clubs, hospitals, libraries, museums, and symphony or-
chestras. They are a guaranteed way of raising money. "I've never
known any organization to lose money on a cookbook," says Mary
Margaret Barile, the author of *Food from the Heart,* a how-to work-
book on the subject. "They're such a sure thing that there are
printers who will wait for their money until you rake the first
proceeds in."

How much money? Amounts vary considerably. The cookbook

of the Wyoming Historical and Geological Society, confusingly located in Wilkes-Barre, Pennsylvania, has averaged returns of a little over a thousand dollars a year since its publication in 1982. *La Piñata,* from the Junior League of McAllen, Texas, consistently pays off ten times that amount annually to community projects. *Charleston Receipts,* the second in sales of the genre, has sold well over six hundred thousand copies. For all my harsh words, I've bought two copies myself.

Securely at the top is *River Road Recipes,* first published in 1959 by the Junior League of Baton Rouge, Louisiana, and now in its sixty-seventh printing of twenty thousand copies each. "If there were community cookbook Academy Awards," wrote *New York Times* food editor Bryan Miller, "the Oscar for best performance would go hands down to *River Road Recipes.*" With sales of *River Road Recipes* and its sequel, *River Road Recipes: A Second Helping,* published in 1976 and now in its twenty-second printing, the League has returned more than two million dollars to Baton Rouge community projects.

Many Baton Rouge cooks lean heavily on *River Road Recipes.* As Thanksgiving and Christmas holidays approach every year, there is a rush on all over town to buy up frozen chopped spinach and jalapeño cheese. Seems the signature recipe of *River Road Recipes,* Spinach Madeleine, is so wildly popular that it causes a minor crisis year after year. "If you can get the spinach for the recipe," Sandy Bezet, the Junior League cookbook chairman, told me, "you can't find the cheese anywhere. And if the cheese is available, the spinach is not to be located. I think people buy up the ingredients weeks ahead of time and just plain hoard them for their holiday parties."

Why do home cooks buy these community cookbooks when there are so many cookbooks from professional food people available? Aside from loyalty to an organization, interest in the place from which the cookbook hails, and interest in the recipes contained, I think there's another, often overlooked reason: simply because community cookbooks are not professional. Some pros might chuckle condescendingly at frozen spinach and jalapeño cheese; home cooks feel that the contributor of this recipe speaks their food language. With the names of the donors, the wide range of cooking styles and interests, the "tips" that range from the sublime to the ridiculous, these books invoke a sense of neighborliness. Cooks do like to congregate, and in these alienated times community cookbooks provide a means of doing so.

When I was a child growing up in Mississippi, my grandmother used to set up a quilting frame in the parlor. There the frame would sit the whole winter, and once a week or so Mama's friends gathered around it to add their stitches to her Double Wedding Ring or Dutch Doll quilt. As they quilted, I listened while they talked, often about how to make "just cooking" a little more adventurous. "Add a half cup of coffee to your chocolate cake batter; it gives it a bite," Miss Ola Wooten might say (all ladies were "Miss," regardless of their marital status). "I grated some rat cheese in the corn bread the other night," Miss Irene Ellard might venture shyly, "and you know my family lapped it right up."

On long summer afternoons, after the dinner dishes were done and a tablecloth spread over the leftovers for supper, my mother would dress my little brother and me in starched playsuits, and the three of us would walk uptown to Miss Ola's and Mr. Luther's "General Mdse" store. Mr. Luther would ceremoniously open a new box of Premium crackers and place it next to the hunk of rat cheese on the block, and all the ladies who gathered would buy Co' Colas. Oh, those old Cokes that burned inside your nose and made your eyes sting! If Mother gave me an extra nickel, I'd put Tom's peanuts in my Co' Cola or buy an ice cream cone. At the bottom of some cones, you might bite into a little paper that read "5 cents," a coupon for a free cone. While my brother and I swung on the hitching post outside the store and angled for extra nickels, Mother and her friends sat and talked. By five o'clock, we would wend our way home for supper, my brother and I dreaming of limitless free ice cream cones, my mother mulling her new ideas for food and life. Exchanging recipes was a communal pleasure.

A move, a wedding, a death, and other events brought home-cooked dishes to the door, and it was considered courteous, when you returned the dish (never empty, the rules said) to ask for the recipe. Then, of course, you would be asked for *your* recipe. Eventually cooks customarily just tucked the recipe in with the food.

This kind of recipe swapping still goes on. Ruby Henderson and her Jackson, Mississippi, neighbors have met over morning coffee every week since 1950, each with a new recipe written on a note card, with a sample for the group to taste. They clip recipes from magazines, get them from friends, or invent them. After all this time, the Henderson recipe collection is as complete as a large library of cookbooks, and every recipe, as Mrs. Henderson says, has "been tested many, many times."

Many of us grew up cooking communally, elsewhere if not at home. Like my mother, Marcia Smith's mother was territorial about the kitchen. Marcia was allowed to set the table, mash the potatoes, pour the iced tea, and dry the dishes, but not to cook. So how did Marcia learn to cook? "The first meal I ever made was in the wilderness, camping out with the Girl Scouts. We made burners by pouring paraffin in an empty tuna can and adding a wick. We slipped that under an overturned coffee can, with a door cut in the side, and poured pancake batter on top of the can. It took hours to cook, as I recall." With her comrades, Marcia learned to make scrambled eggs and cookies to earn a cooking badge.

Community cookbooks, whether you contribute to them, cook from them, or just read them, give you once again that feeling of "we." This subliminal desire for community also helps to explain the consistent popularity of columns like "The Cook's Exchange" in

Bon Appétit and "Sugar and Spice" in *Gourmet,* in which readers supply their own and family recipes for the enjoyment of others. "Creating new recipes for family and friends is a lot of fun," Jim Moss of Atlanta wrote *Bon Appétit.* "I made this salad for a birthday dinner, and everyone loved it. It looks great, too."

About a mashed potato and endive salad, Anthony L. Howell of Colorado Springs confided to *Bon Appétit* readers, "This unusual but terrific side dish has been in my family for generations. My grandmother gave the recipe to my mother, and she passed it on to me. When the time comes, I'll share the recipe with my daughter."

If professional chefs are most often male, home cooks are usually female. Slowly the scales seem to be moving toward balance in both spheres. Though I don't remember men having much to do with our Lafayette Park cookbook, both *River Road* volumes contain sections called "How Men Cook," with recipes contributed by men who practice the art for family and friends. These recipes go far beyond the stereotypical back yard barbecue to such dishes as the Best Corn Casserole in the Whole Wide World and Senator Ellender's Creole Pralines. The community feeling is further broadened with a wide ethnic variety in the recipes contributed to *Gourmet* and *Bon Appétit* by both sexes. The columns I checked at random in the two magazines included moussaka, Louisiana jambalaya, lamb and peanut stew, fruitcake, spicy Thai shrimp soup, vegetable fettuccine, gingerbread, and cabbage soup.

Gourmet strokes egos, or pride of creativity, by running "Sugar and Spice" in a prominent position at the front of the magazine. Another bit of *Gourmet* flattery involves attaching contributors' names to their recipes, so that the column is full of such items as Moussaka Cynthia Gregory, Glazed Turnips Gardenhire, and Chocolate Layer Cake Giorgianni. Readers flatter *Gourmet* right back. No one ever writes in to criticize, apparently; the column is more sugar than spice. Many write largely to claim *Gourmet* kinship.

Because it's older than its competitors, *Gourmet,* which began publication in 1947, often receives letters that say, as one did in 1992, "As far back as I can remember, even as a pre-teen, I have seldom missed one of your issues. My mother read and saved each copy of your magazine as it came out, and I have done likewise."

Maybe the message is that in our highly mobile times, we take community wherever we find it. Most recently Susan Stewart has fallen under another culinary influence, the woman she describes as "our baby sitter—sommelier." According to Susan, the BSS brings copies of *Gourmet* and *Bon Appétit* to work with her and has a life-size grocery-store poster of the Frugal Gourmet in her house. This paragon introduced freshly grated Parmigiano to Susan's family, increased their olive oil consumption dramatically, and caused them to hide their wine coolers in the back of the refrigerator out of embarrassment. "You know," she told Susan last summer, listening to her employers plan a menu for a dinner party, "raspberry vinaigrette has become something of a cliché."

Take it with a grain of salt, the way you should take most everything and certainly community cookbooks. Browsing through a stack of them in the library of the Beard House, I come across some real lulus, but even the lulus are fun to read. *The Y. W. C. A. Cookbook,* from Pine Bluff, Arkansas, includes Billy Goats (date cookies), Heath Bar Pie, Congo Squares, and Japanese Fruit Cake (made Asian, I can only suppose, by the addition of one teaspoon of almond flavoring). "The Ladies of Berkeley" in *Buccaneer Bounty* contribute that classic, Coca Cola cake with miniature marshmallows.

But the biggest lulu comes from my own home state. Throughout *Country Cooking,* published in 1987 by the Mississippi Farm Bureau Federation Women, the slogan "Enjoy Mississippi Products" appears dozens of times. The Federated Women come from towns with colorful names, some familiar to me, some not, like Osyka, Kosciusko, Gore Springs, Gun Town, Hot Coffee, Ittabena.

Surely, I thought, *Country Cooking* will be a book so ethnically correct that even the hard-to-please Nach Waxman will rejoice to contemplate it.

Wrong. "Enjoy Mississippi Products" punctuates recipes for Company Green Peas, with canned peas and canned mushroom soup; Easy Green Bean Bake, with canned green beans, canned celery soup, and, you guessed it, canned French-fried onions; Swiss Bliss, with onion soup mix, canned mushroom soup, and bottled steak sauce. How opening all these cans leads one to "Enjoy Mississippi Products" is beyond me, unless all of Mississippi has turned into a giant canning factory.

Here in *Country Cooking* is Paris Cake, with Paris somehow conjured up by white cake mix and cream cheese. Here is Mm M Mounds Cake (marshmallows and coconut). Here is Sunshine Cake (cake mix and Jell-O). And, consummately, climactically, here is Dump Cake (canned cherry pie filling, canned crushed pineapple, and coconut "dumped" into a pan with cake mix), a recipe of the magnitude of awfulness which until now I had thought possible only in Ernest Matthew Mickler's wonderful parody of community cookbooks, *White Trash Cooking*.

Or is it parody, I find myself wondering? Does someone out there really make Grand Canyon Cake, varicolored cake mix layers stacked and forced open to resemble one of nature's wonders? ("This is a wonderful treat," Mickler writes with a straight face, "for someone that's going to, or just got back from vacationing at, the Grand Canyon. It's also very educational for children.") Is there a real Uncle Willie cheerfully calling the gang in to eat Uncle Willie's Swamp Cabbage Stew? ("If you don't live along the Carolina, Georgia, North Florida coast, Hearts of Palm in a can will work. But don't cook them too long.") *Charleston Receipts* has a recipe for cooter (turtle) soup; *White Trash Cooking* has that, as well as one for mock cooter soup. ("Mrs. Ina Filker of Sandfly, Georgia, says 'Give you a silver dollar if you kin tell the difference.'") Is there a *real* Betty Mae Swilley, to whom the book is dedicated?

And someday will someone with irreverent hands shuffle through Alma's or Renate's papers, find *The Lafayette Park Cookbook* from 1965, and laugh in amazement that there was once a fool woman who made gazpacho in a sausage grinder?

Pipe Dreams

SO THEN WE GOT, like, the brown munchies," I heard, that very first August afternoon, with the mercury hovering at the century mark and the English department line making a long S around Gregory Gym. A tall, skinny boy with a headband around his long locks was talking to the pudgy blond girl hanging on his arm. Both were clad in cutoffs and tank tops, both were sensibly barefoot.

"Where'd you go?" she asked.

"Over to the Night Hawk for double cheeseburgers and a shake. Then we came back and ate the rest of the Oreos and polished off the beer from Jim's party the other night." He grinned, rubbed his flat belly, and licked his hairy lips.

My stomach turned over. I had skipped breakfast and missed lunch to get in this line at the prescribed time. For over an hour I had been standing, sweltering in my nice-young-wife green linen shift and my earnest heels. Now this. I was convinced I had the brown munchies and I might die of them. What I didn't know in my dorkiness was that the prelude to the munchies was dope. You got high and in a kind of haze, a drug-induced euphoria, you had a fine time talking or touching or listening to music. Then you came down, you got the munchies, and you ate.

The year was 1968, the place the University of Texas at Austin, and I was back in school after a decade. It was clear that four years at Belhaven College, a school founded on the rigors of Scottish Presbyterianism, had not prepared me for higher education. Dope I dinna ken.

An unusual innocence for the time. "Of course" was Anna Quindlen's "suggested response for elected officials of a certain age when asked whether they smoked marijuana" after Bill Clinton's convoluted admission during the 1992 Democratic primaries that he had tried marijuana in England but didn't like it and didn't inhale. "Never explain," she advised in her *Times* column. "Saying you smoked dope but didn't inhale is the equivalent of saying you drank beer but didn't swallow it." In the sixties, almost everyone under thirty inhaled. The *New York Times* reported three hundred million marijuana users worldwide and eight million in the United States. Eight years into that magic, manic decade, dope was everywhere. It was certainly at the University of Texas.

About five o'clock that August afternoon, I came out of the gym and struggled back across campus to "The Drag," as Guadalupe Street at the western edge of the campus was known. I bought a bag of Chee-tos and a Coke, freed my hot feet, and sat down barefoot on the curb to satisfy my munchies and to survey the scene. Street peddlers sold beads, headbands, tie-dyed clothes, huaraches, Mexican pottery, handcrafted jewelry, old books, secondhand records, newspapers. All the long-haired, bearded boys and the long-haired, fresh-faced girls wore shorts or jeans, sandals or cowboy boots, and shirts that sprouted slogans — MAKE LOVE, NOT WAR. TAKE A HIPPIE TO LUNCH. I'VE GONE TO POT. LIFE, I LOVE YOU. Someone in jungle fatigues walked by carrying a Vietcong flag.

U.T. was more crowded in the late sixties than ever before or since in its history, with some forty thousand students. Food was plentiful and cheap, both in the numerous student cafeterias on campus and in the fast food joints on The Drag. Dope too was plentiful and cheap. For two or three dollars, you could buy a high on acid, mescaline, or marijuana. For five dollars, you could get stoned and buy a hamburger and fries for the munchies afterward.

Marijuana was the drug of choice. Students smoked grass everywhere, on campus as well as off. "Pot fueled my appetite," one former coed told me recently. "My girlfriends and I would smoke in our dorm rooms, then take the elevator to the Fat Room, where you could buy machine cuisine for munchies." They bought Tab, which came in icy bottles and cost a quarter, to have with their Twinkies or Fritos. "Pizza entered my life in a big way."

Whatever you ate to satisfy the munchies, grass made its flavor more intense. "The term 'getting stoned' is confusing," Charles Reich says in *The Greening of America*. "It implies losing consciousness, rather than a higher awareness. But getting dulled has nothing to do with the psychedelic experience; using marijuana is more like what happens when a person with fuzzy vision puts on glasses." Eating Twinkies, newly conscious of the creamy middle stuff, and of the difference between cake-chocolate and frosting-chocolate, you uttered what Reich calls the "ultimate sign of reverence, vulnerability, and innocence": "Oh wow!"

I heard a lot of "Oh wows" as I got to know the students at Texas. Youngish but definitely of the wrong generation, with a husband and two children waiting for me in the old house we'd bought on Thirty-fifth Street, I found these kids remarkably trusting, even foolhardy. How did they know I wasn't that most hated of creatures, the narc?

Oh, I tried to fit in. Between 1968 and 1970, as one semester flowed into another, I saw *Elvira Madigan,* heard Tom Wolfe speak on campus, bought *Bridge Over Troubled Water,* and played the Stones. I did these things in the same way I would drive on the left in England, drink wine with my meals in France and Italy, say "yes, ma'am" in Mississippi. I was observing the customs of the country, an older woman trying to pass, wearing a gray miniskirt out of polyester as heavy as sheet metal, boots, and a white leather cap, carrying a hot pink notebook embellished with a big daisy. What could be a more perfect narc cover?

Still, the unwary kids talked. The girl next to me in Anti-Intellectualism in American Literature told me she'd picked up a strange guy at the record store, smoked two joints, and "made out with him on the floor all night." I managed just to nod. When my friend Wayne came into class in his usual motorcyclist's outfit, brushing his long hair off a clammy brow, and eased into the seat next to me muttering, "Watch out for me, Jo, I dropped acid this morning," I watched out as diligently as I watched out for my four-year-old at home.

I couldn't really join the culture, but the culture came to me. Vicki, from my Saturday morning poetry seminar, told me about going to a U.T. football game after she had eaten a hash brownie. "It was the scariest experience of my life," she said. "Seventy thousand screaming Longhorn fans, all that carnage on the field, and the announcer saying things like 'Texas takes Baylor apart on the fifty-yard line.' I felt like I was at the Nuremberg rallies." She had managed to last for a while by focusing on her corny dog, which became "cosmic, with purple mustard, and the dog melting into all kinds of colors and spirals," but at the end of the first quarter, she and her date left.

Over lunch at the Union, I heard Wayne's Saturday-night adventures. High on acid, he drove with a carload of like-minded friends up into a deserted section of the hills around Austin. From Mount Bonnell, the highest point, they could see the Colorado River, the campus buildings, the top of the tower from which, a couple of years earlier, Charles Whitman had killed some two dozen people. Stoned, they tried to touch the stars. They talked about Plato, ethics, God, reaching insights that seemed profound and original. At three o'clock in the morning, back on The Drag "from the edge of the universe," they stormed into the Night Hawk to order waffles, sausage, bacon, double orders of cherry pie, gallons of Coke or milk, all for under six dollars. The munchies.

I listened to these tales with some interest, as I observed the political speeches on the front campus; the classroom strikes against the Vietnam War and the campus administration; the haze of marijuana smoke in remote corners of the library stacks; the Save Our Trees campaign, which had students chaining themselves to virgin trees waiting for the bulldozer; the near nudity and the more than near copulation in the grass outside the Union. I fetched doughnuts to the tree huggers after a long night, warned the library smokers when a monitor approached, listened to the speeches, and, though I crossed their picket line, even sympathized with the strikers. But finally these things were less real to me than class. Nothing would have induced me to cut a class, strike or no strike.

My mother warned me about the intensity with which I went into this experience. "It's going to break up your marriage," she said dolefully. I scoffed. She was wrong, I was sure. But in any event, I couldn't really help my intensity. After a decade away from school, when I came back I fell in love — with books, with teachers, with ideas, with the world I was in. And falling in love is intense. Paint the trees greener, the sky bluer, the world brighter. Dismiss Old Man Blues; bring on the dancing girls. Carl Rogers was in vogue, and my grad school friends and I talked jokingly but with an undercurrent of seriousness about being "significant others" to each other as we talked about "I-Thou relationships" and "the thingness of the thing."

To this day I don't know exactly what "the thingness of the thing" meant to Husserl, from whose philosophy it presumably comes. To me, it meant trying to free my mind of preconceptions, to look at the things of the world around me as I would at the unfamiliar array on a well-laden buffet table in an exotic land, as "thingness" to be tasted, enjoyed, relished. The idea itself, as I understood it, inspired a kind of psychedelic consciousness.

If every "thing" was new, all things were joined. "Everything's connected to everything," we read in *The Whole Earth Catalog* in 1968, a statement of the "oneness" of the universe felt under the influence of marijuana and other psychedelics. Behind the fragments of quotidian life lay a "whole earth"; all creatures here below, the world and they that dwell therein, were one entity, an entity visible only to enlightened eyes. Dope was, of course, the shortcut to such enlightenment.

Space travel strengthened this revelation. Stewart Bland's *Whole Earth Catalog* was inspired, we understood, by the space missions. Orbiting the moon, the three astronauts of *Apollo 8* looked back on "the whole earth," and took pictures, televised all over the world, of the planet, so small and vulnerable. That new tenderness toward the earth was the beginning of the modern ecology movement. If the planet was small, as it certainly appeared to be in those pictures from outer space, then obviously it had limited resources. How then could those resources best be used to feed the hungry of the earth, in the present and in the future?

I first began to think about this question through *The Rag,* Austin's underground paper. *The Rag,* in a perpetual state of apoplexy, its thirty or so rackety old typewriters clacking away, was spat out angrily from extremely dirty and jammed offices on The Drag, but was right on target in its antis, I thought: anti-war, anti-Johnson, anti-U.T. administration, anti-Frank Erwin, the macho businessman head of the university's board of regents. So when *The Rag* began to be anti-meat and to favor a diet based on grains, legumes, and vegetables, I paid attention.

If I never hear "You are what you eat" again, it will be too soon. But that was the idea. Want a wholesome, healthy, natural self? Eat wholesome, healthy, natural foods, preferably foods you grow yourself. "Plastic" food, loaded with preservatives and artificial color, made for "plastic" — artificial, pretentious, shallow — people, and *The Graduate* that year would have none of it. Drugs were "natural," said the counterculture. True, LSD was made in a lab, but you could eat nutmeg, mushrooms, morning glory seeds, and get a high. Grass wasn't grass but dried flowers — lovely thought! — of the cannabis plant. Even the scarier drugs were "natural," the prophets said. Opium came from poppies, cocaine from the coca plant, psilocybin from mushrooms, mescaline from the peyote cactus.

Antiwar feeling made the collective gorge rise against any form of butchery. Eating red meat made you aggressive. White bread and white rice, with the nutrients removed, made you barren and bland. Gentled by grass, as turned on by Nature as any Romantic poet, the more idealistic hippies of the period began to eat what came to be called, in the vernacular, "nuts and twigs." That is, they ate the same foods that, in 1969, many of the four hundred thousand bodies sprawled on the thirty-five acres at Woodstock ate — brown rice and vegetables.

Most Texans, indeed most Americans, remained convinced that meat was the best as well as the tastiest source of protein. During my Austin years, I read the emerging evidence for the new way of eating and maybe I cooked a few more pots of pinto beans or spaghetti marinara than I might have otherwise. But no matter how desirable a diet of nuts and twigs, I wasn't quite ready to go whole hog — I guess I should say "whole bean," as hogs were about the worst eating of all, according to the new canon; enemy cops were "pigs" and "pigging out" was a disgusting food orgy.

My husband was even less ready. Bill had grown up in South Texas on barbecue and Tex-Mex, and, after three years in Michigan and Illinois, we were both happy to be back in a place where these delicacies were available in their pure ethnic splendor. So we pigged out regularly on thin, juicy slices of barbecued beef, with a black crusty edge, and a side of white "loaf broad" to soak up the sauce (never, never, never already poured on the meat). We greased our snouts with fat pork sausages with the grill marks on the side or settled for a rush of chopped pork on fat soft buns, with no sauce but meat juice, and a side of cole slaw. And we never missed an opportunity for tacos, enchiladas, and burritos.

Mi Casa was our casa when we could afford it, an upscale pottery- and serape-adorned Mexican restaurant frequented by the politicos from the state capitol. Puffed tacos, the first I'd ever had, topped with a profusion of meat, cheese, guacamole, lettuce, tomato, and sour cream; enchiladas verdes, made with a tomatillo sauce rather than the usual green chilies; flour tortillas as light as the margaritas were serious — after our sojourn in the Nawth, Mi Casa was a dream fulfilled.

Though I've forgotten its name, I also recall with great fondness a little dive in the barrio on the "bad" side of the tracks. From its hole-in-the-wall kitchen poured, to a steady stream of gringo customers lining up outside at noon and night, a steady stream of platters of "the meal." There was no menu. Without being consulted, big and little appetites alike were served, for about three dollars, chips and salsa, two enchiladas, two tacos, two burritos, guacamole, rice, and beans. We ordered Carta Blanca by the pitcher, Cokes for the kids.

Without the children, Bill and I might spend a Friday or Saturday evening sitting at an open-air table at Scholz's Beer Garden. Scholz's was noted for its clientele, Texas liberals like Ronnie Dugger and Greg Olds of *The Texas Observer,* as well as for the graffiti on the rest room walls, considered by the cognoscenti to be the best the Lone Star State offered. I remember "Yossarian is alive and well and living in New York City" and "John Silber" — a detested dean with only one arm — "swims in a circle." And of course there was the poignant, "Hey, hey, LBJ/How many kids have you killed today?" At Scholz's, with our beer we consumed corned beef, rare roast beef, or pastrami sandwiches, not easy to find in Texas.

The kids loved meat. They begged for the "flame-grilled" hamburgers at the Night Hawk. They wanted the steak Bill barbecued on our flagstone patio to be very rare. "Just stun it a little, honey," I would say. When he brought the platter into the kitchen, to the hot meat juices — read "blood" — I would add melted butter, lemon juice, and Worcestershire sauce, and pour this back over the meat. They gobbled down wienies, which I rolled up in white bread, secured with toothpicks, topped with cheese, and toasted. Their favorite TV dinner consisted of a small steak, a few Tater Tots (french-fried mashed potato balls), and a gesture toward vegetables, green beans, I think. And they thought beef fondue was the greatest; tapping their little feet to the Beatles' "Yellow Submarine" or "All You Need Is Love," they gripped the long forks, plunging their own morsels of meat into sizzling oil, then dipping them in a sauce of sour cream and horseradish. Clearly, eating lower on the food chain wasn't made to order for our family.

Nevertheless, we were influenced by the Zeitgeist. After Austin, we moved to Dallas, where Bill joined Jim Lehrer's Channel

Thirteen news team and I began teaching English at Southern Methodist University. If you recall, in the early seventies it was in to drop out. Dropping out meant abandoning conventional life, daring to do the unexpected, following one's star. It meant wearing bell-bottom jeans and an Indian headband. After his beatnik days, as a young father Bill had dressed *old,* in a uniform of black suit, white shirt, and discreet tie, the better to seem sober and responsible. Now in our thirties we both became a part of the bell-bottom revolution. Like our fellow revolutionaries, we wanted to return to the freedom and individualism of an earlier America. The bell-bottoms might be a kind of uniform, but at least they weren't Corporate.

We wanted to grow our own food too. Be careful what you wish for; it may come true. Our wish came true in a section of southeast Dallas called Pecan Heights, where we rented an abandoned farm from late October of 1970 till May of 1973. I remember clearly the day we took a wrong exit off the freeway and came upon it. Bill and I both caught our breath: a two-story white farmhouse, built to last, a porch with a red tile floor across the front, and a big brick chimney on one side. A Sartoris among Snopeses, weathered and vacant but imposing, the house sat across the road from a huddle of small shotgun shacks. Behind its dilapidated white fence lay the romance of the past — an enormous kitchen garden gone to weeds, a screened gazebo nestling in a pear and fig orchard, and a big barn and tidy tack house leading into a gently rolling expanse of prairie.

The front door stood open, which, like the FOR RENT sign in the yard, we interpreted as a sure sign of welcome from the gods. If I'd had any sense, I would have flinched at the primitive kitchen, with its grimy low sink and big old dirty stove. But in my euphoria, I focused on the living room, spacious and airy, and on the octagonal dining room, the prettiest room in the house, with bay windows on four of its sides.

We could have Christmas here the way it should be, we said to each other, and horses, and picnics in the little wood. Never mind, we told ourselves, that the forty acres once the farm's pride had dwindled to a paltry ten. Never mind that along the side of the sloping pasture encroached an ugly row of rental warehouses or that a track for the Texas and Pacific Railroad ran along the back. Never mind, even, that a horse grazing quietly between the barn and the tack house would take its death of fright when a gasoline truck plummeted down the freeway on the west. We were entranced, charmed, felt that we were standing squarely in the middle of a simpler time, a kinder world.

We felt lucky. It was a real farm once, and could be again, we told ourselves, and at least for a time it would be ours. When the toy train thundered across the bottom of the pasture, rattling the windows as it blew its comic whistle, we laughed and mouthed our words: Only in Dallas could we find this overlooked dream. Only us, in Dallas.

We needed some luck; my mother's dire predictions seemed to be coming true. The marriage that housed us all felt a lot less stable than the farmhouse looked. The four of us were excited about living here, the children because of the ponies, cats, dogs, chickens, goats, a whole animal kingdom, that we promised them. Believing that somehow all those animals would stabilize us as two small human children couldn't, Bill and I agreed that finding the farm, so pleasing, so possible, signified that the deities of endurance and permanence were making an appearance for us. With the portentousness of the desperate we named the place Epiphany, and called our first collie pup Pif.

We soon discovered, however, that, with all its charm, for us Epiphany was Cold Comfort Farm. City dwellers who didn't want to be, we were nevertheless a bust as farmers. We harvested our first crop of pecans, baskets and baskets of our favorite nuts, from thirty or forty trees. My head swirled with thoughts of Christmas goodies — fruitcake with *our* pecans, bourbon cake with *our* pecans, fudge and divinity with *our* pecans, and of course that ambrosial confection of my youth, pecan pie, with *our* pecans. But when I began shelling the nuts, a job in itself, I found they were winy and stale. We threw them back out for the squirrels, less picky than we were.

In the spring we raced the greedy birds to the figs and pears, and lost. We either ate the fruit green, or found bird bites and worm holes on every ripe piece. I chopped around these marks of vandals to put up a few tiny jars of fig and pear preserves, a lot of effort for little effect. Another year, we promised, we would cover the trees with sheets or something — surely there was something? What did *real* farmers do, anyway?

We turned to the garden, consulting the almanac and waiting till Easter. We had so much space, row after long row, that we went wild with possibility, planting potatoes, cucumbers, tomatoes, squash, green beans, peppers, even corn. While we waited for our crops to come up so that we could eat off the land, we acquired three horses, gentle old Bess for me, a stallion for my show-off husband, and a Welsh pony, Little Lady, for the children. We fitted out their stalls, filled the feed bins, and put water in the troughs. Then we bought a collie mate, Lochinvar, for Pif. The garden would grow, the dogs would have pups, the fig trees would bear. All would be fertile and we could ride the fences of our Eden on horseback.

Not quite. A mile of potatoes, planted in chunks with eyes, made only greenery, as pretty and unprofitable as the farm itself. A profusion of cucumber vines produced a single giant cucumber, tough and bitter. The horses got out and callously feasted on the succulent tops of the young corn. Big, flat, ugly brown bugs that gave me the shudders covered the squash, and we let them have it. Only the tomatoes didn't know how to give up growing, and the hot peppers, never picked, grew redder and redder under the sizzling sun. The freeway breathed exhaust fumes on all this extravagance, and finally we let the garden go back to weeds.

Temperamentally we just weren't cut out for the quiet life of custom and duty that farming demands. We were creatures of our own time more than we wanted to admit. Our two old cars, laden with the kids and the dogs, were always pulling in and out of the circular driveway, with a screech of tires on the loose gravel, on fictitious and time-wasting errands. But, blind as Milton writing *Paradise Lost,* we continued to love the romance of the farm.

In a gully by the railroad tracks filled with broken Old Crow bottles and rusted Pearl cans, my son and his father found the most momentous sign from the dubiously benign gods: two flat white tombstones speckled gray with age, which they ferried to the house in Winton's red wagon. Sarah Rockett. Edd Rockett. Birth and death dates, that was all. Sarah died in 1933; Edd lived another twenty years or so, died an old man.

The courthouse records told us what we wanted to know. Bill, who loved to find out such things, came home jubilant. Edd and Sarah Rockett had bought forty acres from a man named Thurman in May 1925, and by the end of the year had put up the six-room house, with a big sun porch across the back to face the young pecan and fruit trees they planted, and a five-stall barn. Eight years later Sarah Rockett died of pellagra in the worst year of the Great Depression.

Pellagra. After our failures with the garden, the irony of a farm wife's dying of a nutritional deficiency impressed me. I brooded over it as I moved around the clumsy old-fashioned kitchen and brought pinecones in for the brown Mexican table. Maybe during that impossible winter of 1933 the Rocketts had nothing to eat but the corn saved for livestock. I had heard of such things. But surely Sarah Rockett was a better farm wife than I, and her husband a better farmer than Bill. Why had there been no jars of canned snap beans, peas, and squash? No bright pickles or preserves, with the cucumbers, figs, and pears right outside the door? No crocks of kraut? No hams in the smokehouse or scrawny chickens pecking in the barn grain?

Pellagra. It weighed on me. I took up cooking with a vengeance. Once a week or so, I invited friends for a casual dinner, Bill's cohorts at the station or some of my own new teaching colleagues. In those days, I was supremely cautious about cooking for company. Endlessly I repeated three main dishes — Julia's coq au vin, beef Stroganoff from a recipe I had clipped from a newspaper, and chicken curry — until the kids began to tease me unmercifully. "Erin and I always knew there was going to be company," my son, Winton, told me recently, "by the way the house smelled when we got home from school. We'd play a game we called What's That in the Condiment Tray? Even now, any mention of the words 'Major Grey's Chutney' sends Erin into fits."

Do you wonder that I gave them a break by moving from Betty Crocker Indian to Time-Life Italian, the little Foods of the World spiral in which I set out to master every dish? Coming home from the market on a Saturday morning, piling the sink with mushrooms, tomatoes, onions, garlic, eggplant, zucchini, putting on a big pot of minestrone for the evening's guests, I felt like Sophia Loren. Gnocchi verdi, a dish I had never eaten and did not dare pronounce, sounded close enough to the dumplings I made with chicken to give me confidence. Succulent little balls of spinach and ricotta, they were a hit. I made vitello tonnato for a late spring luncheon in the gazebo. Chicken cacciatore I did well and often. Risotto and polenta seemed impossibly exotic; I hadn't a clue as to how they might taste or even what their texture should be. But my favorite Italian dish was lasagna, which pleased the children, and pleased me because I could do the whole dinner *ahead of time*. That same year, I came into possession of a splendid cheesecake recipe which — answer to my prayers — *had* to be prepared *the night before.* So thrilled was I at the amount of control that these two dishes gave me that one greatly overloaded friend had to advise me that, "Really, Jo, they shouldn't be served at the same meal."

Sometimes I would look around me and realize that I was not in Tuscany but in Texas. Then I prepared bounteous farm meals from food I bought at the supermarket. A brown Mexican pot of pinto beans bubbled at the back of the stove. I simmered turnip and mustard greens with salt pork, fried little circles of fresh okra, mashed potatoes with lots of butter, sliced pale red store-bought tomatoes, pulled iron skillets of hot yellow corn bread out of the old gas oven.

We had our dream Christmas, a wonderful big Christmas with two turkeys and wine. Before Thanksgiving I made a big fruitcake (with store-bought pecans), soaked it in brandy, and wrapped it in cheesecloth and foil. Our tree, decorated with pinecones, popcorn, and cranberries, touched the eighteen-foot-high ceiling of the living room. Winton believed in Santa Claus, but Erin, who was ten, had doubts. One night as I tucked her in, "Mother," she said in the level voice of an adult, "is there a Santa Claus? I want to know. Tell me the truth."

I couldn't lie. "Honey," I told her, "not a flesh-and-blood Santa Claus. He's just, you know, a symbol of the way you love somebody enough to give presents. Don't tell Winton, but your daddy and I really put the presents under the tree."

"Oh," she said thoughtfully. When she woke up the next morning, it was as if I had never spoken. She simply erased all that I'd said from her memory and continued to believe in Santa Claus for at least another year. She liked her pipe dreams, just as I liked mine.

On Christmas Eve, after the children were in bed, while Bill assembled the toys I made pans of corn bread for the next day's dressing, chopped onions, and simmered broth. I ground oranges and cranberries for relish and peeled sweet potatoes. The next morning, Bill and I set up two long tables in the gemlike dining room and loaded them with food and pine boughs and candles. Friends arrived, enough people to fill both tables.

Bill asked the blessing, an earthy old Scottish form he had resurrected from Robert Burns's poetry. Called the Selkirk grace, it lent dignity, Bill thought, without compromising his basic agnosticism. Around the tables, we bowed our heads respectfully while he intoned in his best Highland burr:

> *Some hae meat and canna eat,*
> *And some wad eat that want it,*
> *But we hae meat and we can eat,*
> *And sae the Lord be thankit.*

Laura, a photographer for the television station, took pictures of us all, family and friends, in the candlelight at dusk. Our daughter was a golden child, our son soft and blond, a little boy with curls still. I never covered the windows, so far from neighbors, so everything around their faces was light: crystal and candles and windows' glow. Surveying the scene in the gracious light of the Christmas candles, I remembered the lighting of the candles at the dinner party in *To the Lighthouse,* which I had just taught. For a joyful moment, I *was* Mrs. Ramsay, helping those I loved to "a specially tender piece of eternity."

But the best party we ever gave at the farm was the Jim Lehrer Going Away Party in 1972, when around three hundred people came out to eat barbecue, drink beer, and celebrate Jim's making it into the big time up north. Hart Stilwell came up from San Antonio to help Bill with the barbecue. Hart was a skinny old lizard, a newsman who wanted to be as tough as his old man, the Texas Ranger, had been. Hart was the only man I ever knew who called me a tomato.

For the Jim Lehrer Going Away Party, Hart and Bill cooked half a steer Mexican-style, which involved digging a big pit, drinking a great deal of Jack Daniel's, and sitting up all night under the stars, telling lies and laughing like fools. We arranged a circle of bales of hay in the pasture, got a group called the Possum Trotters to come and play, and asked B. W. Stevenson to sing. I had a red and blue square-dance dress, I remember. We danced to the Possum Trotters, drank beer, ate barbecue, and partied. Late in the evening, old Hart, who in the way of declining macho men felt he wasn't getting enough attention, set fire to one of the bales of hay. We danced attendance on him after that.

It all vanished, of course, as dreams will. Bill left. The kids and I stayed. Pif gave birth to pups with a bird dog look, putting Lochinvar's long collie nose decidedly out of joint. The horses kept getting out of the broken-down fences and straying onto the freeway, and I had to catch them. Several times, Little Lady was picked up on the pavement by the Dallas dogcatcher, and I'd have to pay fifty dollars to bail her out of the pound. Finally, I just jumped the fence myself.

Old Hart died, cussed as ever. Bill and I divorced, and we both married again. Not long after Hart's death, my second husband and I went by the farm to see about a picnic table I'd left behind in my impatience to get away. Tall grass covered every inch of the yard. A commercial Coke machine sat on the front porch. No one was home. The house lay still and quiet in the late afternoon sun; in the paddock, a strange brindle horse looked up benignly from its grazing, grass blades hanging from its long jaw. We walked over to the tack house Bill had used for a study, now empty and sad. Crickets whirred in the dry grass, and a couple of fat yellow cats rubbed against our legs and meowed.

The picnic table was still under the kitchen oak, or part of it was; the legs at one end had been hacked and burned off, maybe for firewood. The back door to the sun porch was open. Followed by the cats, I stepped inside. Like a hippie paradise, the whole house had been divided into separate cubicles with madras bedspreads and tie-dyed sheets. Mattresses lay on the floor, a large hookah beside one. The stove was gone, and a greasy skillet and a stew pot sat on the living room hearth. Dirty dishes and clothes were piled everywhere. The only piece of furniture, a large paint-stained table in the octagonal dining room, was covered with half-finished ceramic pots and bowls. Nice pots. I should at least have taken a pot, I thought, as we drove away. But it had all become someone else's dream.

I sometimes worry that my only mode is nostalgia, my tone the bittersweet, my real theme loss. At first I called it my Scarlett O'Hara syndrome, singing the gone-with-the-wind blues, and blamed my Mississippi birth. But my second husband, a Dutchman, is like that too. He left Holland when he was eight years old, and yet, or therefore, he dreams of it, a Delft blue heaven. Perhaps we are all Southerners of the soul, mourning the past, knowing that we lost something in the War which can never be restored.

·✖·

Strange Fruit

. . . .

IN MY NEXT REINCARNATION, I won't have to get married,"
said my friend Gwynne. "I'll have outgrown all that." As we
were planning my wedding reception at the time, I felt a bit
retarded. I envied her for being able to envision such a state, I
suppose. I couldn't, and I'm not sure I can now. I love being married. Being married for me is like being female, both inevitable and
desirable. For well over half my life, I have been married to one
person or the other.

You know about one person, Bill. The other is Willem Brans,
who gave me his name the year after Bill and I divorced. It was
1974, and lots of people were marrying barefoot in the park and
writing their own wedding vows. Willem and I did neither. We had
a home wedding, predictable right down to the Wedding March
from *Lohengrin*. Wearing a long pink organza dress with white polka
dots and carrying a bouquet of wildflowers, I walked down a make-

shift aisle in Willem's folks' house to an arch of flowers beneath which Willem waited, handsome in his sober suit. Right on schedule, my father cleared his throat emotively and my mother sobbed. Erin, thirteen, also in a long dress, pale blue, and Winton, ten, who had insisted on his favorite tennis shirt, had eyes as round as the dots in my dress as Willem and I exchanged rings and the grand old vows that begin, "Dearly beloved."

After the champagne and cake at Gwynne's house, after a two-day honeymoon in Athens (Texas), we got down to living, and to eating, together. The wedding may have been traditional, but after that came a meeting, and sometimes a collision, of cultures. The family into which I had married had a past incredibly exotic to me and my kids. Willem, his brothers, Jan and Jacobus, called Jay, and his parents, Elly and John, with their dog, Dicky, had immigrated to the United States from the Netherlands on the big ship *Groote Beer* in the years after World War II. Willem's father had spent much of World War II in hiding in Nazi-occupied Holland, in terror of being sent to a Nazi labor camp. Elly's brother, the first Willem, was killed by the Germans. The Branses had stories to tell of fake identities and secret meetings, of cruelty at the hand of Hitler's henchmen, of the trials of surviving in the chaos of postwar Europe, and of poverty and hardship starting over in America.

The family settled first in Maryland, where they took their oaths of citizenship on November 22, 1963. "We were in the courtroom when the judge who administered the oath told everyone that the president had just been murdered," Willem told me. "We almost changed our minds." In the late sixties, a noisy, gregarious, argumentative, game-playing, larger-than-life crowd, the men all six feet tall or over, they moved into the maelstrom, to Dallas, and quickly immersed themselves in the peculiarities of Texas politics and culture. Then in the seventies, the Branses took on my children and me, and we took on the Branses. We were strange fruit for each other.

It can't have been easy for Elly and John. Here was Willem, their brilliant oldest son, with two degrees and a university position, in love with a woman a number of years his senior with two children from a previous marriage. We were married in May. In July, I took up a grant for the remainder of the summer to do research and attend a seminar at the university in Austin. Willem stayed behind in Dallas to teach summer school, peddle encyclopedias door-to-door, and take care of the children he had just inherited.

That summer, he also did most of the cooking, which Erin and Winton found interesting. "Dear Mom, I miss you very much!" Winton wrote me. "The first night you were gone we had slightly burned cutlets, uncooked rice, and boiled parsley? Willem thought it was greens and boiled it!"

I remember quite well a culinary adventure Willem and I had shortly after we were married. The children were with their father for the weekend, and we invited our old buddy John Lampo, Willem's former housemate and the best man at our wedding, for dinner. Willem had been raving about a gourmet dish his grandfather had taught him to make, known fondly to the Brans family as Cod Rotterdam. You sautéed cod fillets ("fresh from the net," in Rotterdam; in Dallas, fresh from the frozen food locker) in butter, topped them with chopped fruit (bananas and oranges? surely not *bananas?*), and topped fish and fruit with a special secret sauce. Willem chopped the fruit and set the fish out to defrost. "I can handle this," he told John and me. "I don't want you to watch me make the sauce; it's a secret. But let's have a drink first."

I made a pitcher of margaritas, and we drank that. Then, what the hell, it's Friday, we said. So I made another pitcher of margaritas, and we drank that. We sat around the table, listening to music, drinking and laughing, having a blast. At some point, Willem went into the kitchen and brought out plates of food. We lapped up the Cod Rotterdam, which seemed exquisite, and tucked into a final pitcher of margaritas to wash it down.

At six in the morning I woke up, with a thirst like all of South Texas. Fully clothed, I was flat on my face on the sofa, with no idea how I got there. Willem lay sleeping on the floor at my side, his head pillowed on a sneaker. John was nowhere to be seen. Later he told us he had let himself out after we had *passed* out. Holding my poor abused head, I stumbled into the kitchen for water. Drinking deeply, I looked around me in dread for the mess, but aside from the nasty, smelly, water-laden, empty frozen fish package, there was none. The skillet in which the fish were to be sautéed was pristine, obviously unused. I let the full horror of the situation settle on my bleary mind. *We had eaten Cod Rotterdam raw.*

Willem must have taken the raw fish out of the package, heaped the fruit on top of each fillet, poured on the secret sauce (which he divulged to be a mixture of ketchup and mayo), and served the plates with a flourish. And we ate that vile raw fish, probably still cold even, with those vile bananas and oranges, maybe even grapes, maybe even berries, and that vile ketchupy mayonnaise — we ate it *all.* Even now the words Cod Rotterdam send me across the Donner Pass, metaphorically speaking.

Not all strange Dutch food was nasty, the children and I soon learned. Some was actually good, and the three of us had an awfully good time being indoctrinated those first years. The time was ripe for such indoctrination. Across America, an interest in other cultures was burgeoning. Woks were a hot item. Numerous Vietnamese, Indian, and Thai restaurants opened, as new waves of immigrants came here. The country tried the exotic ingredients of Moroccan and Japanese food. Szechuan and Hunan restaurants introduced the spicy dishes of those Chinese provinces, a far cry from the blander Chinese foods we were used to. Like Szechuan and Hunan food, the Indonesian sambals and nasi gorengs my new Dutch relatives loved to concoct were a natural for my Texas children, with their long-established affection for chili peppers.

Belatedly, inspired by my hands-across-the-water marriage, I bought Diana Kennedy's definitive *Cuisines of Mexico,* published in 1972, as well as Craig Claiborne's 1971 book, *The New York Times International Cook Book.* Claiborne's fat tome featured recipes not only from the familiar cuisines of France and Italy, but from the very unfamiliar cuisines of such places as Armenia, Tahiti, Barbados, and Dahomey. Where the devil was Dahomey, I wondered, and, in a burst of a newly acquired chauvinism, why wasn't Holland represented?

If Elly and John had reservations about their son's taking on a ready-made family, they never even hinted at them to me. The Branses had — have — a great sense of festivity and celebration, and they warmly welcomed Erin, Winton, and me to the ongoing party of their lives. The kids and I discovered holidays and customs we never knew existed.

I'll never forget the look of startled happiness on Erin's and Winton's greedy little faces the first December 5 that Elly and John showed up bearing armloads of completely unexpected presents. None of us had ever heard of the birthday of Saint Nicholas, or of the traditional treats such as pepernoten, very hard spice cookies tasting faintly of anise, and giant chocolate initials for the first and last names of all four of us. Too big to be eaten at one sitting — though Winton tried — these letters had to be stashed in the refrigerator. You can imagine that this led to a lot of family feeling, most of it rancorous, as we sneaked bites of each other's W or B. "You ate my E," Erin accused Winton, who denied everything. But Erin was so slow, rationing herself to microscopic bites, that Saint

Anthony himself would have eventually nibbled at her tempting, curly, three-tailed E. Willem was the worst culprit. Because Saint Nick's birthday feast was a Dutch custom, he felt proprietary. I know for a fact that for five years running he finished off the curvy bottom of my J.

During the rest of the Christmas season, John, who had apprenticed himself to a baker in Rotterdam while underground during the war, showed off his skill at Dutch breads and pastries. He made kerstkrans, a Christmas ring of flaky puff pastry filled with almond paste and decorated with candied fruits, and kerstbrood, a bread with raisins and other fruit. On New Year's Eve, we indulged in oliebollen, balls of a yeast dough mixed with currants, raisins, and minced apple, which John fried in rolling fat, then covered thickly with powdered sugar.

Some treats were made by Elly. At Christmas, she baked little shells of butter cookie dough, then filled them with flavored whipped cream, topped with fruit. I don't remember the official name for these. The children called them "Elly's little hats" and we all ate them until we nearly croaked. And there was her wonderful dark fruitcake, redolent with wine and brandy — none of my mother's Temperance apple slices used for preserving in this household! — the batter so heavy that Elly had to call John to help stir it. At Easter, Elly formed baskets of ladyfingers covered with chocolate, and packed them with cellophane grass, chocolate eggs, and marzipan bunnies.

In addition to these holiday treats, during those early years of our marriage we also routinely ate Sunday dinner at "the Branses," as the children said. Sitting at their dinner table, Erin nudged Winton to look at the rug with its Oriental pattern which lay under the white cloth and the Dutch plates. The rug had been hooked by Willem's grandfather Treffers and, like the family china, silver, and the big grandfather clock across the room, had been brought over with the family on the *Groote Beer.* These family dinners would begin with John's fresh home-baked bread and Elly's soup. Sometimes it would be chicken noodle soup with big chunks of chicken or homemade tomato soup, like nothing from a can. More frequently, we had thick, creamy Dutch pea soup, laden with bits of sausage or ham. But most of the time it was vegetable soup, a half dozen kinds of vegetables in a beef broth with the unexpected addition of vermicelli and small meatballs. This soup was Elly's specialty and Willem's favorite, and he would often snare a carton of it to take with us as we left. But oh, it was rich, easily a meal in itself, with a way of staying firmly in place for hours after you ate it.

After soup came the wine, passed freely from hand to hand, and the meal proper, maybe steak, or roast beef and potatoes. As in my mother's kitchen, things were done a certain way, a way that often seemed as exotic to me as Hunan chicken. Once when I added garlic to some potatoes I was mashing, John shook his head and corrected me firmly, *"Nutmeg* is for mashed potatoes." In later years, when John retired, he subscribed to *Cook's* magazine and took up gourmet cooking. Under this new dispensation, he became much more flexible in the kitchen and we might be presented with veal medallions with shiitake stuffing or shrimp mousse with a subtle dill sauce. I have to say, though, that I never enjoyed these dishes as much as those early hearty meals, whose subtlety, such as it was, derived from ethnic recipes little known outside Holland or from vegetables unfamiliar to the kids and me, like witloof.

The witloof was cooked to a buttery pulp or covered with kaassaus, a cheese sauce. "Isn't it wonderful?" Elly would say of the witloof, rolling her eyes. Though I pretended otherwise, I didn't like it much at first. Gradually, however, I became as addicted to its bitter tang as I already was to the bitterness of turnip greens and collards, as I have become in the two decades since to radicchio and arugula.

Foreign to us as they were, we all liked the Netherlands specials. The kids especially enjoyed a nameless Dutch dish that was the essence of infrugality. For it, Elly simmered a big beef roast to nothingness, put the meat by for sandwiches, and let us dip up the gravy with big crusty pieces of John's fresh bread. We also loved stimp stamp, which was a mix of potatoes and onions seasoned with beef and its gravy. None of these at-home Dutch dishes was exactly aristocratic. My own favorite, *"aardappelen, sla, en eieren,"* translated by Willem as just a list of the ingredients — boiled potatoes, lettuce, and soft-boiled eggs — Elly considered so lowly as to be embarrassing. Apologizing for this peasant fare, all too seldom she would yield to my pleading. Then our dinner plates were heaped with chopped lettuce, into which we mashed the hot potatoes and eggs, then doused the whole with a vinegary white sauce. Fantastic.

After the salad, dessert might be zwart-wit vla, black and white custard, with vanilla pudding and chocolate pudding poured simultaneously into a parfait dish, as modern chefs now pour two complementary soups. Elly made apple or blueberry pies, and of course there was ice cream for the top. Her pound cake and sugar cookies were memorable. As we could never choose what we wanted her to cook, to please us sometimes she would have two or three desserts — and sometimes I would eat two or three desserts! Is it any wonder that the first year in the Brans family I gained ten pounds? The meal always ended with the Branses' special Irish coffee, after which we grunted our way home for another week of classes.

Although we were eating well, at least on Sundays, on our teachers' salaries Willem and I were very poor. So we were thrilled when, in one of those not-what-you-know-but-who-you-know coups, we were offered part-time work as restaurant reviewers for the local city magazine. What a break! Imagine eating in restaurants night after night, with tablecloths and waiters, with appetizers, entrées, and dessert, on an expense account, with a salary to boot!

Never mind who, the benighted who who offered us the job, our friend and former teaching colleague Charles Matthews. What Willem and I knew was not much. Let's face it, a man who does not recognize parsley is not a food expert. But hiring amateurs as restaurant reviewers was a common practice in the mid-seventies, John Mariani points out in *America Eats Out.* "Too often the aging gardening editor or the sportswriter who liked to eat out got the assignment, whether or not he knew much about food," Mariani says. "Sometimes reviewers were deliberately chosen *because* they had a working man's antagonism to fancy restaurants with fancy food."

Not us. You wouldn't have found an ounce of this antagonism in Willem and me. Though I recognized parsley and was even a fair to middling cook, I was an unrepentant, irredeemable omnivore. Like Browning's duchess, I liked whate'er I looked on and my looks went everywhere. For example, I had a passion for Pop-Tarts; before any automobile trip of more than two hours I would lay in several packages of, preferably, strawberry, in a pinch blueberry. Between us, Willem and I rarely met a meal we didn't like — though, personally, I might exempt Cod Rotterdam.

But restaurant critics shouldn't really like food. A lot of them don't. If you really like food, you can find something to like in every meal, which is what we did. I still remember our first assignment, at a place called élan (that's right, no cap), which was less a restaurant than a glorified "meet market" for singles. "Gable had élan. The kind of place he would enjoy, Dallas enjoys," the magazine ads said. "A club for the dashing."

I suppose Willem and I thought of ourselves as dashing. We gushed on about the food at élan in such fulsome fashion — "the unmatchable shrimp tempura, the to-die-for mushroom quiche, the pièce de résistance, crêpes with lemon sauce" — that it must have been obvious we were rarely allowed out in public. Our worldly, laid-back editor, David Bauer, decided to double-check. What his review talked about mostly was élan's pretentious dress code and silly lowercase spelling.

Our ignorance was vast. If I had thought stimp stamp strange, strange took on new meaning with some of the dishes we encountered, or thought we had encountered, as fledgling restaurant reviewers. Shuffling through *Gourmet* a month or so ago, I came across a fancy suggestion for an Easter luncheon: Asparagus Napoleons with Oriental Black Bean Sauce. Déjà vu smacked me up side the head as I recalled a meal Willem and I reviewed in the seventies in a small Chinese restaurant in a shopping center in North Dallas, where we reached the apex of our misunderstanding of foreign food. We had not been to the restaurant before and were not particularly impressed by its looks.

When the menu came, however, our interest increased. Over and over we noticed references to dishes served with "black bear sauce" — pork with black bear sauce, shrimp with black bear sauce, dumplings with black bear sauce. We were excited and — I am not making this up — a conversation like this ensued:

ME: Black bear sauce? *Fascinating!* I had no idea there were bears in China.
HE: Must be a district of China near Russia.
ME: But wouldn't they be an endangered species?
HE: Well, it's probably pretty barbaric in that region.
ME: So I guess they import the bear meat all this way. Amazing. In quantity too, looks like. I'll try the dumplings if you'll try the pork.

Unfortunately, I've lost most of our restaurant review clips, so I don't know what form our fascination with the black bears of China took when we wrote up our visit, or whether we realized the sauce was made of beans, not bears. Certainly we counted on David to expurgate anything that might prove fatally embarrassing to the magazine. I do know that even after this dramatic misunderstanding, we continued to review restaurants for another year.

We learned on the job. We feasted on Vaccaro family dishes at Mario's and, for the magazine, secured the recipes for saltimbocca and for a scrumptious spinach dish called Frittura Delizia Romana, little fried cheese and spinach balls served with a tomato sauce. Of course, we tried making them at home, as we did the lemon chicken from South China, the rillettes from Chablis, and the mango custard from Javier's.

For one lead review, we ate brunches all over Dallas, with me exclaiming over "an exotic touch that spoke well for the Venetian Room, the first kumquats we'd seen at any Dallas brunch," or, I might have added in all honesty, the first kumquats I'd ever seen anywhere. I'd had to ask the waiter what they were. Willem raved about the "elegant omelette variation with Wisconsin Cheddar, green chilies, and relleno sauce" at a place called Daddy's Money, and waxed sardonic about the Polynesian floor show at Trader Vic's. "As five bored-stiff musicians run through the Arthur Godfrey songbook, three suspiciously American-looking girls dance a dozen or so variations of the hula, with plastic grass skirts, talking hands, the works. There's nothing to do but sip another mai tai." Ho hum, so cool.

We got so fat that, another month, we ate thin for a piece we called "Slim Pickings." Telling our Dallas readers that "if you can eat thin at a Mexican restaurant, you can eat thin anywhere," we tormented ourselves at Chiquita by eating whitefish "with a delicate lemon-herb sauce" instead of the tacos, chalupas, and enchiladas we lusted after, and by passing up Carta Blanca for black coffee. We wasted our tour at the Old Warsaw, one of Dallas's best restaurants, by eating that nonfattening cliché of the period, Dover sole Veronique, more whitefish, this time poached with grapes, accompanied by white asparagus and a salad of endive (my new friend witloof under another name) and Boston lettuce. But we weren't completely mad; for dessert, we splurged with soufflé Grand Marnier. "Man does not live by whitefish alone," we concluded.

Obviously we had fun, eating weird food all over town. But we saw this restaurant reviewing in another light also: it was a way to feed the family. Every place we went, Willem and I agreed, we would do as the magazine wanted and order lots of dishes. But instead of eating everything on every plate, we would just taste everything in order to write the review. Then we would take the leftovers home for our "doggies," Erin and Winton. Thus Willem and I would be fed, but not fat, and the kids could eat too. We figured we could cut our grocery bill in half, really have nothing much to buy except milk, juice, and cereal, since the children ate lunch at school.

Resourceful as this plan was, we had not reckoned on the stubborn intractability of the young. "Escargots *again?*" Erin complained bitterly one night, opening her foil dinner package as Willem and I prepared to go out and bring in more victuals. "Don't they ever send you guys out for hamburgers?"

They did. They also asked us to review cookbooks, which is how I discovered the work of Helen Corbitt, the guiding hand behind the restaurants of Neiman-Marcus and later the Texas spa called the Greenhouse. Though she wrote, I thought, like a garrulous old maid aunt, Helen Corbitt was a fan of Bibb lettuce when other cooks in Dallas were still chopping iceberg with a knife and slathering it with bottled mayo. At Neiman-Marcus's Zodiac Room, she introduced Dallas to steak and kidney pie, popovers, and her special sandwich, the Duke of Windsor, made with buttered toast, Cheddar cheese, chutney, sliced turkey, hot broiled pineapple, and Boston lettuce. Pretty ghoulish, I guess, but it does show spirit.

My favorite Corbitt book, which I acquired by reviewing it, was called *Helen Corbitt Cooks for Company*. In fact, I liked it so much that I bought it for John and Elly, as well as for several other sets of friends. In it, Helen, as I came to call her, provided menus for all kinds of parties — brunches, teas and receptions, luncheons, buffet dinners, formal seated dinners, and picnics. Her idea of a picnic was fresh caviar with hot flageolets and leg of lamb in pastry or cold boiled lobster tail, cold tarragon chicken, and almond cream cake. I stuck with my own favorite fried chicken and potato salad for picnics, but I did a lot of dreaming from Helen's book. And a lot of cooking, too. Even today, nearly twenty years later, my copy of *Company* opens automatically to cold yogurt soup and spinach vichyssoise, to julienne breast of chicken with chanterelles and wild rice with grapes, to mushrooms and watercress crêpes, and to a wonderful little number Helen dubbed Baked Bean Bash, but which I served to scores of my students at the university as Freshman Casserole.

Posh as it is, *Company* does include a chili recipe — it wouldn't be Texan otherwise, or so the natives say. Personally, I have always had mixed success with chili, sometimes sending my guests to perdition with the chili peppers, other times boring them to death. Burt Meyers, a retired journalist, recalls that the chili of his boyhood in New Mexico "had about a fourth of an inch of clear grease floating on top, which was thought to be a necessary part of the dish, perhaps because as it congealed on one's throat, it kept the chili from burning through." Today gobs of sour cream may serve the same purpose.

But the best chili story I know is Charlie Smith's. One year, Charlie and Marcia backpacked across Europe. Before they set out, they arranged in three months' time to spend two weeks at a French village west of Avignon restoring medieval châteaux with an international group of volunteers. To treat the group to a taste of Texas after a hard day of work around the old home château, they planned, as they packed for their trip, that one night they would cook up a batch of real Texas chili. The Smiths figured these international tenderfeet had never had real chili; they would let them know what they had been missing.

"We knew we could get tomatoes, ground beef, and beans about anywhere," Charlie said. "All we needed to take with us was the chili powder for the native touch." On a trip to Santa Fe, they had bought "some hellfire! goddam! shit! that stuff's hotter'n blue blazes! chili powder." They put about a half cup of that in a Ziploc bag, shoved it into a side pocket with other bags containing soap powder, toothpaste, shampoo, and insect repellent, and began their trek across the Old World.

Three months later, they arrived at St. Victor le Coste on schedule, and, like comic strip Texans, began immediately to boast about the real Texas chili they were planning to make for the edification of the troops. "I think it was the adjective that got people interested," Charlie told me. "We began hyping our batch long before we ever got into the kitchen. No, this ain't gonna be none of that goddam mealymouthed, limp-wristed Yankee shit! This here's gonna be *Texas* chili, son!"

People were worried. Will I be able to eat it? they asked. Will you make a vegetarian batch? they asked. Will there be something else just in case? they asked. Hell, no, Charlie told them. Be a man. Be a Texan for once in your goddurned life.

The night before the famous Texas cook-off, the Smiths started their chili, browning the onions and meat, adding the tomatoes. Then out of Marcia's backpack came the precious chili powder, still tightly wrapped. They started to measure it in, then — shucks, this was *Texas* chili — just dumped it all in and let the stew simmer to give it plenty of time to "season." After an hour or so of slow cooking, with great anticipation Charlie took the first taste.

"What hit my tongue," Charlie said, "was something so removed from any food product — ground roaches? snake dookey?

liquid hand cleaner? antifreeze? — that I instantly spat it onto the floor. 'Jesus Christ!' I yelled. 'That's horrible! It doesn't even taste like *food!*' "

"*Savon?*" inquired their French helper upon tasting. Yes, *savon,* they agreed. Soap. It tasted like soap. Snuggling next to those little packets of Tide, the chili powder had lost all of its own flavor and come out with what Charlie describes as a "headily floral, overpowering chemical whang. Our chili was shit — this crud would have poisoned an alligator or a great white shark. Not even a goat would've been tempted by it."

France to the rescue. A miracle worker named Irene poured a bottle of the strong local red into the unfortunate mess, then dumped in "a small thyme bush and a batch of rosemary the size of a Christmas wreath, and salt, a lot of salt. When she had finished, it bore not even a remote resemblance to chili . . . but it did seem vaguely edible, the way, say, the roots of some exotic shrub might seem palatable to a starving man." Strange fruit indeed.

Did people like it, I asked Charlie? "They said, 'So this is Texas chili,'" he told me. "They thought it was good. I thought they were lying. 'I'm glad it's not too hot,' somebody said."

What a thought: all over the world, thanks to Charlie's missionary cooking, members of the group are insisting to their foodie friends that real Texas chili should have the faint but unmistakable flavor of *savon.*

Willem and I ate some really terrible meals in the early days of our marriage. Let me tell you, food writing is not the idylls of the king, even Old King Cole. We ate shrimp with freezer burn and annual rings, green soup so bland the vegetable from which it derived was unidentifiable, meat that fought back. Sometimes cooks trying to be original and inventive sorely tested our powers of endurance; in fact, some of the worst meals we ate were the most pretentious. I particularly remember a trout en croûte — en croûte was big just then — à la Newburg: oily fish in soggy pastry topped with a Newburg sauce made of kerosene and Velveeta.

Being a food writer, however briefly and imperfectly, taught me to hate people who don't like adjectives. I mean all those pseudo Hemingways who demand strong verbs. What strong verbs can a food writer use? *Chomped? Munched?* Problem is, they may tell us something about the eater, but not about what's eaten. To describe food, you need adjectives.

Willem and I quit reviewing restaurants when we ran out of adjectives. One midnight we were sitting up in bed arguing about whether the sauce on the evening's steak Diane was "subtly authoritative" (his) or "authoritatively subtle" (mine) when the absurdity of the whole situation struck us both simultaneously. The truth is, it was neither. The next morning we turned in our halfhearted review and our company credit card. Enough's enough.

Those first years as a couple, we inflicted some subtly authoritative and pretty terrible meals on others. Though we never had a catastrophe of the magnitude of Charlie's Texas chili supper, once, I remember, the magazine asked us to review a selection of cheeses, so I invited our friends Willard and Ken for supper. Then I served nothing but cheese — the old two birds with one stone motif, don-cha know. We began with Brie for our appetizer, then moved on to the solidity of Havarti, bruder basil, and a Dutch roomkas. Our salad was rambol, with walnuts, and reybrier, with pistachio nuts. For dessert we had Stilton, Gorgonzola, and gourmandise. At this point in the proceedings, Willard and Ken were both the pretty pale yellow of a good Vermont Cheddar. When I offered the lagniappe of a nice ripe chèvres, they eagerly declined.

Like Charlie with his chili, like bad restaurants, we did our worst cooking when we were most pretentious. When Adrienne Rich, whose poetry I greatly admired, came to speak at my school's literary festival, I had a dinner party for her. To impress, I decorated the house for the grand event by making bedcovers and curtains of gaily flowered Marimekko sheets. The bath was particularly scruffy, so, when I had fabric left over, I whipped up a matching shower curtain, and even went so far as to cover the bathroom waste can with the final scraps. If the poet needed the facilities, I thought, she couldn't help admiring my creativity. I labored over the meal, too: a costly and fanciful concoction of shrimp and artichoke hearts which I had never made before and have never made since.

"Ah! Just what I prefer," the guest of honor exclaimed as I served the main course. "A simple, light supper." As she ate the dish I had spent the entire afternoon preparing, Ms. Rich, an important figure in the women's movement, praised me because I had just whipped up the meal. She congratulated me on my good values and spoke feelingly of the wasted lives of women. Women spent their most vital energies caring for their children and husbands, she said. They needlessly cleaned ovens, slaved over dinner parties, adorned their bodies and their houses. "You know," she told us sadly, "there are even women who have so little scope for their imaginations that they create *hand-decorated wastebaskets*."

I excused myself to serve the salad. From the kitchen, I slipped quietly into the bathroom and hid my hand-decorated wastebasket behind the handmade shower curtain.

Ambitious for success, Willem and I entered the Ph.D. program at the University of Texas at Dallas. Knowing me to have no Latin and less Greek, the classics professor who would oversee my minor course of study appeared to be particularly resistant to my anxious charms. To win him over, we invited him and his fiancée to dinner. We had been told he was a real gourmet, and we thought we would show him we were gourmets too, completely worthy of his esteem. A dinner of simple elegance, in the Italian manner, with everything served in courses — that's what I planned. A bit of linguine with caviar. A serving of meat. A few leaves of lettuce with good oil. Cheese and fruit. One thing at a time on the plate, simple and elegant, right?

The linguine was good but a very small serving because there was meat to come. The meat, chicken breasts stuffed with prosciutto and fontina cheese, sautéed lightly, then run under the broiler, emerged for some reason as charred clods of jerky. To say they were as tough as shoe leather is to insult footwear. But I had to serve them, and I had absolutely nothing else to go on the plate with them. We sat miserably around the table chomping on our chars, while I watched my chances of academic success plummet.

This experience may explain a dream I had in 1975, after five years of teaching at the university and a year of marriage to Willem. At school, the moment of decision had come for my department. Should they give me tenure? Without it, I couldn't teach beyond the sixth year — that's the rule. This was a hard call for my superiors. They may have wanted to keep me around, but I lacked the proper credentials. I didn't have a Ph.D., I hadn't written a book. The students liked me, but I wasn't heavy, you know?

So, this dream: I am giving a dinner party for the tenure and promotion committee. Things are going well when I go out to the kitchen for dessert — for some inexplicable reason, hot fudge sundaes. Ice cream, hot fudge, nuts, whipped cream, cherry — up and up. Gracefully and competently I pass them around. Surely I deserve tenure for this?

Calmly I survey the candlelit table as I pick up my spoon and look down to see — worms. What I thought were pecans are worms. All around the table people are jumping up in horror, leaving, gagging, covering their mouths.

It's worse than Cod Rotterdam.

·✕·

Nouvelle Is Swell!

. . . .

I N 1990, WILLEM AND I planned a dinner party for July 10,
the day Marcel Proust was born in 1871. Willem, who is now
a consultant for arts organizations, was working on a capital
campaign for the Minneapolis Institute of Arts, so we were tempo-
rarily posted in Minneapolis, a city not very much like Paris. Nevertheless, for the fun and challenge of it, we decided to make our
dinner a birthday party *for* Proust, with costumes, dishes, and service as nearly as possible in our modest apartment like those of Paris
in the time Proust wrote about.

Accordingly, we took all our cues from Proust himself. Our
notes invited twelve friends to dress in their best and come forth, as
Proust wrote, under "a sky of the same pink as the salmon we should
presently be eating." We used table linens of the same salmon pink,
and by the side of each dinner plate, we placed "a carnation, the

stalk of which was wrapped in silver paper." To begin, we served champagne and what the youthful Marcel called "a blackish substance which I then did not know to be caviar." Then followed courses, courses, courses. For the amusement of our guests, Willem made up menus, tied with salmon pink ribbon. In these menus, with the help of Shirley King's marvelous *Dining with Marcel Proust,* we matched each course with lines from *Remembrance of Things Past.*

After "the steaming soup" of watercress and mint came the poached salmon. The fish was followed by boeuf à la mode en gelée, "of which the jelly was enriched by many additional carefully selected bits of meat," Proust says, just as he enriched his narrative with many juicy tidbits. Next came a risotto with wild mushrooms ("'Waiter, some mullets for Madame and a risotto for me'"). We skipped the mullets, so the risotto was accompanied by asparagus vinaigrette, "the asparagus tinged with ultramarine and rosy pink."

Then we refreshed our palates with lemon ice ("The ice need not be at all big"). Dessert was a double chocolate cream cake, "an architectural cake, as gracious and sociable as it was imposing," which, in true French fashion, I purchased from our local pastry chef. Finally we subsided with coffee, mints, and Muscat de Frontignan.

This was not nouvelle cuisine.

Oh, as chief cook and bottle washer, I made some effort to lighten the load for our much imposed upon diners. We served only a couple of hors d'oeuvre, not the full catastrophe that would have been more authentic. I did not put the salmon in a pastry shell, which I might have done (if I'd known how), nor did I cover it with "that sticky glue generally called *sauce blanche.*" The risotto, currently so popular, seems a contemporary touch, though it's right there in Proust. Still, cooking and serving the most elaborate meal I had ever attempted brought home to me the ways in which nouvelle cuisine and its offspring, nouvelle American, have affected me and numerous other American home cooks.

These days, *la nouvelle cuisine* is *le vieux chapeau*. To hear people talk, anyway.

"Adult Pablum. Remember all those parsnip-pear and sweet potato-carrot purées? We'd have starved without a food processor."

"Skimpy. Sauce under the food instead of over. Big deal."

"Some yellowish mush lying in a red puddle, flanked by three sprigs of chives and a gooseberry. Grilled goat heart, in a bed of fiddlehead ferns."

"Pretty, but you'd have to buy a Snickers to get through the rest of the day."

"A pretentious and excessive form of playing with your food."

"Kiwis."

The merest mention of nouvelle cuisine annoys ordinary Americans like the anonymous critics above. Food professionals too have revealed a certain pique on the subject. "I am happy to see that people once again are thinking of putting an honest meal on their tables," gloated Nika Hazelton in the eighties in a *National Review* column entitled "Au Revoir, Nouvelle Cuisine." Even *The New Yorker* gets into the act. In one cartoon, "Chicken with Kiwi Sauce, c. 1979" is displayed under glass in the "Museum of Modern Food"; a museum piece in another is a "Still-Life of New Mexican Grilled Quail with Cilantro and Fennel-Flecked Confit." What's the joke? The joke is that, as Gertrude Stein said of Hemingway's revolutionary prose style, the once revolutionary style of nouvelle cuisine now smells of museums. *Elle est morte, non? Non, non,* a thousand times *non.*

For some reason, nouvelle cuisine has always been an easy target for jokes. In fact, a lot of people who joke about it don't seem to know exactly what it is. To go back to the beginning, the ten commandments of nouvelle cuisine, according to the French food writers

Henri Gault and Christian Millau, who identified and named it in the October 1973 issue of their *Gault-Millau* magazine, are:

1. Avoid unnecessary complications.
2. Shorten cooking times.
3. Shop regularly at the market.
4. Shorten the menu.
5. Don't hang or marinate game.
6. Avoid too-rich sauces.
7. Return to regional cooking.
8. Investigate the latest techniques.
9. Consider diet and health.
10. Invent constantly.

What's amazing here is that, in spite of all the protestations against nouvelle, these commandments are obeyed today. Does anyone still hang game, I wonder? I certainly don't. But, in fact, everything else on this list is au courant also. Fresher produce, shorter menus, lighter sauces, even the "latest techniques" of the microwave and food processor and the "diet and health" considerations of the Eating Right Pyramid — don't these commandments add up to an uncannily accurate description of the best contemporary American cooking?

Nevertheless, something about the phrase *nouvelle cuisine* annoys us. I include myself. Maybe we were annoyed at first because nouvelle was foreign, created by young chefs in France in the sixties and imported to this country some ten years later. In spite of Julia Child, we cherished our chauvinism. Julia *cooked* French, but she was *born* in California. What were Paul Bocuse, Michel Guérard, Roger Vergé, the Troisgros brothers, whose name always reminded me of the Three Little Pigs, to us or us to them? Lacking any native equivalent to the rarefied world of French haute cuisine, American home cooks in the seventies couldn't appreciate the enormity of the break these young Turks made with tradition. To a Frenchman, nouvelle dishes may have been a witty departure from traditional haute cuisine, as Raymond Sokolov has pointed out, a sort of culinary play on food, but the wit was lost on us.

Maybe it was the emphasis on aesthetics which annoyed us. We weren't averse to using a bit of parsley or a radish rose to pretty things up. We put little white shoes on our crown roast of lamb, and pineapple slices and cloves in the diamonds we scored on our baked ham. But these were traditional, *comfortable* garnishes, nothing like the plates of food like minimalist paintings which Willem and I were served when, on a jaunt eastward, we visited the just opened Quilted Giraffe, then considered the best restaurant in New York City. "I don't hold with eating foolishness," an old man once told my grandmother as he raked the meringue off his pie. Nouvelle cuisine was foolishness, sneaking into the meat-and-potatoes heartland through the highfalutin, food-snobby East and West coasts.

I was introduced to the concept of minimalist food in the summer of 1975, when *The New Yorker* published a substantial profile on Michel Guérard. For the first time, I learned about a brotherhood of French chefs who were revolutionizing French cooking. "Some just cannot change their way of thinking," Guérard said. "Bocuse can. The Troisgros brothers can. Vergé can do it." He went on to describe vacations that this band of like-minded cooks all took together, trying out new dishes on each other.

But it was Michel Guérard himself whom Paul Bocuse, the grand seigneur of nouvelle cuisine, called "the most imaginative of us all." With his "cuisine minceur," Guérard had conceived a novel style of preparing the great dishes of France without the usual components of butter, cream, starches, and sugar. In his restaurant at Eugénie-les-Bains, Guérard steamed meat and fish in their own juices, topped them with purées of vegetables, fruits, and herbs rather than with rich sauces, and served them accompanied by creamy vegetable mousses made without cream. Using himself as guinea pig to test these innovations, within two months' time he lost eighteen pounds while never missing a meal, and a delicious meal at that.

I was skeptical but interested enough to buy Guérard's book, *Cuisine Minceur,* "the cuisine of slimness," as the dust jacket put it, when it appeared in 1976. With the instructions of the "chef gourmand — a chef who simply loves to eat," I made fresh tomato soufflés and an onion tart baked in cabbage leaves instead of pastry. But such cooking required new techniques and, as Guérard had warned, new ways of thinking, and at length I put the book on the shelf and forgot about it. In the fall of 1992, a cooking class with the much heralded New York chef David Bouley made me remember *Cuisine Minceur,* and only then did I realize how prescient Guérard had been.

Amateur chefs like me tended to tiptoe toward nouvelle, which, in the beginning, was at home in this country largely in restaurants like Calluaud in Dallas. Before Calluaud, with its sexy French chef Guy Calluaud, opened in the mid-seventies, the hottest restaurant in town had been the Old Warsaw, whose name delineates its menu. Calluaud was a very different sort of place, with fresher-than-life julienned vegetables and such main dishes as filet mignon served with a delicate sprinkling of shallots or salmon scallops with sorrel sauce. I remember a pilaf of mushrooms and chicken livers with wild rice. Willem and I were indoctrinated very quickly and visited as often as we could afford to, as did the rest of the family. To this day, my mother-in-law speaks wistfully of a dessert there, which I don't remember but which she recalls vividly: "Oh, it was like a cathedral or a tent made of threads of spun sugar, with maybe nougat in the center, and some kind of sauce, and whipped cream. I know you had to wait for it, but I never minded a bit." We all remember with great fondness the dessert soufflés, including a truly remarkable one flavored with hazelnut. Somehow, Elly maintains, they seemed more authentic because you had to order them as soon as you sat down so that they would be ready by the end of the meal.

None of us Branses thought of trying to duplicate these effects at home. Only experts in the field, we suspected, knew how to make use of such unfamiliar ingredients as the radicchio and lemongrass which turned up at Calluaud and which I found, to my deep unease, at Simon David, Dallas's most avant-garde market. Willem and I laughed affectionately at our *nouvelle cuisiniste* friend Laura Furman, a transplanted New Yorker, for making fresh whole-wheat pasta and for cultivating arugula in her Texas garden. Alien corn, and just like a New Yorker.

If we distrusted these ingredients singly, that distrust went double for the radical combinations of foods which nouvelle chefs delighted in. As former restaurant reviewers who should have had open minds, in those days we were taken aback in Manhattan to find fresh raspberries on thin slices of rare duck breast and swordfish served with fig mousse. Our distrust was not necessarily misplaced. A little learning is a dangerous thing, as I am not the first to note, and pretentious, ill-informed restaurant cooks ran amuck with exotics. Increasingly, they put already weird things together in weird combinations, without much regard for the harmony of flavors. "Nouvelle cuisine is all too often like bad architecture," David Harris, a caterer in Minneapolis–St. Paul, told me. "Bad nouvelle pays too much attention to topping and too little to structure."

Maybe, at the most profound level, we distrusted nouvelle cuisine because it stressed quality over quantity, which we considered a trait of French rather than good old American cooking. Diners who felt they had feasted not too well on eye of newt and finger bone of toad complained about the meagerness of nouvelle victuals. They wanted what they were used to, that feeling that we always left my mother's table with: "My goodness, I'm full as a tick. I couldn't eat another bite if my life depended on it!" To many, nouvelle cuisine meant leaving the table hungry. As the same old man who raked the foolishness off his pie had said, it was mighty fine, what there was of it. But as a country, we were used to plenty, such as it was.

Today, feeding our nostalgia on mashed potatoes, meat loaf, and Mom's apple pie, we are tempted to recall nouvelle as ephemeral and sissified nonsense, without lasting significance to the American way of eating. "It made food appear too precious," Julee Rosso, the coauthor of *The Silver Palate Cookbook,* told me, "and for that it's gotten a bad rap. Americans tend to take things to an extreme — food, money, anything, and that's what happened with nouvelle, with restaurant dining in the eighties." But beneath the preciousness indulged in by mediocre and imitative cooks eager to get on the nouvelle chuck wagon lie some solid precepts. Nor are the lessons of nouvelle cuisine limited to the food we have learned to order in restaurants. Home entertaining, at least among middle-class foodies, has been changed considerably by the mores of nouvelle cuisine. Let me illustrate with the exception that in my own experience proves the rule.

The essence of nouvelle cooking is spontaneity, with dishes emerging from whatever ingredients are most inviting in the market on a particular day. No doubt some of what then seemed off-the-wall combinations — berries and fish — came into being because both were available in pristine condition, and some freewheeling chef thought, Well, why not? Most of the time, even for guests, I've become accustomed to cooking this way, doing the shopping first and the menu second.

With the Proust dinner, the menu was set in stone (or at least laser printer), so I had to go at the meal in a different fashion. I also had little flexibility in making the individual dishes, especially the beef. A more experienced cook than I might have taken some liberties with the aspic and the decoration, I suppose. Though this menu was certainly not haute cuisine, with its rigid requirements, I felt chained to the recipe and prayed only that what I produced would be recognizably boeuf à la mode en gelée and not some slimy monstrosity. These strictures gave me a sense of the freedom that must have been felt in French kitchens when Bocuse, Guérard, and the Troisgroses broke with tradition with their al dente vegetables, their raw fish and meat, their heavily reduced stock used as sauce instead of the conventional hollandaise or espagnole.

With my deliberations about the Proust party, I also relived in miniature the whole history of table service. At my mother's table, the food was passed family style. In the fifties and sixties, I had commonly served company meals buffet style, placing my enormously heavy Le Creuset pots containing the noodles and beef Stroganoff on the Mexican buffet and asking guests to serve themselves.

Under the influence of nouvelle cuisine, a decade ago I began serving everything on separate plates in the kitchen. No longer did my guests have to stand, holding their plates, waiting for their food "like birds in the wilderness," as we sang at camp. Instead, I could make each plate look pretty. I retired my silver serving spoons from active duty, composed salads in ascending circles on dinner plates, and arranged slices of beef artfully on shredded radicchio.

But what do you do when you have spent the better part of a week preparing perfectly poached beef, straining the stock, allowing it to gel overnight, coating the beef with the aspic, refrigerating it again, coating it again, cutting up cubes of the rest of the aspic, and trimming the whole with aspic cubes and slivers of blanched vegetables? Let me tell you what you do *not* do: you do not serve it up in the kitchen.

So for the Proust party, Willem and I were thrown back on a form called Russian service. Here's how Raymond Sokolov describes it: "The cuisine of our grandparents' time called for edible designs to be executed on serving platters that were brought out from the kitchen, proudly displayed to a table of diners, and then professionally carved or otherwise parceled out to individual diners." Aside from the "professionally," that's what Willem and I did, and a royal pain it was. Not only were there the cooking pots to clean up, but the big serving vessels too: the soup tureen in which we proudly displayed the soup, the covered casserole in which we proudly displayed the risotto, the crystal bowl in which we proudly displayed the salad greens.

All this in order to show off a plate of beef to advantage, as well as somebody else's chocolate cake.

More or less consciously, under the influence of nouvelle, good contemporary cooks avoid unnecessary complications and shorten cooking times. They serve the beef without the aspic, toss the fish in the wok for the twinkling of a newt's eye, and grill the vegetables al dente. And such vegetables, brought in from the market still dewy and tossed on the table! Menus *are* shorter; the traditional American plate lunch of "meat and three" — a slab of meat surrounded by a trio of vegetables, accompanied by bread, butter, and beverage, and followed by dessert — is like dinosaur steak. You do find it in cultural backwaters, I guess, but what supplants it at popular places all over the country is a meal such as pasta and salad. And, of course, dessert — we'll cling to our chocolate cake till the last dingdong of cholesterol doom.

But as for too rich sauces, we avoid them, just like the man said. All over America, we lean heavily on "the latest techniques." At least we use the microwave to heat our frozen food and the food processor to whip up our diet shakes. Certainly we "consider diet and health"; outraged statisticians, if that's not an oxymoron, inform us that we spend millions annually on the subject. As for the command to invent constantly, an amazing diversity and creativity are spoken to by the exuberant outpouring of cookbooks and a sampling of restaurant menus across the country — of which more later.

Yet so dishonored has the term *nouvelle cuisine* become that few cooks today will fly its flag. Take David Harris, who interests me because he bridges the gap between home and restaurant cooking. David is a professional musician with years of kitchen training and expertise who supports his music habit by cooking. For a price, if he approves of you, David will plan your menu, shop all over Minneapolis and St. Paul for the ingredients, then come to your house and in your very own kitchen cook dinner for you and two, or two hundred, of your dearest friends. David insists that his main interest is in Mediterranean cuisine, especially the cooking of the French provinces. Still, as a cook he epitomizes the best precepts of nouvelle cuisine, as I learned when I signed on with him as sous-chef for one gig.

David began his professional training with a year in a Japanese restaurant, "dealing with immaculately fresh produce and the tender loving care that goes into preparing it so that it will be equally wonderful for each day's meals." Specifically he learned to chop. His Japanese overseer had rigid visual requirements for each dish. David was set to work chopping onions. "If the onion was cut improperly for that dish, the dish wasn't right, even though the taste was identical." For some dishes he minced the onions, cutting them in small squares. For others, he cut slender half moons; just how slender mattered. Onions that didn't pass muster were thrown unceremoniously into the stockpot.

Raymond Sokolov, among others, has pointed out that, even in xenophobic France, nouvelle chefs were influenced by Japanese cuisine. "Bocuse himself," says Sokolov, "traveled so often to Japan that diners complained the master was abandoning his own stove." David's year with the Japanese was the ideal preliminary for his next stint, The New French Cafe in Minneapolis.

Like Calluaud in Dallas, L'Espalier in Boston, and Le Bec Fin in Philadelphia, The New French Cafe has been identified by John Mariani in *America Eats Out* as one of the early nouvelle restaurants in this country. At The New French, David once again found emphasis on visual appeal but "with far more room for individual creativity," circumstances under which he flourished. He started at the very bottom of the kitchen as a salad boy. Eventually he became responsible for designing the day's specials. Ultimately, at the end of his five years there, it was David who designed the four seasonal menus which, except for the specials, dictated what The New French Cafe would serve during the entire year.

Along the way, he learned a lot more about the use of the knife, such as the different methods of fileting a wide assortment of whole fishes. He learned how to intensify flavor through the use of stocks, wine, herbs, and "time-honored seasoning constellations, like garlic-fennel-orange zest." David also learned the joy of departing from those time-honored ways of seasoning in the creation of something he termed Halibut en Chemise, or Halibut in a Shirt. For this dish, he pressed fennel seeds into the flesh of a filet of halibut, wrapped it in Boston lettuce, and steamed it in white wine. We might well call it Halibut Nouvelle.

What I attribute to this nouvelle background is that David could cook an interesting, inventive dinner in four hours for sixty people, whereas cooking Proust's birthday dinner, using written recipes and old-fashioned methods, had taken me at least twenty hours for fourteen people. Of course, David had a sous-chef — me — and I didn't, but I bought dessert already prepared and he didn't. It hurts to confess that he assured me that, valuable as my assistance was (his tactful words), he could have prepared the meal alone in about the same amount of time and usually did.

The hard day's night I worked with David began shortly after noon when David picked me up to shop for the party to be held that evening at the home of Rody Hall. The occasion was a house blessing, complete with the celebration of the Eucharist, for a new addition that Rody Hall, an Episcopal priest, and her husband, Ted, had built to their house.

At Roots and Fruits, David and I bought the tenderest, tiniest fresh asparagus. I nearly fainted when that alone cost eighty-four dollars. We also bought lemons, baby lettuces, spinach, mushrooms. At Johnson's meat market, we bought fifteen pounds of chicken breasts and three whole chickens, and smoked shrimp and mussels at Coastal Seafoods. That morning, David had already bought butter, onions, garlic, cream, raisins, eggs, basmati rice, and some spices.

By the time we arrived at the Halls', unloaded the provisions, and prepared to start the cooking, it was three o'clock, the guests were due at seven, and I was a basket case. How could we ever finish on time? David was as cool as the seafood. He set me to work washing and picking the Adirondacks of spinach, which overflowed the double sink. Meanwhile, he put the whole chickens into cold water for stock, made mushroom duxelles, and made the pastry, from scratch, for six large lemon curd tarts.

When I finished, at last, with the spinach, I was allowed to trim the asparagus, all eighty-four dollars' worth. David rapidly constructed a huge terrine with the steamed spinach and mushroom duxelles. Then I washed the baby lettuce while David prepared the lemon curd and made a madly fragrant curry sauce. By this time, it was after five, and he had done nothing with the fifteen pounds of chicken breasts. David made a dressing for the salad and a light vinaigrette for the asparagus. Then we both set to work on the onerous job of boning the chicken breasts, removing all the fat, and cutting them into slivers. David inspected my slivers every bit as critically as any Japanese overboss he'd ever complained about. By this time it was seven o'clock and the guests were arriving.

The service of the blessing began. In the dining room, I could hear Father Byrd, the celebrant, intoning, "The living God gave you from heaven rain and fruitful seasons, satisfying your hearts with food and gladness. He brings forth food from the earth and wine to gladden our hearts."

Contemplating the huge, slithery mass of uncooked chicken, I thought if there were to be any food for the sixty strong who responded, "All to make a cheerful countenance, and bread to strengthen the heart," it would have to come from the earth. With the hubbub we were in, I certainly didn't see how it would ever come at any decent hour from this kitchen.

But a miracle occurred. David dropped the chicken slivers into the simmering sauce, where, since they were cut so uniformly, they cooked in an instant. As the service ended, the meal was being served up for the happy worshippers. God, the earth, and David Harris had gladdened their hearts. Dinner was glorious, as even I could see from my seat among the cinders. The curry was a holy coupling of sweet and pungent on its bed of basmati rice, the asparagus cut to perfection, if I do say so myself, the guests appreciative, the hostess touchingly grateful. David was the soul of aplomb, and I was an exhausted, sweaty, chicken-reeking, foot-aching wreck. If I'd ever had any illusions about the glamour of being a food professional, I lost them chopping that chicken.

But I could see how David's kitchen skills exemplified the tenets of nouvelle cuisine. Perhaps the menu was a bit ambitious, but then it was a very special party. On the other hand, the dishes were simple and inventive, the ingredients absolutely fresh, and we had certainly shortened the cooking time!

After any successful revolution, the once radical elements become the norm, taken for granted. In America, over the last fifteen years or so, the mixture of disparate elements typical of nouvelle cuisine has been as seamlessly planted in our dining habits as arugula amid the turnip greens and pattypan squash in Laura's Texas garden. If this were not so, how could the downtown Minneapolis café Tejas feature as popular take-out lunches, "perfect for meetings, conferences, and office gatherings," such items as Grilled Chicken Salad with Cilantro Pesto Mayonnaise on Grilled Brioche or Yellowfin Tuna Salad Sandwich on Black Pepper–Olive Focaccia with Smoked Pepper–Mint Marigold Mayonnaise? To eat in, Tejas offers entrées like Grilled Duck Breast with Pumpkin Seed–Goat Cheese Empanaditas and Citrus-Ginger Sauce or Hot Smoked Beef Sirloin with Guajillo Whipped Potatoes, Barbecued Corn, and Poblano Aioli.

Back in New York after our Minnesota sojourn, one summer night in 1992 we ran into Stephen Pyles, the food genius behind Tejas, at the James Beard House. How, I asked him, had he persuaded those cold Nordic types in Minneapolis to accept the hot stuff, the chilies and ginger with which much of his food is peppered? "Oh, they were ready for it," Stephen told me. "When we opened Tejas, we began with mild food. But before long we realized that our customers could take the heat. There's a big Vietnamese population in the Twin Cities, and lots of Vietnamese restaurants, so they were used to peppers and ginger. They like food hot."

Chili peppers and ginger, not to mention cilantro, pesto, brioche, focaccia, empanaditas, guajillo, poblano, and aioli, surely constitute a confusing and sophisticated mixture. Yet every day at Tejas, secretaries and salesclerks, buyers and bosses, order these delicacies with no perceptible flinching, just as they do at Baby Routh in Dallas or the Zuni Café in San Francisco. How brave they are, without a backward thought consuming blithe combinations of French, Italian, Mexican, Vietnamese, Indochinese, African, Caribbean, Japanese, and American food. My debonair countrymen, courageous as Columbus, setting their sails for a nouvelle world!

·✕·

Silver Palate
in My Mouth

. . . .

OVER THE LAST TWENTY YEARS, I have interviewed
some pretty famous people. Most were writers of works of
fiction I so revere that the prospect of talking to their creators filled me at once with delight and terror. Saul Bellow, John
Cheever, Eudora Welty, Iris Murdoch, Margaret Drabble: I felt myself honored beyond all imagining to be in the actual living presence
of such giants.

Yet I can truly say that never have I approached interviews with
more of that delight and terror than I did those with the coauthors
of *The Silver Palate Cookbook,* Julee Rosso and Sheila Lukins. Julee
and Sheila, creators of Chicken Marbella! Julee and Sheila, whose
recipes worked! Julee and Sheila, slavishly worshipped coast to
coast! Julee and Sheila, who taught me about aioli, balsamic vine-

gar, and tomato coulis! Julee and Sheila, who understood my fears of failure and gave me courage in the kitchen! Julee and Sheila, whom I trusted so completely that I dared their dishes for guests *without a dress rehearsal!* Now Julee and Sheila, that dynamic duo, newly elected members to the Who's Who of American Cooking, were to be met in the flesh!

Though they remain good friends, the dynamic duo are no longer working together. Julee has married and moved to Michigan, where she runs an inn part-time and works on a low-fat, low-cholesterol, low-sodium cookbook to be published in the spring of 1993. Sheila too is tackling a cookbook alone; hers will be international in scope. Traveling to all points of the globe, from Cuba to Russia, she has immersed herself in the food of other regions and is in the process of adapting recipes for American kitchens.

Julee was in New York on this May morning in 1992 for events surrounding the tenth anniversary edition of *The Silver Palate Cookbook.* The book, with some two million copies in print, had just been elected to the James Beard Foundation's Cookbook Hall of Fame. This rare honor, received by only fourteen predecessors, places Julee and Sheila in the company of such illustrious cookbook creators as Fannie Farmer, Craig Claiborne, Betty Crocker, Julia Child, and James Beard himself.

At ten-thirty, Julee and I were scheduled to meet at E.A.T., Eli Zabar's den of costly indulgences on Madison. Awestruck at my opportunity, I arrived at ten-fifteen, positioned myself at a back table, ordered iced coffee, and checked out my tape recorder. Then I watched the door. I was worried over the fact that I literally did not know whom to expect to walk through its portals.

It was not for lack of trying. For several days before, I had pored over *The Silver Palate Cookbook,* published in 1982, its sequel, *The Silver Palate Good Times Cookbook,* which appeared in 1985, and their giant 1989 opus, *The New Basics Cookbook,* as well as my extensive collection of press clippings. Julee and Sheila were a personable pair, I thought, studying the black and white photos for the hundredth time. The only problem was that I wasn't sure which was Julee and which Sheila.

In most of my clippings, the press had used the same picture of the two of them, the picture on the back of the original cookbook, in which both wore black and white, both brandished cooking utensils, both had twinkly eyes and wide smiles. The most readily definable difference between the two, in this picture at least, seemed to be that one had a tumult of dark curly hair, the other a more streamlined coif. Well, I would look at the hair, I thought. The hair was the key. But sometimes Curly Hair was identified as Julee, sometimes as Sheila.

So now, as I sipped my iced coffee at E.A.T., I did not remember feeling so much anticipation watching a door since I had read "The Lady or the Tiger" in the fifth grade. Which one was Julee, anyway? Who would come through the door, the Lady, with the smooth hair, or the Tiger, with her vampish curls?

In she came, tall, curvy, well turned out in what looked like Armani to me. She glanced around for the stranger with the tape recorder. Then a big smile, and over she came: the Lady. Dark, glossy hair, not curly, framed the serene oval face of a Fra Angelico Madonna. But I mustn't get carried away. Forget the medieval Madonna. "What a good idea," Julee said of my iced coffee. "Let's splurge and have raspberry muffins too." In manner Julee Rosso is as friendly, lively, and practical as her cookbooks.

So is Sheila Lukins, as I discovered a week later. I had to brave the prices at E.A.T. to meet Julee. To meet Sheila, I had to scale the walls of the castle. Which is to say, I had to present myself at the Dakota, the massive apartment building on Central Park West the whole world knows as the home of Yoko Ono. In that impressive hulk, which would be a perfect setting for Morticia and her brood, I was required to say the password at the guardhouse, pass through the electric eye of the huge iron gate, cross the cobbled courtyard, and ascend several flights of ornate stairs to the apartment where Sheila and her husband, Richard, have lived for more than a quarter century. The couple has two daughters, Annabel and Molly.

Sheila may have always lived in the castle, but she's no Morticia. So small-boned and tiny that, from my own less than grand height of five three, I could look *down* on the crown of her mahogany mop, she met me wearing leggings, a big sweater, white running shoes, and socks. Huge glasses magnified her alert, amused, quizzical eyes. Her long hair was tied back with a colorful scarf. We sat for a few moments in the bright living room, filled with flowers, books, and plants. Then by mutual consent we drifted back to the homey kitchen, rather like the opening illustration Sheila drew for *The New Basics.* We put our elbows on a large scrubbed butcher-block table in the center of the room and I looked around. Over the stove hangs a sign reading THE GOODS ARE HERE. A pegboard on one wall holds pot lids, skillets, and several Le Creuset pieces just like mine. I felt right at home.

Sheila made me feel at home. The thing is, Julee and Sheila are *both* ladies, in the nicest sense of that somewhat discredited term. That's the right word: *nice.* Julee and Sheila are nice. You would enjoy having them in your kitchen. "I think the best compliment we ever get," Julee told me, "is when people say *The Silver Palate Cookbook* is like having a friend in the kitchen beside you."

To this Betty Crocker comfort is joined a high level of culinary sophistication and style. Like so many American women of their particular generation — both are now in their late forties — Julee and Sheila are also tigers, in energy, in ambition, in business acumen. In 1977, with an initial investment of $21,000, Sheila Lukins, the owner of The Other Woman, a catering service, and Julee

Rosso, an advertising executive, opened The Silver Palate, a minuscule take-out shop on Manhattan's not yet trendy Upper West Side. They quickly added a catering service, then began distributing Silver Palate products, elegantly packaged mustards, sauces, chutneys, and vinegars, through other stores.

We're talking high cotton here. Since 1986, when they took over the mantle of their distinguished predecessor Julia Child, the two women have reached more than seventy million readers every week through their food column in *Parade.* Before they sold the Silver Palate business in 1988, by then a ten-million-dollar enterprise, they had marketed their specialty foods worldwide, opened a second shop in Tokyo, written two enormously successful cookbooks on evenings and weekends, and were ready to begin testing hundreds of new recipes for a third. In 1992, four million copies of their three cookbooks were in print. Their cultural influence is equally immense. As the syndicated food columnist Barbara Kafka says on their latest book jacket, Rosso and Lukins have "changed the way America cooks."

In the beginning, they were less interested in teaching America to cook than in providing good food-to-go for those too busy with, as they wrote in the preface to the first book, "school schedules, business appointments, political activities, art projects, sculpting classes, movie going, exercising, theater, chamber music concerts, tennis, squash, weekends in the country or at the beach, friends, family, fund raisers, books to read, shopping" to have time to cook. What Sheila cooked in her Dakota kitchen and Julee sold in the two hundred−minus square feet on Columbus Avenue was "good simple food prepared in a special way."

When Dean and Deluca opened in SoHo about the same time, they worried that there wouldn't be enough business for both shops. But take-out caught on like mad in the Me Decade, as Tom Wolfe called the seventies, and Julee and Sheila rode in to the yuppiedom of the eighties on the crest of the wave. "A lot of people described *The Silver Palate Cookbook* as 'the yuppie book,' which irritated us to death," Julee told me. "When we had the store, we called the same dishes 'survival food.'

"They had to survive from Sheila's kitchen, where she began cooking early every morning, sometimes still in her nightgown, by messenger to the store around the corner, where I sold them. Then they survived the trip home with our customers to be reheated. Sometimes they even survived for leftovers the next day." She learned from a pleased client that leftovers from their first main dish, which she calls "the indestructible Chicken Marbella," made a terrific chicken salad.

The food also helped busy people, and perhaps some marriages, to survive, of course. I missed all the fun until 1984, when Willem and I moved from Dallas to Manhattan. During those early settling-in days, while Willem tackled his difficult duties as executive director of a struggling orchestra and I tried to get a book off the ground, we lived out of packing crates. Unwisely, we had moved the contents of a spacious, gentrified 1910 farmhouse into seven hundred square feet of Manhattan property and we didn't have room to unpack! I became the queen of take-out. I even remember — something I would never have done in Dallas — serving our first dinner guest, Peter McLean, the headhunter who'd brought us to town, with take-out food. I'd like to brag it was from the Silver Palate, but in truth it was Chinese food from one of the Hunans across the street. What did I know?

It didn't take me long to learn. I had already heard the Silver Palate mentioned back in Dallas by Laurie Colwin, a New York novelist. During a week-long literary festival at the university a year or so before, Laurie, who later published a funny, touching book, *Home Cooking,* about her adventures in the kitchen, talked to one of my classes about fiction, and, off the cuff, about food. Among other surprising things, she told my students that if they wouldn't read *Anna Karenina* for any other reason, they should at least read it for the food, especially the descriptions of Russian banquets. Leaving them stunned, she asked *me* if I had read Elizabeth David and if I had heard of the Silver Palate. I don't know if my students made a run on Tolstoy, but I made a mental note. Imagine my joy to find the Silver Palate within walking distance of our new home.

But I never really bought much at Julee and Sheila's shop because no sooner had I tasted the delicious food at the Silver Palate than I discovered *The Silver Palate Cookbook.* We moved to a larger place on the other side of the park, I unpacked my pots and pans, and for three or four years afterward, the Silver Palate books were almost the only cookbooks I used. Sitting at E.A.T., I told Julee this. "And I have friends who say the same thing. Aside from the reliability of your recipes, what do you think the appeal of your books is?"

"We made cooking fun, and we made it taste good," she answered. "We were doing peasant cooking, bistro cooking, ten years before it became popular. Good plain food with just a little bit of sophistication, international in origin, eclectic. We're good home cooks who like flavors that make you stand up and take notice, say 'Wow!' with each bite."

She spooned raspberry jam on her raspberry muffin. "I'm loving these raspberries. These muffins are wonderful."

As I watched her with her double dose of raspberries, I thought of all the raspberry dishes the Silver Palate books had introduced me to. From the first book, I had learned to marinate carrots in raspberry vinegar, and had concocted a fabulous fresh raspberry pie with lemon juice and crème de cassis, as well as a fig and raspberry tart — a combination I'd certainly never have thought of on my own. From the *Good Times* book, I had learned to serve fresh raspberries with a sprinkling of sugar and balsamic vinegar for dessert; to use fresh raspberries and raspberry vinegar as a marinade for poultry; to make wonderful raspberry tarts with pignoli — all these new dishes based on just one ingredient.

Multiply that by the numerous ingredients I had never tried at all before my introduction to the Silver Palate books — phyllo dough, sorrel, fiddlehead ferns, fennel, fruit vinegars — and I must acknowledge that the books really have changed my cooking more radically than anyone since Julia Child. Glancing through my grease-spattered, dog-eared, broken-spined volumes, I see on every page reminders of past dinners I cooked from these books, almost all pleasing to my family and our guests. I wish I had kept a record during the eighties, as I do now. Still, some occasions stick in my mind.

On her way to Stockholm for the Nobel Prize festivities, Muriel Seldin, an old friend from Dallas, stopped off in New York for a visit. Her husband, Dr. Donald Seldin, now retired but then the head of internal medicine at Southwestern Medical School, had already gone on to Sweden because a couple of his star doctors were to receive a Nobel. The night before she was to dance with the king or whatever one does in Stockholm, here was Muriel, prepared to sleep in our "guest room," a futon under the grand piano in the living room.

Muriel has been important in my life. She saw me through the divorce from Bill, introduced Willem to me, even coached me when I tried to learn to read French. But when I think of Muriel, as when I think of so much else, I think of food. I remember the Oriental chicken salad she whipped up before we read French better than I do the French. I recall her fondness for anything broiled to blackness, like Cornish hens split and broiled, with a side of chutney, or English muffins topped with cheese and Worcestershire sauce and charred. When I think of her marvelous parties, rather than the music or the dancing or the talk, I recall the escargots with garlic butter, the Velvet Hammers, the individual omelet prepared for every departing guest at dawn on New Year's Day. She had given a party for Willem and me when we were leaving Dallas, and now I was to cook a reunion dinner for Muriel, her two New York daughters, and a couple of other friends.

Dinner that night began with salmon mousse, a much-favored Silver Palate recipe I have probably made a couple of hundred times; it never fails to make guests relax and count on being fed. The pièce de résistance was a veal and onion stew, with ten cloves of garlic and two pounds of white pearl onions, a dish new to me. With the veal, I served puréed broccoli with crème fraîche (I made my own crème fraîche from Silver Palate instructions) and a risotto porcini casserole from *Good Times.* Then a salad, followed by a raspberry soufflé, made with frozen raspberries flavored with framboise, which looks hard but is actually very easy to prepare.

I really wanted Muriel, sophisticated and elegant, to approve, even to be impressed. So I was overjoyed when she called the stew the best veal dish she had ever tasted, and for several months afterward I made it for *everyone.* The risotto porcini casserole, miraculously a sort of risotto which can be made ahead and which in my experience would feed an army, also became a staple, with the veal or with a roast. When I gave up red meat, I sometimes served it with a roast chicken; later still I served it as the main dish, with a soup before and a salad after. It's fabulous.

And of course I was most pleased of all when, spooning up the last drops of cream, framboise, and raspberry juice from her soufflé, Muriel looked at me obliquely and inquired, "But my dear, did *you* really make this heavenly thing?" My dear, thanks to the Silver Palate tiger ladies, I really did.

On another occasion, for young friends who were getting married, I did a Mexican Mediterranean buffet for thirty, with all the dishes that weren't from the folklore of Texas coming straight out of

The Silver Palate Cookbook. Beef stew with cumin seed was the surprise hit of the evening because I hadn't cooked it before, and cumin is not a spice I'm intimate with. But I said a prayer, cooked it, and they loved it.

With it, I served black beans with cilantro and ham, guacamole with tortilla chips, Mexican rice, and jalapeño corn bread. After years in Texas, I didn't need recipes for these. But the leeks Niçoise were of *Silver Palate* origin, as were the bread pudding with bourbon sauce and the lime and macadamia tarts. The Tex Mex Sheet Cake came from a recipe straight off the Eagle Brand condensed milk wrapper, and mighty fine it was too. Carta Blanca and jug wine to wash it all down, music and dancing. Fun.

You can see I used these books. And I showered copies on my friends. But were there other devotees, I wondered? I first gained an inkling of how widespread the Silver Palate cult actually was — is — when I was on a book tour of several cities in 1987, being met by a guide, usually a woman, in each. To make small talk in Boston, I asked my guide, a charming young woman with two small children and a lawyer husband, if she ever used *The Silver Palate Cookbook*. Bingo. Her eyes lit up. So then, out of curiosity, I asked the same question in Philadelphia, in Washington, in Houston — I forget where else, wherever I went. To a woman, each guide had the same reaction.

My young friend Sarah Ziegler, who has been a food professional for years, told me that caterers use the Silver Palate cookbooks a lot. Sarah is not easily impressed, with cooks or their guests. At a Washington party she catered, she teased one of the guests about his pants, "hysterical bell bottoms with ducks on them, what a bozo," only to discover within minutes that the bozo was Dick Cheney, Secretary of Defense in the Bush administration. "I don't care," she said. "He was still a goofus."

But cool Sarah is very much impressed with the Silver Palate cookbooks. "The recipes work, but they're also imaginative, with unexpected ingredients and garnishes. They can make a caterer's reputation."

"Lots of caterers, lots of restaurants," said Julee Rosso, when I asked her about this. She was still seething at the yuppie label. "You get out there and you see that using our books are young college guys cooking their way through school; little grandmothers who have gotten bored, are tired of cooking, and want some new ideas; men who have retired and are taking up cooking for fun."

Not everyone who cooks from the Silver Palate books acknowledges the source. At a potluck supper Willem and I attended in Minneapolis, I raved about a chicken dish one of the guests had brought, a highly memorable combination of chicken, garlic, prunes, and olives, served at room temperature. "It's from *The Silver Palate Cookbook,* isn't it?" I asked the person who had brought it.

"Oh, no," she said. "I never use cookbooks. My friend Betsy gave me the recipe. I'll send you a copy." When the recipe came, I saw that, with some minor changes, it was one of the best-known Silver Palate dishes. The indestructible Chicken Marbella had entered the realm of folk cuisine.

Julee told me a story that indicates the way a popular, dependable dish like Chicken Marbella becomes folklore. Christmas 1989, when *The New Basics* first came out, two sisters came up to Julee and Sheila at a book signing and said, "Would you please sign this book for our mother? She cooks everything out of *The Silver Palate Cookbook,* and she won't admit it. She pretends they're her own creations. But we're not stupid. We have those books too. We're cooking the same things."

So Julee and Sheila inscribed the gift book with "Caught you!" or "The jig's up!" Julee remembered. "Or something like that. I hope she laughed."

"Nothing is original," Sheila said when I asked her about this story. Both she and Julee pointed to the importance of the examples of cooking grandmothers in the development of their own palates and cooking skills. Sheila's Russian grandmother just "danced around the kitchen," rolling out blinis, making paskha, stirring up borscht. "She never used a recipe and never measured, but I learned a lot watching her."

"What amazes me," Julee said, "is for someone to take a classic and make it sound as if he just invented it. I'm not sure it's even possible to invent something completely new." For example, during the time they were working on *The New Basics,* they decided to try something completely different, a gazpacho salad. Many months later, they discovered Mrs. Beeton had done it — in 1861.

Another time, Julee "created" a potato aioli, "thinking it was entirely original," she said, and later found one almost like it in a James Beard book. What did she do? "I just said, 'Ai-ai-ai-aioli!'"

If the two have been influenced, consciously and sometimes unconsciously, by cooks of the past, other forces have also fostered their ingenious, exciting ideas about food. Sheila credits two major influences on her cooking. One was the time she has spent in other countries. As a young woman, she studied at the Cordon Bleu in London, meanwhile doing graphic design for a London theater. Then she lived in Paris for a year, continuing to study both art and food, and after that lived for a time in the wine country of Bordeaux. "Those years abroad were what really shaped me as a cook," she told me.

Alone and with her husband, she has traveled extensively since. What impresses her most about life in Europe is "the glory of fresh produce": in Greece, pulling figs fresh off the tree for breakfast; in Italy, picking perfect tomatoes and chopping them up for a sauce. "You don't need meat with vegetables as good as they have there."

The other continuing influence on Sheila's cooking has been her two daughters. Of Molly, born in 1973, and Annabel, in 1975,

Sheila said, "I not only nursed my children until they were a year old, I made every morsel of food that was put into their mouths for the first couple of years of their lives." She made soup and puréed it; she puréed vegetables and froze them in ice cube trays. "The ice cube was a perfect serving size." She continued this good-mother feeding even after she and Julee opened the shop, putting up vats of tomato sauce every summer "because Molly and Annabel don't eat commercial canned stuff." So her emphasis as a cook has always been on beautiful, fresh, seasonal produce.

One of the things I have always appreciated most about the Silver Palate books is the menus. I'm a little intimidated at the prospect of making a menu for a company dinner, especially if I'm preparing a new dish. How am I going to know what will be good with it?

Julee and Sheila both had the same tip for me. "Stay with the seasons," Sheila said. "The flavors from a season complement each other naturally. It's hard to go wrong when you go to the market and you see salmon and asparagus and strawberries. There's your menu. If you use really good, fresh ingredients, you aren't going to make many mistakes."

What else intimidates home cooks? "Herbs," Julee told me. "It's a great luxury to have fresh herbs in this country, and they still scare people. Now home cooks are growing them, and I think they will become a lot more confident. It's fun being spontaneous with herbs, not having to follow those charts that say lobster needs tarragon and tomatoes need basil. Try tomatoes with tarragon. They're terrific."

To preserve herself from herbal madness, she depends on the criticism of her husband and her mother, both middle-of-the-road eaters who are her toughest critics. "That's very important for a cook," Julee said emphatically. "It keeps you from becoming precious. They never lie, and if they say something is great, it's great."

Herbs they call weeds. "Do we have to have weeds in everything?" one or the other will ask plaintively. Sometimes they enjoy weeds. Other times, they will request a weedless meal, and Julee complies.

But that a meat and potatoes man will eat weeds at all indicates something about the vast changes that have taken place in the national consciousness — and conscience — in the decade between 1982, when *The Silver Palate Cookbook* first appeared, and the tenth anniversary edition. "Now if I don't eat a vegetable every twelve hours," Susan Stewart wrote me from Detroit, "I feel disgusting. This is not discipline; it is middle age." As the whole population leans toward middle age, particularly the Yuppie Generation — I know, I know, Julee, it's not a yuppie book! — the large amounts of cream and butter in *The Silver Palate Cookbook* make us feel guilty.

Don't feel guilty, the authors advise. Instead, feel free to make healthful changes in your favorite recipes. These days, Julee might make the dilled blanquette de veau with a little chicken stock and thicken it with a vegetable purée instead of using butter and heavy cream. "A lot of the flavors are the same," she told me.

Sheila has lost twenty-five pounds recently by eating fish, vegetables, and grains instead of meat, and by cutting back on fat and dairy products. Julee compared eating habits to a checking account. "It's the way you use your checkbook. You spend your calories and your fat the way you spend your dollars. You monitor it to your own level. Have a big lunch, make dinner lighter. After a heavy day, make the next one light."

As she made this striking analogy, she finished off her E.A.T. raspberry muffin. Our time was up. I looked down at the still uneaten half of mine. "Don't leave that," Julee exclaimed. "It probably cost about eighteen dollars. Get them to wrap it up."

So I did as the tiger lady advised. What better conclusion to a Silver Palate interview than eating your cake and having it too?

·✗·

Rabbit Stew

. . . .

WHAT DOES RABBIT STEW ABOUT? His diet. In *Rabbit at Rest,* John Updike's quintessential novel of the eighties, Rabbit Angstrom has "a typical American heart . . . tired and stiff and full of crud." In 1989, at the age of fifty-six, Rabbit barely survives a major heart attack brought on by "the spicy pork sausage he was raised on, or scrapple drenched in maple syrup, or apple pie," and by a lifetime of eating "steak and hamburger, which is what he usually orders, though he doesn't mind a breaded pork chop or piece of veal, or a slice of ham with a pineapple ring or some moon-shaped snitzes of baked apple and on the side some greasy Dutch fries."

In addition to such heavy nostalgia food, Rabbit is also a junk food addict. Over the course of the novel he scarfs down Planter's Original Peanut Bars, cherry Danishes, vanilla Cameos, Sunshine pretzels, macadamia nuts, and Oreos, as well as Fritos, Doritos, Nibs, Good & Plentys, dry-roasted peanuts, and butter pecan ice cream. He'll eat anything from a machine, even, by mistake, pellets of dry bird food.

Afterward, he repents, "retastes the acid pellets and the yellow-and-red glop McDonald's puts on hamburgers, with the little green pickle, and wishes to God he could stop eating." On one level, *Rabbit at Rest* describes an ordinary American's futile attempt to clean up his act and his arteries before he literally eats himself to death.

E pluribus unum. As Rabbit goes, so goes America. Lest we miss the point, midway through the novel Rabbit even becomes Uncle Sam. Still popping Nitrostat for his heart, he dons the familiar top hat, swallowtail coat, and red-striped trousers for a Fourth of July parade. Thus he turns himself into the national symbol of "the happiest fucking country the world has ever seen."

Happy and fat. If you doubt me, drive across the heartland today and check out the citizenry. You'll see, in towns and cities, on farms and ranches, whole families glistening with fat like prize porkers and still chomping, chomping, chomping. The American melting pot has become the national potbelly. Torn between hedonism and health, like Rabbit we wish to God we could stop eating. "If you live in America," the nutritionist Jane Brody wrote, "chances are you have been on a diet."

American food since the eighties has been called schizophrenic, but I'd diagnose it as a case of multiple personalities. Diet food, gourmet food, fast food, comfort food, junk food, soul food, organic food, and nostalgia food are all striving for control of the body politic. How sweet the memory of Mom's meat loaf and mashed potatoes, we sigh wistfully, while holding a double cheeseburger with fries in one hand and a bottle of Evian in the other.

What does America want, dear God, what does America want?

Like Rabbit, most of us want contrarieties. We want to be good *and* to be satiated, to live right *and* to live it up, to look lean *and* to eat fat. Take Charlie Smith, who in middle age is lean and healthy. "I've long since given up fried foods," he told me, "almost all pork, real mayonnaise, butter, and actual ice cream, and I do feel better, okay, sure, yes, I'm participating in this new wave of 'stay healthy' eating."

But Charlie hasn't quit yearning. Guess what he misses? Spam. He yearns for Spam, fried brown and crisp like bacon, with a side of Kraft macaroni and cheese from the box and canned peas. "I still pause now and then as I pass it when I'm shopping. They've made it in smaller cans now — twelve ounces. What could *twelve ounces* hurt?"

Susan Stewart also stews in the bitter juices of ambivalence. Guilt drives her to vegetables, but she shares Rabbit's love of vending machines. She also likes SpaghettiOs, eaten cold from a can. "You spear the Os on your fork in interesting patterns."

Before they had children, Susan and her husband spent a lot of eighties evenings in front of the TV set. "He held a two-liter bottle of Coke between his knees. I held a two-liter bottle of Diet Coke between mine. The chips were on the floor between us. This was dinner."

Later, with the responsibility of two children, Susan tried to be good. "I like to think we cover the dietary waterfront," she told me. "We grow basil, and mix it with Potato Buds."

But, as she tells it, children introduce temptations as well as responsibilities into a household. One night while watching "Northern Exposure" after the children had gone to bed, Susan climbed on a chair and got the Halloween candy off the shelf.

"Don't you feel guilty," her husband asked, "eating *their* loot?

After all, it was their holiday. They are the ones who walked up to the neighbors' doors with their little hands outstretched."

Susan unwrapped a Fun-Size Snickers. "*They,*" she said, "would not be walking on this earth were it not for *me.* And they weigh one-fourth of what I weigh. They shouldn't have this candy. I'm just doing my job as a mother."

"Pass it over here," her husband said.

By the end of the decade, Susan had adopted for everyday eating what she called "the yuppie solution of bland and soul-less urban food stripped of its ethnic origins along with its fat and calories." In her Michigan kitchen, she produces skinless chicken breasts with stir-fried vegetables, fat-free fajitas, vats of lentil soup. Not thrilling, to hear her tell it, but "I cook this stuff all the time."

Maybe increasingly tasteless food is the answer to our dietary dilemma in this country. Think how thin we'd all be if we couldn't taste. I have read accounts of people whom illness has left in such a state, however, and they seemed less than grateful. Among my own circle in New York, there's the example of Michael Dunne, who on a visit to his parents in Houston was mugged. The experience left him with, among other injuries, a broken jaw. The doctors wired it shut and put him, for some months, on a steady diet of Ensure-Plus, a high-calorie, fully nutritious drink.

Fully nutritious, but not fully delicious. Michael, who prides himself anyway on being "a stoical eater," opted for even more stoicism by having only *vanilla* Ensure-Plus. "The lack of flavor diversity seemed to make even the one flavor disappear after a while, and the only motivation for eating that remained was pure physical hunger," he told me.

Michael's highly selective diet was forced upon him. Most of us, even the very poor, select our own diets; beans cost less than frankfurters, after all. For all the carping of nutritionists and ecologists,

American food is anything but a wasteland. Mixing memory and desire, as Eliot puts it, we can eat what our parents ate, or what we have discovered for ourselves. We can eat to be thin, and we can eat to be healthy, which may or may not be the same thing. We can eat what's convenient, or we can eat what's cheap, certainly not the same thing. We can eat for status (Kobe beef) or for the status quo (Mom's meat loaf). We can eat to be happy. We can choose.

Choosing is hard work, especially for those who eat to be thin. Every day, in every way, I always think of food, but in writing this book I've had to think of food even more, for duty as well as for pleasure. So naturally I have gained five ugly pounds, which are located directly south of my ribs and north of my hipbones, neither of which I can feel just at the moment. I choose to lose those pounds. Every morning, lying in bed, I choose to lose them. This is the first day of the rest of my life, I tell myself. This is the day that I will eat nothing. In fact, I rhapsodize, I will eat nothing for several days, for as many days as it takes to feel those bones again. If I eat nothing, those five pounds will go away. It's as simple as that.

Oh, yeah? Out of bed, I drift toward the kitchen and herb tea, then find myself staring longingly at the cereal box. Breakfast is mandatory, I tell myself; all the experts say so. Weight Watchers says so. Thin people never skip breakfast. I am a thin person, I say, psyching myself up and moving resolutely toward the cereal box. Therefore I will not skip breakfast. This diet is off to a good start.

After the cereal, I may last until lunch, and then again, if we have any of Eli Zabar's raisin nut rolls in the freezer, as we usually do, I may not. Lunch is a highly virtuous salad, with Healthy Choice blue cheese dressing. So what if I'm eating? I am choosing and I am choosing right.

Then, after lunch, as I sip another mug of herb tea, my eyes get (I'm sure) that faraway look as I fixate on the jar of peanut butter which I know is in the cabinet behind me. I love peanut butter. A home without peanut butter is a hell on earth. "The only thing my mother eats peanut butter on," my son once remarked, "is a spoon." Not today. In a blind, stubborn, angry delirium on this first day of the rest of my life, I smear peanut butter on five Stoned Wheat Thins and wash them down with a nice fresh Coke. After that it's Sodom and Gomorrah all the way.

Even if I were to succeed in my desire to lose weight, there's no guarantee the success would be permanent. Quite the opposite, in fact. Most people who take weight off don't keep it off. Abstinence makes the heart grow fonder, somebody said. Ninety-five percent of people who lose weight gain most or all of it back; sometimes they gain more than they lost. Losing weight is a losing proposition. Nevertheless, millions of people, especially women, diet. Female *children* diet. According to the 1991 film *The Famine Within,* eighty percent of fourth-grade girls have already been on their first diets. By conservative estimate, a tenth, most of them female, of all seniors in American high schools have some kind of serious eating disorder.

Win some, lose some. Experts are quick to point out that the ideal of thinness for women often accompanies female gains of some kind. As early as 1985, my first year in New York, *Vogue* anticipated the thesis of Naomi Wolf's 1991 book, *The Beauty Myth,* by linking this female obsession with weight loss to other social factors. Wolf calls it a societal trade-off for power; as women become more powerful in the marketplace, society requires them to be more "beautiful" — for "beautiful," read "thin." In the eighties, rigorous dieting was seen as a trade-off for the sexual liberation of the seventies. *Vogue* quoted Dr. William Bennett, the editor of the *Harvard Medical School Health Letter,* as saying, "In order for women to show that they're mature, capable, adult human beings, in this bizarre way they're being asked to demonstrate another kind of control over their bodies."

Thanks to my genes, if I'm fairly reasonable in my expectations (and if I don't look at the pictures of models in that very same *Vogue*), I rarely need to lose more than five pounds, and there are those who believe those five pounds are between my ears instead of where I know them to be, right here where I'm patting. We are old foes, those five pounds and I. Sometimes they win, sometimes I do. I've tried fasting. I've tried running. But what I like more than fasting or running is eating, and therein lies the problem.

Out in California, Charles Matthews refuses to go along with the trend toward dieting and guilt-free eating. "I have neither the time nor the spirit to be in tune with the Zeitgeist," he told me, "so I guess that makes me a rogue when it comes to vogue." Carried away by poetry, he went on, "In a crunch, I lunch. When in stress, I *fress*. My metabolism is such that I faint and fall if I don't feed."

Like Charles, under stress I *fress* — Yiddish for "pig out" — just as I too lunch in a crunch. Even when I'm unhappy, I rarely lose my appetite. Charles and I both descend from Algernon in *The Importance of Being Earnest,* who philosophized, "When I am in trouble, eating is the only thing that consoles me. Indeed, when I am in really great trouble, as anyone who knows me intimately will tell you, I refuse everything except food and drink."

Oh, when my first husband and I divorced, long years ago, I got very thin, but Willem refuses to leave me just so I can lose five pounds. For less than monumental crises, for the small vicissitudes of life, I keep my eating up to speed.

Sometimes I even pick up the pace. To wit: The first year we were in New York, I had left my teaching job, my family, and my friends back in Dallas. All day long it was just me, the word processor, and the refrigerator. I was lonely, yes. Some women take lovers, others hit the cooking sherry. I hit the cookies. For consolation I acquired, let's face it, a potbelly.

At length I decided to try Weight Watchers. What better, I

thought, than to find a group of people to talk to and to lose my pot at the same time? I longed for popularity, but, let me tell you, you don't know what unpopularity is until you go to a Weight Watchers meeting and announce that you want to lose five pounds.

The branch I chose met at five o'clock on Tuesdays in the antiseptic quarters of a hospital just up the street from me. When I arrived, a line had already formed of some two dozen women and a gent or two, all waiting like complacent cows to be weighed in. They were a cheerful group, exchanging pleasantries and tips, congratulating, gossiping, giggling, as they ritualistically removed heavy jewelry, suit coats, sweaters, and shoes on the way to the scale. I felt that I could find friends here.

I climbed on the scale nervously, feeling like a freshman during rush week, or like an inductee into a rather pudgy army. I smiled at the counselor and managed a timid joke. "Do I pass the physical, sarge?"

The counselor looked at the scale, then sharply at me. "You can't join Weight Watchers," she said brusquely and much too loudly. "To join, you have to be at least ten pounds overweight, and you're not."

Silence fell in the ranks. The giggling horde stopped giggling. I didn't argue, but slunk away, feeling looks of raw hatred piercing my insufficiently padded back. At home, I drooped around morosely for the rest of the week. I had been rejected by Weight Watchers. Rejected by Weight Watchers! I had never before heard of *anyone* being rejected by Weight Watchers, but I had been. It hurt.

When Tuesday rolled around again, I had a plan. At four-thirty, I donned two sweaters, a heavy coat, woolen socks, lined boots, a battery of bracelets, and a faux fur hat, and presented myself to my draft board again. Weighing in, I sweated but I passed. And, friends, today I am a lifetime member of Weight Watchers International, with a gold key to prove that I attained my goal weight.

If I stay within two pounds of my goal weight, and check in every month, I can attend Weight Watchers meetings anywhere in the world free of charge for the rest of my life.

There's only one catch: those five pounds between my ribs and my hipbones are back. And you know what? I'm hungry, and I'm thinking there's an Eli's roll in the freezer.

Lusting after Eli, I'm in good company these days. At the turn of the decade, a backlash rose among the ranks of the starved and surly. No less than two national magazines ran humorous features in 1991 entitled "Spa, Humbug!" and women across the country echoed them. In an antidiet movement reminiscent of the sixties, women who had perhaps once burned their bras now formed support groups and trashed their bathroom scales, carrying banners that read, SCALES ARE FOR FISH, NOT FOR WOMEN.

This as yet minirevolution was fueled in part by two films. *The Famine Within,* a documentary produced by Katherine Gilday, took a hard, cold look at the physical, emotional, and social dangers to women of the cult of the body — such dangers as anorexia and bulimia, low self-esteem, and the loss of power and self-definition. Henry Jaglom's *Eating* focused on the food neuroses of thirty-eight women gathered for a birthday party in which the celebratory cake goes mostly uneaten.

For Jaglom's women, food substitutes for all the good things in life that they are missing and arouses the guilt that once was reserved for sex. In fact, the best line in the film compares food and sex, to sex's detriment: "I think I'm still looking for a man who could excite me as much as a baked potato." Serving as the control figure for Jaglom's send-up of food silliness is an older woman played by Frances Bergen, Murphy Brown's real-life mother, for whom food is simply another of the many pleasures of a rich life.

Not everyone who diets is concerned with appearance. In the eighties, many people became concerned with health as the nation reeled with blow after blow to their favorites of what Warren Belasco, the author of *Appetite for Change,* calls the American Standard diet. American Standard is not rabbit food, but Rabbit food: iceberg lettuce with Thousand Island dressing, roast beef, mashed potatoes, apple pie à la mode — the diet that engenders Rabbit's "typical American heart." Even in the health-conscious eighties, plenty of people still indulged in American Standard.

According to Susan Orlean in her book *Saturday Night,* for example, in 1989, the year of Rabbit's odyssey through the intensive care ward, the Hilltop Steak House in Saugus, Massachusetts, fed two and a half million people on steak, potatoes, and salad with Italian dressing. That year the restaurant grossed forty-seven million dollars by serving some forty-five thousand pounds of beef during an average week.

At the other extreme, Orlean spent a Saturday night at the Pritikin Longevity Center in Miami Beach. Here the overweight enrollees, many of whom had heart problems, signed up for a two- or four-week stay. To get in, they must agree to go on a diet that includes virtually no salt, fat, or protein. Even at the Pritikin Center, however, human nature, American style, will out. Like Rabbit with his corn chips, the Pritikin disciples eat light but talk heavy, constantly shmoozing about steaks, fried chicken, jelly beans, potato chips, pasta, bread, sausages, crab, and corned beef. Some of them cheat. Try as we will, the Old Nick in us surfaces.

Sheila Lukins, my Silver Palate friend, sat up in her hospital bed after an operation, demanding that her startled family fetch her an order of nachos grandes, pronto. And Cecilia deWolf, a nurse whom I know, told me of a woman on her deathbed, no longer able to eat anything, who asked for, and got, a pizza. "She took one bite, but she had her pizza," Ceci said. We want what we want.

For all our backsliding, we became smarter eaters, though not necessarily better eaters, in the eighties. Between 1983 and 1988, according to Food and Drug Administration surveys, the general public became half again as knowledgeable about the link between heart disease and fat. But pretty is as pretty does, my mother used to say, and we didn't do all that pretty. Over the decade, we still ate nearly twice as much red meat as poultry and fish combined. We cut back on eggs, butter, and pork rind, but stepped up our consumption of potato chips, pizza, and soft drinks. You may remember that Ronald Reagan defined ketchup as a vegetable for the school lunch program; his countrymen defined potatoes, including French fries, as our favorite vegetable, accounting for a third to a half of all vegetables eaten by the populace.

Everything went "lite" under the Teflon president. Charlie Smith told me there was even lite Spam. A common misconception was that by eating "lite" — bread, mayonnaise, lunch meat, yogurt, cookies — one was eating well. But the point of major recommendations from food experts throughout the decade, culminating in the new Eating Right Pyramid issued jointly by the United States Department of Agriculture and the Department of Health and Human Services in 1992, was that for good health, one's diet should consist largely of vegetables, fruits, and whole grains. A healthy diet means adding as well as subtracting; man does not live by "lite" alone.

Still, we continue to struggle to get it right, or some of us do. It's not easy. All these food rules and regulations are hard to keep in mind and even harder to follow for *me,* with all the time in the world and with everything I've learned writing this book. Think what they must be like for my daughter, Erin, a single parent with a demanding job.

Two years ago, separated from her husband, Erin became heavily embroiled in a custody battle for her then four-year-old daughter, Bailey, my only grandchild. It was a nasty and extended fight, and for the ten days of the trial — a jury trial, to add to the stress — I was on hand to lend support in what was undoubtedly the worst week of my daughter's life.

Mothers being what they are, and me being what I am, picture me on the sleepless midnight before the first day of the trial, in the kitchen of Erin's apartment, defrosting the refrigerator. And writers being what they are, as Joan Didion once wrote, always selling someone out, I am taking mental note of the contents. And in fact I find the contents of the freezer compartment soothing: four Swanson pies, my own old favorite, three of macaroni and cheese and one of beef; fish sticks, of course — how would kids ever reach adulthood without fish sticks?; five of something called Lean Pockets; one of those rectangular packages of ocean perch, I'd guess never to be eaten; something else called Border Breakfasts, with egg and cheese tacos and sausage; and the usual complement of frozen vegetables.

I scrub and scrub, wishing lives were as easy to clean up as refrigerators. The bottom part of the fridge comforts me further: skimmed milk, tamales, designer water, three kinds of juices — V-8, apple, and grape — plastic packages of Jell-O pudding, dinosaur SpaghettiOs. Erin comes in on her way to bed as I am on my knees with my head poked deep into the vegetable bin, scouting the mushrooms, bean sprouts, broccoli, cucumbers, lettuce, and green onions for even further reassurance. "Mom, what on earth," she exclaims, a grin crossing her pretty, tired, worried face. "What on earth are you doing?"

"Oh, just a little straightening out," I say, getting to my feet shamefacedly. Is this, I wonder briefly, the equivalent of reading her diary? "Just sort of seeing what we'll have to eat this week."

Here's what we ate, the three of us, Erin and four-year-old Bailey and I, between trips to the courthouse and the nursery school and the lawyer's office, between tears and rage and laughter. Here's what we ate the worst week of Erin's life. Oatmeal and three kinds of dry cereal. Teenage Mutant Ninja Turtles Fruit Snacks. Broccoli sandwiches with mustard and bean sprouts on whole-wheat pita. An enchilada casserole, with chips and salsa. An angel food cake with candles on top. What Bailey calls "pusghetti" with garlic, butter, and Parmesan cheese. Bananas. Teddy-Os. Elfkins, which I learn are bite-sized chocolate sandwich cookies. In short, Rabbit stew.

At a café near the courthouse, Erin and I eat lunch with her lawyer. Lee, a tall, impressive woman with a beautiful chiseled face and black hair, has the grilled chicken breast and two orders of mashed potatoes with lots of gravy. We urge her to eat more, and more. I find myself wishing, in spite of my burgeoning vegetarian sentiments, that she were gnawing red meat running with blood. I want her tough. I want her mean.

The night before the jury is to bring in their decision, Erin makes baked apples for the three of us. That night, in the bed we're sharing for the first time since she was a little girl, "Good night, Mom," she says firmly. "I'm going to sleep now."

"Don't talk anymore," I say. "*I'm* going to sleep."

And I am just about asleep when she speaks again. "I remember once coming home sick when I was living in that apartment over on Gaston," she says. "I had a high fever. And you brought me juice and crackers, soup, Jell-O. And I could hear you puttering around in the house, humming, talking to the cat — and I just felt so safe."

My mind goes back over the decades, and I remember being sick as a child, throwing up in the middle of the night, and at early light my own mother offering me a cracker with a bit of mayonnaise spread on it, her sleepy face in the faint light from the fireplace behind her, and the immense comfort in that cracker. What we must teach the experts is that food is more than fuel, chosen like gas just to match our engines. It is the very stuff of life.

I began with a Rabbit and I'll end with a bunny. In one of her columns, like any good mother, Anna Quindlen broods over the evil significance of the Easter Bunny. "The Easter Bunny stands for sugar," she writes, ultimately capitulating in a way that Erin, Susan Stewart, and all mothers everywhere will probably understand. "I support candy manufacturing," she says.

> The only part of a chocolate rabbit I have no use for is the empty space in the center and those little sugar eyes they put on them. Everyone knows the best part of Easter is eating your children's candy while they are sleeping and then trying to convince them the next morning that the chocolate rabbit came with one ear.
>
> But all this is very confusing to today's children, who are always being fed things like kale. They meander along, living their whole-wheat lives, and then one Sunday they wake up and discover there is nothing on the menu but jellybeans and ham. . . .
>
> Once a year some child has the wit to say: "Cool! He brought all the stuff that she never lets us eat!"

May every granddaughter be that child, happy with fish sticks and pusghetti from her mother's kitchen, and may she grow into a woman who recognizes the immense subtleties of the Rabbit stew in which we live and move and have our being.

How Would You Feel
If a Cow Ate *You?*

. . . .

I'M SEXY. *Psychology Today* said so. Sexier than gourmets, health-food fans, fast-food devotees, and synthetic-food users. That's because I am, more or less, a vegetarian.

Some time ago, a couple of psychology professors, Edward Sadalla and Jeffrey Burroughs, set out to determine whether eating preferences had anything to do with how people see themselves, with how others see them, and with how they really are. In three studies, Sadalla and Burroughs performed experiments on some seven hundred college students. They reported, among other things:

1. If you don't eat meat, you regard yourself as sexy.
2. If you don't eat meat, others regard you as sexy.
3. If you don't eat meat, you really *are* sexy.

As a vegetarian, you are also, according to this study, serious, peace-loving, and artistic. You eagerly take on "difficult, challenging tasks of an intellectual nature," but are not inclined to compete aggressively with others. More recent studies show that, compared to meat eaters of your age and socioeconomic level, you probably have a lower cholesterol level, lower blood pressure, fewer cancers of the breast, colon, and prostate, less body fat, and a healthier heart. Which means that you will probably be sexy, artistic, and all that other good stuff *longer* than your carnivore cousins.

So why isn't everyone a vegetarian? First of all, because, as the whole world knows, Americans love meat. They especially love beef. They especially love steak. In November 1991, a Gallup Poll reported that the menu for a typical American's ideal meal would look like this:

Shrimp Cocktail or Other Seafood Appetizer
Green Salad
Potatoes and Broccoli
Steak
Bread
Cheesecake or Ice Cream
Tea

Steak, you will note, is the center of this meal.

Carl Shaver, who owns a consulting firm in Manhattan, told me a story about the link in the world's eyes between Americans and beef. He and his wife lived for several years in Lausanne, where they ate frequently at La Grappa d'Or. "So frequently," Carl said, "that our two favorite young waiters became quite aware of our tastes."

Several years after the Shavers left Switzerland, they were in Bermuda on a holiday and stopped at the Princess Hotel in Hamilton for lunch. As they entered the restaurant, two familiar-looking waiters stared at them and began whispering excitedly. Suddenly, beaming with pleasure, the waiters cried out exuberantly and rushed over to the Shavers.

What were they exclaiming so exuberantly? They were of course the two waiters from La Grappa d'Or, and they were exclaiming, "Ah, m'sieur, madame, filet de boeuf, filet de boeuf, filet de boeuf!"

"Needless to say, we had fine service at our lunch at the Princess," Carl said, "but we *didn't* order filet de boeuf."

In addition to this national love for beef, Americans don't take readily to vegetarianism because virtually every boy and girl in the country grew up with a traditional food chart. The graphic for this chart was a pie that encouraged daily infusions of nutrition from the Four Basic Food Groups, which were represented by equal slices. The four were meat, fish, and poultry; dairy products; grains; and fruits and vegetables, usually lumped together.

In that old standby of millions of American housewives, *Betty Crocker's Picture Cook Book,* the basic four were refined to the basic seven in Betty's "circle of Good Nutrition" — refinements such as you wouldn't believe. For example, one of Betty's basic seven is butter or margarine. Just that. In this circle, for "complete or abundant meals," everyone ate three or four eggs a week, at least one serving of meat, poultry, or fish every day, as well as butter, cheese, and a pint to a quart of milk daily.

"Meat and potatoes" was invariably the center of dinner, some sort of protein-heavy "main dish" the center of lunch. Ed Allen, an amateur historian, likes his steak but was quick to remind me that the potatoes alone would sustain life. "Millions of Irish peasants in the nineteenth century subsisted almost exclusively on potatoes," Ed said. "No dieticians were around to tell them that this was unhealthy, so in the main they were reasonably active and pink-cheeked until the potato blight struck in 1845 and again in subsequent years." But for better or worse, in this country we did have our dieticians for whom meat was every meal's prime factor. Around the stability of this central axis circulated the green and yellow vegetables, bread and butter, fruit and sweets, that made up the remainder of a nutritious diet.

Because of this early and ongoing indoctrination, we remain a nation of meat eaters. For us, beginning with meat makes meal planning easy. Time was when everyone knew steak required baked potatoes, broccoli, and green salad with blue cheese dressing. Meat loaf required mashed potatoes, green peas, maybe carrots or Waldorf salad. Barbecue required French fries and cole slaw. Easy as, well, pie, which Betty Crocker considered "as American as the Fourth of July." A lot of people still think this way. The ideal meal of steak, potatoes, and embellishments is a meal Americans can understand. It hits all four food groups, and everything *goes together*. Nutritious as well as delicious, right? As we said here in the summer of 1992, *not*.

But, for pete's sake, who knows *what* goes with bulgur, tofu, or a bean casserole? To become vegetarians, and even to eat nutritiously, we may have to learn, if we take seriously the Eating Right Pyramid recently advanced by the United States government.

This pyramid has a tiny peak of fats, oils, and sweets, and comes with the recommendation to "Use Sparingly." Under that is a thinnish slab of dairy, meat, eggs, and other protein. Beneath that is a hefty wedge of vegetables and fruit. At bottom, undergirding the structure is a solid hunk of bread, cereal, rice and pasta, with instructions to eat "6–11 Servings" daily.

Such a picture sends a message that a thousand words cannot convey. As Bonnie Liebman, a nutritionist for the Center for Science in the Public Interest, told *The Wall Street Journal,* "It has a tremendous power to convey at a glance that fruit and vegetables and grains should make up the bulk of the average American's diet to reduce the risk of heart diseases and cancer."

In spite of the pictorial strength of the pyramid, it's still a big step for the typical American from eating meat in moderation — "it's still legal as a garnish," Susan Stewart said — to eating meat not at all. Still, it's a step many people have taken over the years. Among performers, Madonna is a vegetarian. Candice Bergen is a vegetarian, possibly Murphy Brown as well. Paul McCartney and George Harrison are vegetarians; Ringo Starr was, briefly, but he couldn't give up fish and chips. Among other artists, vegetarians can point to Plutarch, Leonardo, Tolstoy, Shelley, Shaw, and most recently Isaac Bashevis Singer. Buddha was, Gandhi was, and there's even a theory that Jesus was. And some twelve million Americans are, or consider themselves to be, vegetarians.

Or, like me, "more or less" vegetarians. "More" are the vegans (pronounced vee-gans), who eat nothing of animal origin. Also in the "more" camp with these vegan saints are lacto-ovo vegetarians, who eat dairy products and eggs, but no meat; lacto-vegetarians, who give up eggs but eat dairy, and ovo-vegetarians, who give up dairy but eat eggs. In the "less" camp are those who eat fish, chicken, eggs, and dairy products, but refuse red meat, as well as those who refuse both red meat and chicken.

To make the whole thing even more confusing, it's possible to categorize vegetarians also on the basis of motive. Some, highly vocal, eschew meat for reasons of principle having to do with health, ecology, or animal rights. In his 1992 book, *Beyond Beef: The Rise and Fall of the Cattle Culture,* Jeremy Rifkin enlarges on the concern, raised by Frances Moore Lappé in 1971 in her groundbreaking *Diet for a Small Planet,* that we are killing ourselves and the rest of the world by eating beef. Through its high fat content and heavy residues of pesticide, beef endangers the health of those who eat it. It endangers the rest of the world because tons of grain that could completely wipe out human hunger are used to feed beef cattle.

Some ideologies are less specific. Jackie Rushing, who worked in Vietnam for the State Department between 1968 and 1970, gave up meat for a while after the war was over. "You might once have called me a lacto-ovo-vegetarian," she told me. "I didn't think in those terms. My criterion was simple: I wanted nothing taken by violence or fear. Vietnam had provided me with an excess of both." She couldn't change the past, she realized, but she hoped by giving up meat retroactively to pay respect to the memory of "friends and strangers who died so bloodily."

Others abstain because of personal repugnance at the thought of a bloody carcass. In *The Vegetarian Epicure,* Anna Thomas says, "Good food is a celebration of life, and it seems absurd to me that in celebrating life we should take life. That is why I don't eat flesh. I see no need for killing." Isaac Bashevis Singer advanced the same idea more succinctly, remarking that he gave up chicken not for his own health, "but for the health of the chicken."

But many drift into vegetarianism from a complex and inextricable intertwining of motives. To say you're a vegetarian inevitably means defining your terms. "What do you immediately think when you hear the word *vegetarian?*" I asked a sampling of my friends, none of them vegetarians. A number saw vegetarianism as the moral high road.

"Morally superior. Healthy. Less 'different' than it used to be. Something I should aspire to."

"Highly appealing. Virtuous."

"Good health."

Others were less positive. "All of my sons' girlfriends," answered the mother of three of mating age. "I understand that there are no more elegant evening meals at the sorority house because the girls are all anorexic and only eat small cups of yogurt before bingeing on pizza at midnight." But she went on to praise the city green-markets "that bring us new and exotic organic vegetables daily, and the city newspaper columns that tell us how to cook them."

Others also rhapsodized about vegetables. Jackie Rushing recalled a tomato in her mother's garden, "a bright tomato-red tomato, big and heavy. It wasn't perfectly round. The stem end was flattened, with bumps arranged symmetrically around the stem scar." She still remembers its scent and its juice that flowed down her face and dripped on the ground. "If I had dropped that tomato, it would've burst like a geyser — real tomatoes don't bounce."

"My neighbors are finally convinced that they needn't hide the pork chops when I drop in at dinnertime, because I am not 'against' eating meat," says the chef and food writer Martha Rose Shulman. In *The Vegetarian Feast,* Shulman explains that over time, because of the plenitude of vegetables and the declining quality of meat, she gradually lost interest in meat. "I didn't really *decide* to give it up."

Nanette Fodell recalled a huge garden that she cultivated while she lived on a farm in Miller Grove, Texas. She made wine from pears, canned her own tomato sauce and apple jelly, and "learned to start the pot boiling before I picked the corn. I'd race from the field and blanch the ears before the kernels started turning to sugar and losing their flavor."

Her country neighbors were less enthusiastic about their plenitude of homegrown produce than Nanette, the city slicker. Add a little Jell-O to her fresh figs, they advised, and they'd taste just like store-bought strawberry preserves. "They gooped up the simplest garden delights with tons of sugar and food coloring." And being typical Texas-Americans, they liked their beef. Nanette swears that one recipe in the Miller Grove community cookbook lists as an ingredient "a bowl of meat." Generic to the genus, you see.

Only one of my friends, Jim Hyatt, had a flatly negative reaction to vegetarianism. "Vegetarian? Food kooks and anorexic women," he said. I'm certainly not anorexic, so I must be a food kook.

Let me say that I've heard the food kook jokes, as you have, and even as a "more or less" vegetarian I find them pretty funny. The funniest summation I've seen of attitudes by food kooks like me was in a piece called "Was It Ethical for You Too?" which Colin McEnroe wrote for *Mirabella*. I can't resist quoting at length:

> Dinner parties are a challenge. The Snodgrasses will only eat veal if it's range-fed and had access to a lap pool. The Plunts will only eat chicken if somebody picked it up and hugged it once in a while. The Kaldenbores are vegatonementarians, which means that they can eat anything as long as they feel guilty afterwards. The Serafinos are fruitarians, which means that they bring their own tomato plants and wait for one to fall off the vine on its own before they eat it. Sometimes they're up all night.
>
> The Plunts threw a bash where they gave you your own live lobster, and you had to figure out what to do about killing it. One option was this little lobster-sized Kevorkian suicide machine. . . . Another choice was a device that consisted of a little trap door over a steaming pit of water. There was a little lever near the door, and when your lobster, in the course of aimless claw-waving, hit the lever, it dropped into the water. So it wasn't really you.
>
> Of course, a lot of people bonded with their lobsters and just ate the chickpeas.

Ask me to define my terms when I say I'm "more or less" a vegetarian and I would have to answer that I have bonded with my lobster. I really hate to go all soft on you, but when it comes to motive, I'm undeniably in the Singer camp: I abstain from chicken not for my own health but for the health of the chicken.

My own health I'm pretty casual about, probably too casual. To me cholesterol and pesticide residues have one thing in common: you can't see them. I'm sure I wouldn't give up meat because of anything I couldn't see. For that reason, though I'm told ice cream is bad for me, my idea of fun is still to eat a pint of Ben and Jerry's Coffee Heath Bar Crunch at a single sitting. Scotch shortbread with real butter, pecan pie with four eggs, Brie with sixty percent butterfat, I hardly ever push away. But if I were to, it would be because of visible rather than invisible fat — fat on me, not in them. If cows or chickens find constantly giving milk or constantly laying eggs unpleasant, as the vegans claim, that's too bad. But we all have to sacrifice, and at least they're not being eaten. No, if over the years I've felt my lust for meat gradually weaken and wither away, it's because some of my best friends have been animals. I'm not keen to gobble down a creature to whom I could buddy up.

I was not born finicky or in a finicky family. When I was a little girl, many times I saw my mother step lightly out into the chicken yard at my grandmother's country house, snatch up a passing pullet or fryer, and deftly twist off its head with three or four wide circles of her swinging arm. The body flew out in the yard and bounced around for a few wild seconds till she gathered it up, pulled out its feathers, cleaned out its guts, and put it on for dinner. I ate as heartily as anyone.

My grandparents kept a few hogs every year, fattening them up through the spring and summer to butcher during the first cold snap in the fall. They were fat, lazy, ugly creatures whom I don't recall in much detail, though my first husband, Bill, used to reminisce with affection about a prize hog whom he'd raised from a tiny piglet. What I remember is the excitement of their slaughter. A Mr. Martin came to preside, like a hired executioner, and I can still smell the big wash pot out in the barnyard where the fat was rendered and see the stretched skin from which the bristles were scraped for crackling and salt pork pieces for seasoning. Soon enough, the hogs were pork chops on the table, hams and a side or two of bacon in the smokehouse.

I always had pet animals, at one time nine cats, mothers and grown children, forbidden the house by my father. At night, by design I closed my bedroom door and left my window open. In the morning I would wake up with six or eight cats draped artistically around my bed. They were not at all disturbed by the presence of my spitz mix, Poochie, who was legally in my bedroom but not legally under the covers, where she invariably slept. When Poochie crawled out to greet a new day, out the window the cats flew before the rest of the house stirred.

When I began to make a connection between my pets and other, edible animals, I don't know for sure. It may have been when my younger brother, Ken, was given a tiny, featherheaded, yellow duckling for Easter one year. This particular duckling, named Mr. Porter for the friend who had brought him to Ken, did not conveniently off himself as such tiny, featherheaded, yellow creatures usually do. He grew into a lean adolescent duck, then in a couple of years into a fine portly fellow with the same shape and waddling gait as the original Mr. Porter.

Porter was a gregarious soul. He followed us around the back yard and garden in a friendly fashion, nipping at our heels as we hung sheets on the line. When we offered him treats — he particularly liked cold corn sticks — he spread his wings joyfully and uttered squawks that sounded to me like a laugh: "Har, har, har." Strangers often asked if we planned to have him for Christmas dinner. We would as soon have thought of eating Ken. Mr. Porter finally died when a pack of renegade dogs didn't share our scruples, and the whole family went into mourning.

Probably the next phase of this slow slide into vegetarianism came with Sissy. One cold October afternoon in 1966 when Bill, the kids, and I lived on a ranch in the Texas hill country, we were scouting for arrowheads when we came across a tiny white kid standing by herself in the dubious protection of a mesquite tree. We left her, but she followed, running after us on wobbly baby legs, bleating plaintively. Erin bleated back and the kid kept coming. There was no sign of a herd or a mama goat.

"She'll starve, Mother, I know she will," Erin begged, as we got in the car to drive back to the house. She began crying, "How will she eat? She's too little to eat grass, and there's no grass around here now anyway."

So we took her home with us. I knew it was a mistake, but what could we do? We fed her with a bottle, put her in diapers, and gave her the run of the house. It was just too cold to put her out. She became Sissy, by spring a beautiful white *jeune fille* with elegant manners and the intelligence and loyalty of a pet dog. When we left to go somewhere in the car, she waited on the ranch house porch till we returned. When she wanted to see us, she ran from door to door of the house calling for us until we came out or brought her in. When we took a walk, she followed at our heels.

That spring before we left the ranch for good, Mexican friends invited us to a going-away feast. The main dish was a meat I wasn't familiar with, something called *cabrito*. When I called to thank our host the next day, I asked for the recipe, which began, "Kill a baby goat." That was definitely a turning point in the development of my palate.

From the ranch we moved to Chicago. We gave Sissy away, to a neighboring rancher who promised not to butcher her. None of us felt good about this decision, but we didn't see any way Sissy could fit in the back yard of a house in a middle-class neighborhood in Evanston. Maybe we should never have adopted her in the first place. I don't know.

I suppose I could use some kind of argument like that to quiet my qualms about eating meat, the instinctive recoil I feel these days when I realize that what is before me is *flesh,* the flesh of some animal, like Sissy and, yes, like me. Linda McCartney has spoken of her memory of eating a leg of lamb with her husband, Paul, while their pet lamb gamboled with their children on the lawn outside the window. "I realized I was eating someone's leg," Linda said.

Other vegetarians define this recoil in various ways. I don't eat anything that has a face. I don't eat anything that has a mother. I don't eat anything that runs away from me. Or, like Jackie Rushing, anything taken by violence or fear. If I could look at Sissy and know what she felt about me, seeing that feeling made visible in her eyes, how can I be sure that cows and pigs don't have that same ability?

I can still stomach seafood, I suppose because it's hard to feel intimate with a shrimp, an oyster, or a scallop. However, the last time I brought lobsters back from Maine and thrust them into boiling water, I couldn't eat mine. There's this sound they make, you know, between a whistle and a scream. People have told me that's just the air escaping from the shell or something, but these are the same people who don't seem to have any trouble with veal, which is *baby calf*.

My cousin Reid told me a story about a crawfish boil he and his wife, Sarah, attended at an oil conference in Houston which gave me a new concern for crawfish. "What a feast!" Reid said. "You would fill your paper plate with hot boiled crawfish, draw a beer, and get to work peeling the hulls off the crawfish tails.

"We were eating away on our fourth or fifth plateful when we heard a commotion behind us at a table occupied by a dozen or more Japanese visitors. They were excitedly jabbering in Japanese and pointing at the center of the table. One crawfish had survived the boiling water and was backing his way across the table."

Gulp. And George Bernard Shaw wondered if even vegetables feel pain when they are eaten. It's all a damned nuisance, isn't it?

God knows, I don't want to be a vegetarian, and if you invite me to your house for dinner — and I hope you will — you probably won't know that I am. Miss Manners says, "By law, guests of any age enjoy doing and eating whatever their hosts want them to do and to eat. . . . The clever guest admits to no food dislikes, short of things that give him violent physical reactions — and those should be explained at the time of accepting the invitation."

I'm a sexy vegetarian, but I'm also a clever guest. I will not identify my prejudices for you, lest you should think it imperative to bake an acorn squash for me or something. How embarrassing. What I will do is fill my plate sky-high with vegetables, rice, pasta, and bread, if I'm allowed to serve myself; shove the meat around a bit if you put it on my plate; and eat dessert like there's no tomorrow.

·✗·

Food Fanatic
in New York

. . . .

IT DOESN'T GET ANY BETTER THAN THIS," my husband
said. Willem and I were sitting on the curb on Ninth Avenue
in Hell's Kitchen, eating warm slices of Pennsylvania funnel
cake. "I'm having an epiphany. I'm as happy as I expect to be in
this life."

I licked the powdered sugar from my fingers and looked at him.
"Don't tell me you want to go home already," I said.

With some nine hundred thousand other nibblers, we were celebrating Manhattan's Ninth Avenue Food Festival on a perfect Sunday
in May, with sun, light breezes, music, happy strollers, and food,
food, food. Willem and I had walked from Fifty-seventh Street
down to Thirty-seventh, the entire length of the festival, on the
west side of the avenue. We had eaten our way through vegetable

fritters, wedges of spinach pie, manicotti stuffed with three kinds of cheese, pizza, empanadas, and something called arepas, vegetables stuffed in pita-like bread.

We had seen the mayor and a marching band. A whole suckling pig on a spit. A couple eating toward each other from each end of a six-foot-long hero. Pretty girls in brightly colored dresses and turbans doing African dances. Mariachis, skaters, and people from Queens. At Thirty-seventh Street, we sat down to rest with our funnel cake and glasses of freshly squeezed lemonade.

Willem wanted a nap.

"How can you think of sleep when there's all this food?" I asked. I wanted to walk back up toward home on the east side of the avenue. "Let's try that French apple tart or some apple-walnut pie, some kind of pie anyway. Maybe a couple of Mexican cookies or a Good Humor bar. And something chocolate. Definitely something chocolate."

"Aren't you sleepy?"

"The Food Fanatic never sleeps," I said.

And the Food Fanatic is right at home in New York, the city that never sleeps. Manhattan is simply the most indulgent place in America for a food lover like me, and here's my chance to describe for you some of the indulgences I've had living here. The last part of the meal I've almost always regarded as the best, and as an eater I can give this city no higher praise than to say that, like this chapter, it is *dessert*.

First, you can always find a good place to eat and probably someone to eat with you. Oh, to eat at a hot restaurant between seven and ten on a given night you may have to book four months in advance, but look at the compensations. At two o'clock in the morning, you can get a hot pastrami on rye with Russian dressing at the Carnegie Deli or a burger and the hot fudge brownie at the Hard Rock Cafe. You can rub shoulders with cool SoHo at Lucky

Strike or reminisce about Dylan Thomas at the White Horse Tavern, where he ate his last meal, or watch for Woody Allen at Elaine's or Mike Wallace at Gino's. Any hour, day or night, you can find food and fellow travelers at the Empire Diner. And at all of these places, and hundreds of others, you're a lucky eater.

The luckiest occasion for me may have been a special performance sponsored by *Bon Appétit* magazine at CSC Repertory of *Bon Appétit!* starring Jean Stapleton. I find I may have difficulty describing this play, a one-woman musical monologue based virtually line for line on one of Julia Child's 1961 "French Chef" programs during which the redoubtable, inimitable Julia baked a chocolate cake. Jean Stapleton, best known as Edith Bunker in "All in the Family," sang — not very well — a musical score — not very good — by Lee Hoiby, an opera composer. There! Do you get the picture?

Inferior dramatically, the evening was superlative gustatorily. Four top New York restaurants, Le Cirque, Felidia, Mondrian, and the Union Square Cafe, as well as the cooks at *Bon Appétit,* provided special "chocolate creations" for the edification of the audience, along with many other chocolate goodies. Perrier-Jouët sent champagne, much champagne, and Martell donated cognac.

Not only that. After the performance, the magazine held a drawing for six dinners for two to be given away at the restaurants, and I won the one at Mondrian. A couple of weeks later, Willem and I feasted on smoked salmon, a ragoût of mixed seafood, duck breast with foie gras (my vegetarianism sometimes gives way under pressure), and yet another chocolate ganache with grape, passion fruit, and ginger sorbet. When the bill that would have been over three hundred dollars was presented and we waved it away with our award letter, I realized that *Bon Appétit!* may have been the best play I had ever seen.

New Yorkers are especially lucky in the international flavor of the city. Dozens and dozens of Italian restaurants, some as good as those in Rome or Florence, dozens of Chinese and Japanese and French. Blocks from my apartment, a hungry person can sample every ethnicity from Afghan to Vietnamese, even Czech and Tibetan, as well as exotic combinations like Cuban-Chinese. And of course there are all the Americans, South, Central, Standard, and nouvelle.

New Yorkers eat not only whenever and whatever, but wherever. They have whole meals — pizza, falafel, hot dogs, salads, sandwiches, fruit, ice cream — on the go. Aside from these peripatetic meals, you can sit at a restaurant table inside, outside, in the clouds, in a tunnel, on the water.

Some people even eat at home. Willem and I prize good restaurant meals all the more because we mostly eat at our own table. I like to cook, and Willem thinks I'm better at it than I used to be, thanks to this Food Fanatics' town. I'm definitely not a food professional, just an ordinary American who likes to eat. Nevertheless, a year or so ago, I climbed two long flights of very steep stairs up to Peter Kump's New York Cooking School on East Ninety-second Street, where demonstration classes are open to the nonprofessional public. There I watched a dozen people, mostly young women, clad in chef's white jackets and armed with decorating tubes, pipe fondant roses onto a cake.

After the class, they laid down their tubes, picked up cups of black coffee, and sat around a long table talking knowledgeably about trends for the nineties. Less meat and more beans, grains, and vegetables, they said. Fewer fussy dishes and more peasant and comfort food. What good news to find that, as a member of the comfortable, peasant, vegetarian persuasion, I'm also trendy.

Many people don't bother to entertain in a space as small as ours with a kitchen that can be described, kindly, only as a galley, but I like to feed my friends. We have held on to our Dallas table that seats ten, and once or twice a month we have people in. Instead of the veal stew or boeuf bourguignon of my unregenerate days, I offer pasta or polenta. Though the occasional carnivore will sharpen his knife and wait expectantly for the roast, most have learned by now that there is to be no roast. Pragmatically — I hope not resignedly or bitterly — they take another helping of pasta and wait for dessert.

There I try not to disappoint. I have never considered it fair of a hostess to offer fruit in lieu of what the English call "pudding." Engraved on my heart are the immortal words of a friend settling happily into her chocolate chocolate chip ice cream with hot fudge sauce, "Don't you love it when dessert comes? And don't you hate it when it's not chocolate?" If the dessert I serve forth is not chocolate — personally I love raspberry and lemon just as much, and I don't sneer at ginger, banana, pistachio, vanilla, or rum — I will follow it with After Eights or truffles for those who need their fix.

To Tim Allis, a writer for *People,* who at thirty-one lives alone and eats out seven nights a week "by a conservative estimate," the Big Apple offers maybe too many possibilities for what he calls the "fiscally overextended, socially overstimulated, gastronomically overindulged restaurant addicts like me." Listen in to a typical phone conversation between Tim and one of his regular dinner companions. It's about eleven A.M. on Wednesday, or Thursday, or any day you like.

Where do we want to eat tonight?
Oh, God. There's nowhere.
Cheap, right?
Right, cheap.
Chinese?
[*Moan*]
That barbecue place on Houston.
Sue's a vegetarian.
Thai?

Did it last night.
The new one on Prince, with all the models.
Too trendy.
Jerry's?
It's so . . . so . . . so . . .
SoHo.
Exactly. How about Two Boots?
Not trendy enough.
Right. How about whatsit? On Gansevoort?
Florent. But it's French. I have a problem with French.
Uptown?
John's phobic.
Upper West?
I'm phobic.
Upper East?
They're phobic.
How about the West Village? A million great places there.
Right. Name one.
I can't.
[Phone beep] That's my other line. Wanna decide later?
Perfect.

Spoiled, spoiled, spoiled, I said after Tim's recitation. He ac-
knowledged that his expectations were high. "The perfect New
York restaurant, to me," he admitted, "is dark, in a light sort of
way, cheapish with an expensive feel, lively yet subdued, close to
home (but don't make me eat in my neighborhood again!), old but
fresh, dependable yet startling, in short unpretentiously glamorous
and merely fabulous. Maybe with good food. I've heard such a place
exists in Santa Fe."

I agree that Manhattan doesn't have everything. Though Willem and I have trekked all over the city in our quest, we haven't

found good Tex-Mex food. Just swallow that tip you're about to give me about El Coyote, Juanita's, Santa Fe, the Border Cafe, whatever. I'm telling you, we've tried them all, and by Texas standards they're lousy. Something execrable happens to every taco or enchilada or guacamole tostado on its way to our table. Usually it gets doused with raw chili powder or bottled hot sauce or something equally unthinkable. Plenty of times, on evenings when we crave a really fine green enchilada, made with tomatillos instead of chilies, we've longed to be back in Dallas at the Blue Goose on Greenville tucking into the $5.95 combination plate. There is excellent Mex-Mex at Zarela's, Mi Cocina, or Rosa Mexicano, but that's another story.

Yet here I stand, crying in my beer, in the center of Mecca to food pilgrims. New Yorkers concentrate on food with an intensity unmatched in the rest of the country. A New York telephone operator was asked the number of the Yellow Rose Cafe, Patricia Morrisroe reported in *New York* magazine in 1984. "It's 595-8760," the operator said. "Order the pork chops." Things have lightened up some since the eighties, I guess, but not much.

Take the first half of 1992. Did you know that in January, New York City talk radio began broadcasting a hot line for foodies? During the lunch hour every weekday, Arthur Schwartz, a cookbook writer and restaurant critic, took up the microphone on "Food Talk" (WOR, 710 on the AM dial) to address concerns about everything from a roach in a restaurant salad to the proper way to clean copper pots.

In April, a record crowd turned out at Symphony Space on Upper Broadway to hear Roy Blount, Jr., and Nora Ephron, among others, present *Le Menu,* from *la soupe* to *le dessert,* of readings on food. *Un petit poisson* was, appropriately enough, a selection from M. F. K. Fisher, *le plat principal* "The Hunger Artist" from Franz Kafka.

On May Day, some completely benighted citizens wandered

into a new gallery on Lower Broadway to see, like a poached salmon on a bed of watercress, a naked man lying on a bed of pears, artichokes, squid, strawberries, and roasted rabbits and piglets. You won't find a sight like that in Dubuque.

On the why-go-out-for-hamburger-when-you-can-get-steak-at-home premise, I didn't go to see the naked man, but during the month of the naked man, I attended five cooking classes, free of charge, presented by Le Cordon Bleu at Galeries Lafayette, the new French department store on Fifty-seventh Street. Raffish in his toque and charming accent, Chef Jean-Claude Terrettaz coached forty of us in Cordon Bleu techniques required to make *croustillant de rouget au fenouil, poêle de langoustines au porto, salade Niçoise,* and other wonders of Provence.

And that same May, Willem and I celebrated our eighteenth wedding anniversary with dinner and a movie at Robert De Niro's TriBeCa Grill, after learning that Liza Minelli had celebrated her tenth wedding anniversary there. "We're not really a romantic restaurant," the woman taking reservations demurred faintly when we requested the most romantic table in the place, "but we'll do our best."

Their best was fine. After our dinner of homemade cheese ravioli with roasted tomatoes followed by soft-shell crabs, our dessert came, warm brioche with a peach and berry compote and lemon verbena ice cream for Willem, chocolate torte with a layer of chocolate mousse in the center for me. Each dessert was alight with candles and presented on a plate with "Happy Anniversary" written in chocolate sauce at the top.

After dinner, we moseyed upstairs to the private screening room for a showing, included in the price of dinner, of the movie *Delicatessen.* Not exactly the usual anniversary fare, I guess. Romance may be in the eye of the beholder for some, but I'd say it's in the tummy for us, and we went home happy.

New Yorkers scored a coup during the Democratic Convention in July 1992 which gave new meaning to the word *lucky*. During the recession of the early nineties, there was, you may recall, a great deal of talk about "paring down" in the Big Apple. Numerous stories appeared in the *Times* and elsewhere, touting the attempts of restaurateurs to cut costs and the stratagems of customers to manage "fine dining on a budget," as one *Times* headline put it. Some of the "stratagems" were less strategy than sacrifice. I might be willing to split an appetizer, as Eric Asimov suggested, but divvy up the fabulous banana tart at Union Square Cafe? Not on your life. Keep your piratical fork to yourself.

The one manifestation of paring down I wholeheartedly approve of occurred during the convention when well over a hundred of the best — and most expensive — New York restaurants offered special lunches for $19.92 in addition to their regular menus. The now defunct Quilted Giraffe promised to serve exactly the same prix fixe lunch for which it normally charges $45. Here, listed in the *Times* for the eyes of an incredulous New York, were the likes of Le Cirque and Montrachet. Here were Petrossian, Provence, and the TriBeCa Grill. Here was Bouley.

Bouley. I must say a word about Bouley (pronounced Boo-lay). In 1990, Bryan Miller of the *New York Times* awarded Bouley its rare four stars. "David Bouley's rabid zeal for fresh regional ingredients, his cerebral approach to textures and flavors, and his obvious delight in wowing customers make this one of the most exciting restaurants in New York City," Miller declared.

By 1991, Bouley was the best in the city, according to seven thousand volunteer restaurant goers, people like you and me, who voted the little piece of France in TriBeCa the city's best in overall quality of food, decor, service, and popularity in the Zagat restaurant survey. That same year, the James Beard Foundation declared Bouley the best restaurant in the United States.

Again in 1992, Bouley defeated one thousand other New York restaurants for the top two titles in Zagat. At one point, the Zagat crowd was asked where they would like to have the last meal of their lives and overwhelmingly they responded, "Bouley." Count me in. When I heard Bouley was doing a $19.92 lunch, I cheerfully spent most of a day listening to a busy signal to snare a place for what was, if not the last, surely the best meal of my life.

I went alone. Those unimaginative sheep who bleat that they must eat alone deserve no sympathy in my book. All by myself, I easily turn into the eating scene from *Tom Jones*. For me, eating alone, whether it's the last piece of lemon meringue pie devoured in bed late at night or four gorgeous courses at Bouley, is the most exquisite, the most orgasmic, of pleasures.

First of all, Bouley is beautiful, a feast for the eyes. A huge hand-carved wooden door imported from Provence invited me into a bucolic setting from that sunny land itself, redolent with the heavenly smell of fresh fruit and flowers. Everywhere I looked there were Impressionist landscapes; window boxes and pots of wildflowers; big baskets of golden pears and apples; tables set with blue, white, and pastel crockery and glowing with tiny lights; dark, mellow French provincial furniture; and happy, mellow American faces.

Then there's the service. On this particular occasion, perhaps because I was alone and looking hungry and hopeful, I was given a large table in the center of the room, and offered, instead of the regular lunch, a sampling menu. The sampling menu, of course, I said, whereupon four or five waiters proceeded to bring me four or five of the most delectable tidbits that ever passed my lips. Between tidbits, the waiters hovered, with more bread, more water, and many smiles. Hovering is far too rare in the service world. I *go* for hovering.

Good hovering. Eating thin slices of roasted breast of guinea hen and their entourage of tiny translucent discs of broccoli and potatoes, I inquired about two small leaves on one side of the plate. Was it sage, I asked? Oh, no, madam, said Jean-Luc, organic basil, so fresh, so potent, so puissant, as to be nothing like the usual nongarden variety. I will show you sage, he said. And back he trotted with the prettiest little stalk of green and white streaked leaves of sage, as well as a sprig of lavender and a pinch of rosemary, all from plants hanging in the kitchen. Now that's hovering raised to an art.

Finally and foremost, there was the food, which began with perfect ingredients painstakingly chosen by David Bouley himself. The preparation I suppose you'd call cuisine minceur. Every dish is healthy because Bouley uses very little cream and butter, preferring flavorful juices, herb oils, and reduced vegetables to sweeten and thicken. Every dish is also gorgeous. Bouley himself does the fish, and fortunately for my principles and for my palate, most of the dishes on that afternoon of the best meal of my life were seafood.

First came a little medallion of sashimi-cured tuna, its buttery softness enhanced by an anise-flavored dressing, on a bed of puréed celery root. With this, and what was to follow, I ate warm rolls baked in the kitchen from which Jean-Luc and the others moved smoothly back and forth; one was sourdough with a little brownish *chapeau;* another with a sweet crust was studded with hazelnuts.

What followed were tiny seared brook trout in a shallow estuary of herb oil and balsamic vinegar. They were topped with toasted pignoli and surrounded by a mesclun salad, with fresh tarragon and dill.

After the trout swam down my throat, Jean-Luc brought in a plateful of, I thought, delicate but chewy rings of pasta. No, he said, baby squid. I've never had great hopes for squid, but these were smaller and lighter than I had ever thought squid could be, served with a creamy vinaigrette flavored with tarragon, like a béarnaise without eggs. I asked about a couple of crunchy, tasty, golden garnishes. The heads, Jean-Luc said, as I ate the last bite. Oh.

Then there was Bouley's famous Maine skate, procured from a marine biologist in Camden, who fishes for a rare variety that's the tenderest of all the sixty species of skate on the Atlantic Coast. With the skate were organic peas the size of a butterfly's eye, just warmed in a bit of butter with their crunch still intact.

Then the hen, for which I forsook my principles, and at last, and none too soon, dessert. I was given a choice of hot chocolate soufflé or wild cherry tart. How to choose? Well, the tart, because more unusual, though heaven knows I hated to forgo chocolate. The tart was served in a pool of cherry sauce and garnished with raspberries, blackberries, tiny wild strawberries — the exquisite fraises des bois — and a stem of crystal red beads of currants.

But David Bouley is a wise man. After the coffee, with the bill, came a small wooden box sealed with a gold seal and tied with an iridescent green bow, which, when untied, revealed a box of miniature chocolates, truffles, and one white chocolate mouse with a long purple satin tail.

The bill was $19.92.

It doesn't get any better than this.

Notes

Epigraph

William Shakespeare, *Pericles,* I, iv, 107. *The Complete Signet Classic Shakespeare,* ed. Sylvan Barnet (New York: Harcourt Brace Jovanovich, 1972), 1424.

Eudora Welty, "June Recital," *The Golden Apples* (New York: Harcourt, Brace and World, 1949), 94.

A Love Affair with Food

PAGE

3 The average American ate: "Changes in What We Eat," *U.S. News & World Report* (February 4, 1985), 52.

4 In 1960, 49 new cookbooks: Figures provided by the New York Public Library.

5 "Why describe, as if you were changing a tire": Jo Brans, "The Fragrance of Morality: An Interview with John Cheever," *Listen to the Voices: Conversations with Contemporary Writers* (Dallas: Southern Methodist University Press, 1988), 44.

At My Mother's Table

9 "I think any child of the thirties": Quoted in John Edgerton, *Southern Food* (New York: Knopf, 1987), 198–99.
19 Eudora Welty once wrote: See "The Flavor of Jackson" in *The Eye of the Story* (New York: Random House, 1978), 325.

The Way We Ate

27 "If you grow up in a family with strong rituals": Steven J. Wolin, quoted in Daniel Goleman, "Family Rituals May Promote Better Emotional Adjustment," *New York Times,* March 11, 1992.
31 Maybe Lin Yutang was right: Quoted in *The Viking Book of Aphorisms,* ed. W. H. Auden and Louis Kronenberger (New York: Penguin, 1983), 369.

Kooking in the Kamera Kitchen

36 "It began with curry": Nora Ephron, "Critics in the World of the Rising Soufflé," *New York* (September 30, 1968), 35.
   "especially elegant": *Betty Crocker's Picture Cook Book,* 1st ed. (New York: McGraw Hill, 1950), 387–88.
37 Considered the Queen of Square: Jane and Michael Stern, *Square Meals* (New York: Knopf, 1984). See 41–42, 162, 199–200, 228.
41 Who was this welcome interloper, anyway?: Facts about Betty Crocker come from General Mills archives.
42 "Dear Miss Crocker": General Mills archives. Quoted by Jane Simon,

"Mix Trust, Blend Ease, Cook till Sales Are High," *Compass* (November 1990), 36.

44 "Where the male factor": General Mills archives.

45 "Keeping a personal relationship": Ibid.
"It's best to use ingredients": *Betty Crocker's Picture Cook Book,* 2d ed. (New York: McGraw Hill, 1956), 17.

47 "In winter people eat stew and mashed potatoes": Anna Quindlen, "Summer Reading Lists" ("Public and Private"), *New York Times,* July 15, 1991.

Eatniks

51 "There is no sun without shadow": Albert Camus, *The Myth of Sisyphus,* trans. Justin O'Brien (New York: Knopf, 1955), 91.

52 "the force that through the green fuse drives the flower": Dylan Thomas, "The Force That Through the Green Fuse Drives the Flower," *Modern Poems,* ed. Richard Ellman and Robert O'Clair (New York: Norton, 1973), 335.

53 "all the food of San Francisco": Jack Kerouac, *On the Road,* ed. Scott Donaldson (New York: Viking, 1979), 173–74.

55 "I knew it was nutritious": Ibid., 15–16.
"rear glows like a peach": Quoted in *This Fabulous Century,* Vol. VI, 1950–1960, ed. Ezra Bowen (New York: Time-Life Books, 1970), 222.

57 "All my New York friends": Kerouac, *On the Road,* 10.

59 "The cafeteria concept struck just the proper balance": John Mariani, *America Eats Out* (New York: William Morrow, 1991), 119.
In 1961, McDonald's had sold five hundred million hamburgers: Ibid., 169.

60 "As for the Beat Generation": Kenneth Rexroth, "Beat Sequence," *The Village Voice Reader,* ed. Daniel Wolf and Edwin Fancher (New York: Doubleday, 1962), 337.
"Should I get married?": Gregory Corso, "Marriage," *The Norton Anthology of Modern Poetry* (New York: Norton, 1973), 1257–59.

63 "The Beard House is like having Beethoven's house": Promotional material from the James Beard Foundation.

64 "It's a combination culinary Mount Vernon": Ibid.

66 "astonish the bellies of New York": James Beard, *Delights and Prejudices* (New York: Atheneum, 1964), 280.

67 "first gastronomic adventure": Ibid., 4.

"Forceful and fearless": Ibid., 9–10.

thrown out in his freshman year: Barbara Kafka, "A James Beard Memoir," in the James Beard Foundation, *The James Beard Celebration Cookbook: Memories and Recipes from His Friends,* ed. Barbara Kafka (New York: William Morrow, 1990), 34.

68 "a gastronomic gigolo": Beard, *Delights and Prejudices,* 279.

69 "And now, the table is set": Beard, *Hors d'Oeuvre and Canapés* (New York: Quill, 1984), 18.

"Food is very much theater": James Beard, quoted in Evan Jones, *Epicurean Delight* (New York: Knopf, 1990), 105.

"opera dinner": James Villas, *Villas at Table: A Passion for Food and Drink* (New York: Harper and Row, 1988), 42–44.

70 "I can close my eyes and see him forever": Gael Greene in *Celebration,* 265.

"I'm a butter boy": Cornelius O'Donnell, ibid., 121.

71 "The key word that distinguishes the saint": Donald Attwater, *The Penguin Dictionary of Saints* (Harmondsworth, England: Penguin, 1965), 10–11.

"I have come to realize": Raymond Sokolov, *Why We Eat What We Eat* (New York: Summit, 1991), 148.

72 "This is quite delicious": Christopher Idone in *Celebration,* 216.

he regaled his student Mark Caraluzzi: Mark Caraluzzi, ibid., 45.

73 "Gourmet has become a hideous term": Stern and Stern, *American Gourmet,* 227.

74 "cooked the way he dressed": Joe Baum, *Celebration,* 93.

"He practically said so what": Jones, 143.

"Was it fun?": Larry Forgione in *Celebration,* 98.

hired an inexperienced cook to make the soufflés: Stern and Stern, *American Gourmet,* 182.

A Servantless American Cook

77 "cobwebbed bottles": Julia Child, Simone Beck, and Louisette Bertholle, *Mastering the Art of French Cooking, Volume I* (New York: Knopf, 1961), vii.

80 "It really doesn't matter": Peg Bracken, *The I Hate to Cook Book* (New York: Harcourt Brace, 1960), 5.

81 "This is a book for the servantless": *Mastering,* vii.

82 "1½ cups sauce Mornay": Ibid., 243.

"I started cooking because I was housebound": Leslie Newman to Nora Ephron, "In Praise of Home Cooking," *New York Times Magazine,* November 4, 1990.

84 "Vichyssoise is not pronounced veeshy-swah!": Craig Claiborne, *The New York Times Cook Book* (New York: Harper and Row, 1961), 83.

"is like telling a small boy": Bracken, 71.

85 "There was an unbelievably elaborate recipe": Leslie Newman to Nora Ephron, "In Praise of Home Cooking."

Gazpacho in a Sausage Grinder

106 "Dis-yah de way de buckra like": The Junior League of Charleston, Inc., *Charleston Receipts* (Charleston, S.C.: Walker, Evans and Cogswell, 1950), 323.

108 "Best Ever Rum Cake": Mickey (Mrs. Gerald) Sandridge, *Sharing Our Best* (Olive Branch, Miss.: Bethel Presbyterian Church, 1990), 144.

112 Ruby Henderson and her Jackson, Mississippi, neighbors: Clarion-Ledger/Jackson Daily News, *A Cook's Tour of Mississippi* (Jackson, Miss.: Hederman Brothers, 1980), 181.

113 "Creating new recipes": "The Cook's Exchange," *Bon Appétit* (February 1992), 156.

"This unusual but terrific side dish": Ibid. (March 1992), 120.

114 "As far back as I can remember": "Sugar and Spice," *Gourmet* (March 1992), 34.

115 "This is a wonderful treat": Ernest Matthew Mickler, *White Trash Cooking* (Winston-Salem, N.C.: The Jargon Society, 1986), 87.
"If you don't live": Ibid., 11.
"Mrs. Ina Filker": Ibid., 57.

Pipe Dreams

118 "Of course": Quindlen, "Just Say Yes" ("Public and Private"), *New York Times,* March 29, 1992.
The *New York Times* reported: Figures came from a series on drugs in the *New York Times,* January 1968.

119 "The term 'getting stoned' is confusing": Charles A. Reich, *The Greening of America* (New York: Random House, 1970), 258–59.
"ultimate sign of reverence": Ibid., 263.

132 "a specially tender piece of eternity": Virginia Woolf, *To the Lighthouse* (New York: Harcourt, Brace and World, 1927), 158.

Strange Fruit

143 "Too often the aging gardening editor": Mariani, 226.

Nouvelle Is Swell!

153 Accordingly, we took all our cues from Proust himself: Most of the quotations, as well as suggestions for the dishes, came from Shirley King, *Dining with Marcel Proust: A Practical Guide to French Cuisine of the Belle Epoque* (London: Thames and Hudson, 1979).

155 "I am happy to see": Nika Hazelton, "Au Revoir, Nouvelle Cuisine," *National Review* (June 6, 1986), 60.

156 "Avoid unnecessary complications": Quoted in Mariani, *America Eats Out,* 234.

157 "Some just cannot change": Joseph Wechsberg, "La Nature des Choses," *The New Yorker* (July 28, 1975), 38.

158 "chef gourmand": Michel Guérard, *Cuisine Minceur,* trans. Narcisse Chamberlain (New York: William Morrow, 1976), 5.

161 "The cuisine of our grandparents' time": Sokolov, 230.

163 "Bocuse himself": Ibid., 225.

Silver Palate in My Mouth

168 Over the last twenty years: See Brans, *Listen to the Voices.*

172 "school schedules, business appointments": Julee Rosso and Sheila Lukins, *The Silver Palate Cookbook* (New York: Workman, 1982), xi.

Rabbit Stew

182 "a typical American heart": John Updike, *Rabbit at Rest* (New York: Knopf, 1990), 166.
"the spicy pork sausage": Ibid., 81.

183 "retastes the acid pellets": Ibid., 105.
"the happiest fucking country": Ibid., 371.
"If you live in America": Jane Brody, "Personal Health," *New York Times,* July 3, 1991.

187 "In order for women to show": Kathleen Madden, "Women and Food: The Consuming Passion," *Vogue* (May 1985), 306.

188 "When I am in trouble": Oscar Wilde, *The Importance of Being Earnest,* in *The Victorian Age,* ed. J. W. Bowyer and J. L. Brooks (New York: Appleton-Century-Crofts, 1954), 813.

190 In an antidiet movement: Molly O'Neill, "A Growing Movement Fights Diets Instead of Fat," *New York Times,* April 12, 1992.

191 American Standard: Warren Belasco cites this menu in "The Two Taste Cultures," *Psychology Today* (December 1989), 29.
the Hilltop Steak House: Susan Orlean, *Saturday Night* (New York: Knopf, 1990), 112–29.
Pritikin Longevity Center: Ibid., 130–41.

Cecilia deWolf: Brans, *Take Two* (New York: Doubleday, 1989), 28.

195 "The Easter Bunny stands for sugar": Quindlen, "Rabbit Punch," *New York Times,* April 15, 1992.

How Would You Feel If a Cow Ate You?

197 "difficult, challenging tasks": Edward Sadalla and Jeffrey Burroughs, "Profiles in Eating: Sexy Vegetarians and Other Diet-Based Social Stereotypes," *Psychology Today* (October 1981), 54.
Gallup Poll: Reported in *New York Times,* July 26, 1992.

198 "circle of Good Nutrition": *Betty Crocker's Picture Cook Book,* 1st ed., 31–33.

199 "as American as the Fourth of July": Ibid., 295.
"It has a tremendous power": Bruce Ingersoll, "U.S. Picks Pyramid to Show How to Eat," *The Wall Street Journal,* October 28, 1991.

200 there's even a theory that Jesus was: Rynn Berry, *Famous Vegetarians & Their Recipes* (Los Angeles: Panjandrum Books, 1990), 21–24.

201 "Good food is a celebration": Anna Thomas, *The Vegetarian Epicure* (New York: Vintage, 1972), 3.

202 "My neighbors are finally convinced": Martha Rose Shulman, *The Vegetarian Feast* (New York: Harper and Row, 1979), ix.

203 "Dinner parties are a challenge": Colin McEnroe, "Was It Ethical for You Too?" *Mirabella* (November 1990), 130.

207 "By law, guests of any age": Judith Martin, *Miss Manners' Guide to Excruciatingly Correct Behavior* (New York: Atheneum, 1982), 65.

Food Fanatic in New York

215 "It's 595-8760": Patricia Morrisroe, "Sex, Exercise, and Apartment Hunting Can't Match Restaurant Madness," *New York,* November 26, 1984.

217 "fine dining on a budget": Eric Asimov, "Fine Dining on a Budget: Stratagems for the 1990's," *New York Times,* July 31, 1992.
"David Bouley's rabid zeal": Bryan Miller, "Restaurants," *New York Times,* August 3, 1990.